A Probus Guide to World Markets

•

INNOVATION AND TECHNOLOGY IN THE MARKETS

A Reordering
of the World's
Capital Market
Systems

•

DANIEL R. SIEGEL
EDITOR

Preparation of this book was supported jointly by
The Annenberg Washington Program in
Communications Policy Studies of Northwestern University
and
J.L. Kellogg Graduate School of Management,
Northwestern University

PROBUS PUBLISHING COMPANY
Chicago, Illinois

Library of Congress Cataloging-in-Publication Data Available

ISBN 1-55738-120-8

Printed in the United States of America

1   2   3   4   5   6   7   8   9   0

Contents

About the Contributors   vii

Foreword   xiii
    Newton N. Minow, Northwestern University

PART 1   AN OVERVIEW   1

    Chapter 1   **The Competitive World of Electronic Trading**   3
                Daniel R. Siegel, University of Washington

    Chapter 2   **The Intersection of Technology and Financial Services**   13
                Paul F. Glaser, Citicorp

    Chapter 3   **An Overview of Automation of Information Dissemination**
                and Trading in U.S. Securities Markets   23
                David S. Ruder,
                   U.S. Securities and Exchange Commission
                Alden S. Adkins,
                   U.S. Securities and Exchange Commission

PART 2   THE ECONOMICS OF THE IMPACT OF TECHNOLOGY
           ON FINANCIAL MARKETS   45

    Chapter 4   **Trading Technology and Financial Market Stability**   47
                Sanford Grossman, The Wharton School

    Chapter 5   **Before and After October 19: Structural Changes in**
                U.S. Financial Markets   59
                Louis Margolis, Salomon Brothers

Chapter 6   **Market Making in the Electronic Age**   71
Junius W. Peake,
Peake/Ryerson Consulting Group, Inc.

Chapter 7   **How Automated Trade Execution Systems Affect Trading, Price Discovery and Quantity Determination**   89
Ian Domowitz, Northwestern University
Wayne Gardner, Loyola University

Chapter 8   **Order Routing: A Technological and Economic Perspective**   117
Rajiv M. Dewan, Northwestern University

PART 3   **REGULATORY ISSUES**   131

Chapter 9   **Regulation and the Automation of Information Dissemination and Trading in the U.S. Securities Markets**   133
David S. Ruder,
U.S. Securities and Exchange Commission
Alden S. Adkins,
U.S. Securities and Exchange Commission

Chapter 10   **When Financial Markets Work Too Well: A Case for a Securities Transaction Tax**   151
Lawrence H. Summers, Harvard University
Victoria P. Summers, Harvard University

Chapter 11   **When is a Marketplace a Market? Automated Trade Execution in the Futures Market**   183
Ian Domowitz, Northwestern University

Chapter 12   **International Securities Regulation in a Global Electronic Environment**   197
Alger B. Chapman,
Chicago Board Options Exchange

PART 4   **THE CONTRIBUTION OF TECHNOLOGY TO SPECIFIC MARKETS**   209

Chapter 13   **The Contribution of Technology to Financial Markets: A View from NASDAQ**   211
John Wall,
National Association of Securities Dealers, Inc.

Chapter 14   Two Systems in Transition: Open Outcry and
               Electronic Trading   219
                 William J. Brodsky, Chicago Mercantile Exchange

Chapter 15   The Future of Financial Markets and the Role of
               Technology: The Impact of the GLOBEX System   225
                 Paul A. Tattersall, Reuters Plc.

Index   231

About the Contributors

Alden S. Adkins is Senior Special Counsel with the Division of Market Regulation of the U.S. Securities and Exchange Commission. He graduated magna cum laude from the Washington College of Law of the American University in 1981. From 1987 until 1989 he served as Special Counsel to Chairman Ruder.

William J. Brodsky joined the Chicago Mercantile Exchange in 1982 as Executive Vice President and Chief Operating Officer. In 1985, he succeeded Clayton Yeutter as President and Chief Executive Officer. Prior to joining the CME, Mr. Brodsky was with the American Stock Exchange from 1974 to 1982 and held the title of Executive Vice President for Operations between 1979 and 1982. From 1968 to 1974, Mr. Brodsky was an attorney with the New York investment banking and securities brokerage firm of Model, Roland and Company. Mr. Brodsky received an A.B. degree from Syracuse University in 1965 and a J.D. degree from the Syracuse University College of Law in 1968. He is a member of the bar in New York and Illinois. At Syracuse University, Mr. Brodsky serves on the Board of Trustees, the Endowment Committee and the Board of Visitors of its College of Law. Currently, he is a Board Member of the Chicago Council on Foreign Relations, J.L. Kellogg Graduate School of Management and the Chicago Association of Commerce and Industry, where he is the Vice President for the World Trade Division. He is a member of the Commercial Club of Chicago and The Economic Club of Chicago. He also serves on the boards of the Japan American Society of Chicago, the Swiss Commodities, Futures and Options Association, and the International Futures and Commodities Institute in Geneva.

Alger B. "Duke" Chapman has been Chairman and Chief Executive Officer of the Chicago Board Options Exchange since 1986. Before joining CBOE, he was Vice Chairman of American Express Bank Ltd. in London. Chapman came to

American Express through Shearson Hamill & Co., which he joined in 1966. He was elected President and Chief Operating Officer of Shearson Hamill in 1970 and C.E.O. three years later. When Shearson Hamill merged with Hayden Stone in 1974, Chapman became Co-chairman. The firm later became Shearson Loeb Rhoades and was acquired by American Express in 1981. Chapman served as Vice Chairman until 1982 when he became Vice Chairman of American Express Bank. From 1960 to 1966, Chapman was Vice President for Civic, Legal, Government and Industry Affairs for the New York Stock Exchange. Previously, he was an attorney for the Securities and Exchange Commission in Washington. Chapman holds a bachelor's degree from Williams College and a law degree from Columbia University School of Law. He is a member of the board of visitors of the Columbia University School of Law, an Associate of Northwestern University and member of the board of the National Council on Alcoholism.

Rajiv M. Dewan is an Assistant Professor of Information Management at Northwestern University's J.L. Kellogg Graduate School of Management. He received his Ph.D. in Information Management from the Simon School of Business at the University of Rochester. His research interests include telecommunication network design, the economics of information systems, and applications of information technology to financial markets.

Ian Domowitz is currently the Household International Research Professor of Economics and Statistics at Northwestern University. His principal areas of research and expertise include time-series analysis and forecasting, industrial organization and its link with the nation's economy, law and economics, and finance. Domowitz received his Ph.D. in Economics from the University of California, and has published extensively in various professional journals and books. He has served as a consultant to major industrial, financial, and government organizations.

Wayne Gardner is pursuing a law degree at Loyola University in Chicago. He graduated with honors in Economics from Northwestern University in 1989. Mr. Gardner was awarded the Frederick S. Deibler Prize in Economics for his work on the automation of financial markets while a senior at Northwestern.

Paul F. Glaser is Chairman of Citicorp's Corporate Technology Committee, and a member of Citibank's Policy Committee. He is responsible for establishing technology policy and standards, for the introduction of new technologies, for evaluating the quality and direction of systems efforts and for defining technology-driven future business directions. Since joining Citibank in 1973, he has been responsible for business planning, development and operation of advanced electronic systems and transaction processing networks for delivering financial and information services to Citibank and Citicorp customers. From 1973 to 1984, Mr. Glaser was Chairman of Citibank's wholly-owned subsidiary, Transaction Technology, Inc. Prior to joining Citibank, Mr. Glaser was with TRW, Inc. for 15 years as Vice President and General Manager of TRW Electronic Systems Division and President of TRW Colorado Electronics. Mr. Glaser's external activities include membership of the Board and Executive Committee of the Corporation for Open Systems, membership of the Board and Executive Committee of the American National Standards Institute, membership of the Board of Volunteers in Technical Assistance, Chairman of the Office of Technology Assessment Panel on Securities Markets and Information Technology, membership of the Scientific Advisory Board for the Institute for Cancer and Blood Research, membership of the Electrical Engineering Advisory Council for Cal State Long Beach, and membership of the Advisory Board for the Graduate School of the City University of New York. Mr. Glaser holds Bachelors and Masters degrees in electrical engineering from New York University. He has authored numerous articles and lectured on electronic banking, information management, computer systems, communications and space technology.

Sanford Grossman is the Trustee Professor of Finance at The Wharton School, University of Pennsylvania. He has been an economist with the Board of Governors of the Federal Reserve System, and has taught at Stanford University, the University of Pennsylvania, the University of Chicago, and Princeton University. His current research topics include takeover bids, securities trading subject to transactions costs, the determinants of market liquidity, tactical asset allocation, the analysis of program trading subject to transactions costs, the determinants of market liquidity, tactical asset allocation, and the analysis of program trading and portfolio insurance. The American Economic Association awarded him the John Bates Clark Medal at its December, 1987 annual meeting. The Q-Group awarded him first prize in The Roger F. Murray Prize competition for his paper "An Analysis of the Implications for Stock and Futures Price Volatility of Program Trading and Dynamic Hedging Strategies." The Editorial Board of Financial Analysts Journal awarded Sanford Grossman the 1988 Graham and Dodd Scroll for his paper "Program Trading and Market Volatility: A Report on Interday Relationships." In 1988 he was elected Director of the American Finance Association.

Louis Margolis is a Managing Director of Salomon Brothers Inc. and Manager of the firm's Equity Options & Futures Department. He joined the firm in 1979 in Institutional Option Sales. Margolis is now a member of the Chicago Mercantile Exchange Financial Products Advisory Committee and its Board of Governors, the Commodities Futures Trading Commission's Financial Products Advisory Committee, the Board of Directors of the National Options and Futures Society, and the Securities Industry Association's Option and Futures Committee. He participated in the Securities Exchange Commission's Program Trading Round Table in July 1986. Born in New York City, Margolis received a B.A. degree in Economics from Columbia University in 1967.

Junius W. Peake is Chairman of the Peake/Ryerson Consulting Group Incorporated and is an authority on the functioning, structure and operations of the financial services industry, including capital markets and clearing and depository systems. An executive in the financial services industry for many years, he has served as a consultant to it since 1973. Prior to that time he was a senior officer of a major brokerage firm, where he was responsible for all operational, administration, data processing and compliance functions. Mr. Peake has consulted for banks, brokerage firms, and exchanges, as well as for the regulatory organizations which supervise the securities and banking industries. He served as Governor and Vice Chairman of the National Association of Securities Dealers, Inc., and has been a member of committees of the New York and American Stock Exchanges, the Securities Industry Association and the Public Securities Association. He was also a founder and director of the National Clearing Corporation (now the National Securities Clearing Corporation) and has lectured at leading American business schools. He is a member of the Bond Club of New York and the International Operations Association and serves on the Panel of Arbitrators of the National Association of Securities Dealers, Inc.

David S. Ruder was sworn in as the 23rd Chairman of the U.S. Securities and Exchange Commission in August, 1987, two months before the October, 1987 market break focused increased attention on the role of the Commission in addressing securities market problems. During the week of October 19th, Ruder initiated the Commission's staff study of the market break. He took an active role concerning market problems through Congressional testimony, Commission legislative proposals, oversight of the Commission's Division of Market Regulation, discussions with self-regulatory organizations and industry leaders, and participation in the President's Working Group on Financial Markets. Before his nomination to the Commission, Ruder was a faculty member of Northwestern University School of Law from 1961 to 1987 and its Dean from 1977 to 1985. In 1989, Ruder returned to Northwestern University. Ruder received a bachelor's degree, cum laude, in 1951 from Williams College, where he was a member of Phi Beta Kappa. He received his law degree with honors in 1957 from the University of Wisconsin, where he received the Salmon W. Dalberg Prize as the outstanding graduating student. He was editor-in-chief of the Wisconsin Law Review. Ruder served in the U.S. Army from 1951 to 1954, attaining the rank of First Lieutenant. From 1957 to 1961, he was an associate with the Milwaukee law firm of Quarles & Brady.

Daniel R. Siegel is the Paul Pigott/PACCAR Professor of Business Administration at the University of Washington. He is the Director of the Technology and Financial Markets Program of the Annenberg Washington Program. His research and teaching interests include options, futures, corporate finance, and the impact of technology on financial markets. His articles have appeared in leading academic journals, trade publications, and the financial press. Siegel has recently co-authored (with Diane Siegel) *The Futures Markets: Arbitrage, Risk Management, and Portfolio Strategies*. Before coming to the University of Washington, Siegel was an Associate Professor of Finance at Northwestern University's J.L. Kellogg Graduate School of Management. He received his Ph.D. from the Massachusetts Institute of Technology and a B.A. from Reed College.

Lawrence H. Summers is the Nathaniel Ropes Professor of Political Economy at Harvard University, where he specializes in macroeconomics and the economics of taxation. He served as Domestic Policy Economist on the President's Council of Economic Advisors during 1982-83. He has recently published two books, *The Asset Price Approach to Capital Taxation* and *Understanding Unemployment*. Summers received his B.S. degree from the Massachusetts Institute of Technology (M.I.T.) in 1975 and his Ph.D. from Harvard in 1982. Prior to joining the Harvard faculty in 1983, he taught economics at M.I.T. In 1987, he was the first social scientist to receive the National Science Foundation's $500,000 Alan T. Waterman Award. He was also elected as a fellow of the American Academy of Arts and Sciences. Summers has served as a consultant to the Department of Labor and the Treasury in the United States as well as to the governments of Jamaica, Indonesia and Mexico and a number of major U.S. corporations. He is the editor of *The Quarterly Journal of Economics*, a member of the Brookings Panel of Economic Activity, and a Research Associate of the National Bureau of Economic Research. In addition to his academic research, Summers writes a monthly newspaper column on economic policy.

Victoria P. Summers is currently the Deputy Director of the Harvard International Tax Program and a Lecturer on Law at the Harvard Law School. She received a B.A. degree, summa cum laude, from Yale University in 1978 and a J.D., cum laude, from the Harvard Law School in 1982. Prior to assuming her present position, she was a member of the Boston law firm of Hale and Dorr, specializing in income taxation. She is also affiliated with the Harvard Institute for International Development. In this capacity, she is presently involved in advising the governments of Malawi and Indonesia with respect to income tax reform. Her other research in the past year has included an analysis of the taxation of debt in the financial climate of the 1980s.

Paul A. Tattersall is Vice President of Reuters America, Inc. for the Globex Project. While Tattersall was President of the Minneapolis Grain Exchange from 1982 to 1987, he became an advocate of on-line electronic trading. Prior to that he was employed by the *Minneapolis Star and Tribune* from 1975 to 1982 as a Senior Vice President responsible for six subsidiaries in the newspaper and television business. Between 1971 and 1975 he was employed by *The Washington Post* in data processing and general management positions. He worked for IBM from 1958 through 1971 with experience in systems, marketing and management. Tattersall has been a member of the Board of Directors of the Minnesota Grain Exchange, the National Futures Association and the Minnesota Orchestra. He received a B.A. from Wesleyan University in 1956 and an M.B.A. from Columbia University Graduate School of Business in 1958.

John Wall has been Executive Vice President, Marketing and Market Operations of the National Association of Securities Dealers, Inc. (NASD) since 1982. He is responsible for the overall development of the markets for securities through NASD services to investors, issuers and the securities industry. He heads the NASDAQ market, the second largest securities market in the U.S. and the third largest in the world and is charged with market policy dealing with the recently proposed Electronic Bulletin Board and the International PORTAL Market for dealing in non-registered securities. Wall began his career with the NASD in 1965 as an Examiner and subsequently became the Associate Director of the New York office. He was transferred in 1973 to run the new Department of Enforcement (which encompassed activities relating to SIPC, Market Surveillance, Anti-Fraud, and Automated Financial Reporting) in addition to directing the operations of the NASD's District Offices throughout the country. In October 1974, he became Vice President of the Surveillance Department, and then in July 1976 became Senior Vice President of the newly created Compliance Division. Prior to joining the NASD, Wall worked in the field of public relations and on Wall Street. He is an alumnus of the University of Notre Dame. He serves on the Board of Directors of the Options Clearing Corporation.

Foreword

Since the dawn of the Information Age, midway through this century, technology has begun a worldwide upheaval as complete as the transformation brought by the Industrial Revolution in the last century.

Those who lived through the Industrial Revolution were ambivalent about the way it changed their lives. They welcomed rising wages and the greater availability of consumer goods, but worried about the social dislocations that accompanied the benefits. Most troubling was the general feeling that these changes were beyond the control of the people affected. Technology seemed to control change.

We can detect important parallels today, as the new communications and computing technologies change finance and nearly every other aspect of society. Workers and consumers enjoy the speed, convenience and low cost of networked computing. Technology allows participants in financial markets to gather information in real time, analyze it quickly and act on that information by tapping a keyboard—all at a fraction of the cost of a few years ago.

Like earlier technological advances, however, the networking of the economy seems to bring as many disadvantages as benefits. While traders are now able to buy or sell at any hour that suits them, communicating with markets around the world, they are also "on call" 24 hours a day, reacting to market movements that will not wait until nine o'clock Monday. At a geopolitical level, the interconnected markets undercut old notions of national sovereignty, as Walter Wriston has observed.

> Our new international financial regime differs radically from its precursors in that it was not built by politicians, economists, central bankers or finance ministers, nor did high-level international conferences produce a master plan. It was built by technology . . .
>
> The entire globe is linked electronically, with no place to hide. Finance ministers who believe in sound monetary and fiscal policies are starting to

perceive that the new technology is on their side. And politicians who wish to evade responsibility for their imprudent actions on fiscal and monetary matters correctly perceive that the new Information Standard will punish them.

As the Industrial Revolution did, the advent of the Information Standard makes many people feel that life is plunging ahead, out of control. The public perceives that technology ran amok in the Crash of 1987. In the news media, computerized trading is a standard explanation for large movements of market prices. Fate and fortune seem to depend on electronic blips over high-speed transmission lines.

In 1988, The Annenberg Washington Program in Communications Policy Studies and the J.L. Kellogg Graduate School of Management, both of Northwestern University, commenced a project to dig beneath these perceptions and study the actual impact of communications and computing technologies on the financial markets. We brought together leading members of the financial, regulatory and academic communities. This volume represents their thinking. As might be expected, they did not arrive at a consensus. But I am sure that you will find the authors' views controversial, informative and insightful.

Newton N. Minow
Director
The Annenberg Washington Program
of Northwestern University
May 1990

AN OVERVIEW

The Competitive World of Electronic Trading

Daniel R. Siegel
University of Washington

The world's financial markets are undergoing profound changes stemming from advances in communications and computing technologies. Older trading systems that rely on personal contact between traders are being replaced by computer networks, in which traders throughout the world communicate and trade over microwaves and optical fibers. GLOBEX traders in Chicago can execute trades as easily with traders in Europe and Asia as they can with traders sitting in the next office. The move toward electronic trading appears inexorable. Over the last decade, there has been a proliferation of new financial markets throughout the world. Very few of these markets have chosen to use older trading methods based upon personal contract between traders. Similarly, established markets such as the New York Stock Exchange (NYSE), the Chicago Mercantile Exchange (CME), and the Chicago Board of Trade (CBOT) are spending millions of dollars to automate their markets. There is also a great deal of diversity in the types of trading systems being introduced. This diversity involves everything from the level of anonymity of traders to the level of automation in execution. Unfortunately, the diversity in types of trading systems results not necessarily from a diversity of needs, but from great uncertainty about how communications and computing technologies can best facilitate the trading process. Because of this, the 1990s will see a fiercely competitive environment, in which a few surviving systems will best meet the needs of the financial world.

Economic Forces Behind Automation

The trend toward the use of advanced communications and computing technologies in financial markets is apparent throughout the world and across financial instruments. On GLOBEX, traders can execute buy and sell orders for futures from terminals throughout the world. Electronic futures trading also takes place on the Tokyo Stock Exchange through the Computer Assisted Order Routing and Execution System (CORES). Similarly, the Tokyo International Financial Futures Exchange (TIFFE), the Swiss Options and Financial Futures Exchange (SOFFEX), the London Futures and Options Exchange (FOX), and the New Zealand Futures Exchange are automated.

Automation is hardly confined to futures trading. On the NYSE, traders can submit buy and sell orders for equities electronically, through the SUPER-DOT (Designated Order Turnaround) system. The system also executes small orders. The Tokyo Stock Exchange uses its CORES to trade all but the most highly capitalized stocks and the Toronto Stock Exchange (TSE) has a similar system called the Computer Assisted Trading System (CATS). On the Chicago Board Options Exchange (CBOE), there is automatic execution through the Retail Automatic Execution System (RAES) for small orders for options on equities. A similar system, called Auto-Ex is used to execute small options orders on the American Stock Exchange (Amex). Every year, exchanges add new systems to this orgy of acronyms.

Automation is also not confined to exchanges. The National Association of Securities Dealers Automated Quotation (NASDAQ) system uses a complex communications and computer network to link market-makers in over-the-counter equities and to execute small orders. Similarly, stocks (from around the world) are traded in London using the Stock Exchange Automation Quotation (SEAQ) system. With the Reuters Dealing 2000 system, traders can execute foreign exchange spot and forward transactions over a computer network. Reuters also maintains a system called Instinet, over which institutional investors trade blocks of equities.

Why has there been such a rush to automate the trading in financial instruments in recent years? The major reason for the existence of exchanges is that they make it easy for those who wish to trade to find each other and then trade. This involves routing orders to the exchange, executing them, and disseminating price information to potential traders. The costs of any resources used in this process are ultimately borne by those who trade and any exchange adopting technologies that reduce these costs will gain an advantage in attracting business. Similar advantages will accrue to any exchange adopting technologies that more efficiently inform potential traders of its trading activity.

The adoption of new technologies to facilitate trade is a recurring story. The invention of the telegraph greatly increased the speed and accuracy of routing orders to Wall Street. Perhaps more importantly, it opened the markets to potential traders all over the U.S. and ultimately the world. Similarly, by facilitating dissemination of prices over the ticker tape, the telegraph gave potential traders more up-to-date information with which to make their decisions. The telephone, by allowing instantaneous two-way communication between broker and customer and broker and exchange floor, continued the trend toward automation of order routing. Computers have for several decades revolutionized the "back-office" function, so that it is easier to keep track of the trading that occurs for clearing and accounting; any errors and inefficiencies in record-keeping hamper the trading function of exchanges.

While the use of sophisticated communications and computing technologies in the order routing and back-office functions of trading in financial instruments is well-established, it is only recently that exchanges have begun to experiment with automating the function of matching buyers and sellers: order execution. Consider the case of the futures markets in Chicago and New York, where trading occurs in pits on the exchange floor through a system called open outcry. An institutional client considering a futures trade can see the price of the last trade in his office on a computer screen. However, to find the current bid (sell) and ask (buy) prices, he must call his broker, who is sitting at a desk on the exchange floor. The broker then determines, through hand signals to a partner in the trading pit, the bid and ask prices and relays this information to the client. If the client chooses to trade at the current price, he tells the broker, who writes up an order slip and time-stamps it. The broker then uses hand signals to relay the order to another broker who is in the actual trading pit. This pit broker presents the order to other traders in the pit by voice and hand signals. If another trader agrees to take the opposite side of the transaction, then both traders write down the quantity and price on a card, along with the initials of the other trader (taken from a large badge worn by each trader). The pit broker then tells an exchange official in the pit of the trade and signals a confirmation to the broker at the desk. The desk broker confirms the trade with the client and the exchange official relays the information to a clerk, who sends the information to a network connected to information vendors such as Reuters and Telerate. The price for the trade is then sent to computer screens throughout the world. Periodically, each brokerage firm collects the cards from its pit brokers and inputs the trades into its computers. These computers manage the brokerage firm's paper work and are linked directly to the computers of the organization that clears and settles the trades, the clearinghouse.

Thus, while the order routing (to the broker's desk on the floor), information dissemination, and back-office functions use modern communications and computing technologies, the actual trading takes place in a technologically primitive manner. Similarly, trading in equities on the major exchanges takes place in large part between brokers on an exchange floor.

How have such apparently primitive systems of trading survived? For the most part, they have worked extraordinarily well. For example, while the process of executing a futures order appears to be cumbersome and labor-intensive, it is extremely efficient. The entire process takes only a matter of seconds. As a result, huge volumes of orders can be handled using the existing system.

That the current floor-based order execution systems have as a whole performed well does not, however, mean that they are the best of all possible systems. These systems are not the result of a planning process in which designers produced the optimal system from scratch, taking into account current trading volumes and the available technology. Both the futures and equity systems now in place have evolved from other systems that were designed in a different era, with different trading volumes and different (and more primitive) technologies.

What will continue to spur the development of electronic order execution is that even very small cost advantages in trading are of value to users of the market. A small per contract or per share savings can add up very quickly given the massive portfolios managed by today's institutional investors. For example, a common question that prospective futures clients ask brokers is the location of the broker's desk on the trading floor. Sight-lines into the pit are critical because they determine how quickly a broker will be able to operate when markets are moving quickly.

And there are trading costs associated with current order execution systems that are much larger than the cost of losing several seconds because of bad sight-lines on a trading floor. On the NYSE, there was great dissatisfaction with the performance of the specialist system during the week of October 19, 1987. On the futures exchanges, there is the chronic problem of out-trades, which occur when the clearinghouse cannot locate trading cards making up both sides of a transaction. Recently, there have been allegations that traders manipulate the open outcry futures trading system to skim profits from customers. Finally, there is the inefficiency of large numbers of people, each drawing a salary, performing the various functions of trading. All of these inefficiencies create costs ultimately borne by the trading public.

Diversity and Competition

The potential cost advantages of automating trading have been noticed by nearly every exchange in the world. As mentioned earlier, several stock exchanges have added automated order execution to their order routing systems for small orders. The most exciting trend, however, is that many exchanges are asking how systems can be designed from scratch that will optimally use modern technologies to trade modern instruments with today's (and tomorrow's) volumes.

Consider GLOBEX. GLOBEX seamlessly integrates order routing, order execution, back-office functions, and information dissemination. A institutional trader with a GLOBEX screen can see the current bid and ask prices from around the world and then place an order from the keyboard. A computer sends the order into the system and executes it according to price and time priority. Upon execution, the trader receives a confirmation and the information is sent to the clearinghouse and the trader's broker. Finally, the information is sent out to all GLOBEX terminals as well as to other information vendors.

Comparing this with our description of the open outcry system, many potential advantages become clear. First, there can be no out-trades, because the computer will not allow a trade to occur unless both sides of the transaction present themselves over the network. Second, many of the alleged trading violations under the open outcry system are impossible with GLOBEX. Further, there is an automatic audit trail that allows investigators to follow the trades of any individual. Third, the number of human hands through which the trade passes goes to zero. This is important, because while the costs of communications and computing will continue to drop, the price of manpower is likely to rise. Fourth, the speed of the execution will also continue to increase over time with technological improvement, while the human-based system has probably reached its limit.

The electronic trading systems that other exchanges are developing throughout the world are also taking advantage of technology to lower the costs of trading. Here are some of the most important issues that designers of electronic trading systems are facing.

Anonymity

There is disagreement among designers of electronic systems as to the whether trading should be anonymous. Orders entered into GLOBEX and SOFFEX carry no indication of who placed the order. At the other extreme, the CATS system on the Toronto Stock Exchange includes a code number for the broker in each order. Similarly, with the AURORA system being developed by the CBOT and the Automated Pit Trading (APT) system being developed by the London International Financial Futures Exchange (LIFFE), traders will consummate trades on a computer screen by moving a mouse over to an electronic "badge" with the initials a specific trader. The Tokyo Stock Exchange's CORES provides information on aggregate trading activity for each trader. Those advocating anonymous trading claim that a fairer system will result from "blind" trading, because everyone will have a fair shot at any trade. Those advocating revealing trader information counter that traders feel more comfortable knowing who is on the other side of the trade. Each side claims that their approach will attract more traders.

Large Order Execution

A major worry of a trader considering taking part in a large trade is that the opposite party is trading on information. This is especially true in the equity markets where there is great potential for specialized information about a firm's stock. As a result, it is common in the equity markets for those offering large blocks of stock to use brokers to find opposite parties with which to trade. Part of the "mating dance" involves telephone conversations in which both parties try to establish the trading motives of the other side. Many believe that an equity market that does not allow this type of negotiation will fail. This does not appear to be as large a problem in futures markets, where the potential for specialized information is smaller.

Access

An important issue is who will have access to the computer that matches bids and offers. In principle, every potential trader could have a terminal and directly enter trades. GLOBEX allows a select group of institutional investors access to trade for their own accounts. Most exchanges, however, have chosen to limit access to brokers and exchange members. In many ways this is a turf battle. Brokers bristle at the possibility that they will no longer be needed in the trading process and exchange members like the trading edge that comes from direct access to the system.

Order Book Display

While some orders (called market orders) from clients direct the broker to trade as quickly as possible, many orders specify that a trade should occur only if prices move to a certain point. For example, a client may enter an order to buy 100 Treasury Bond futures contracts if the price rises to 95. While there are quite a number of these types of orders, they all have the characteristic that they direct action only at prices away from the current market price. The collection of these orders is called the order book. One issue that designers of automated trading systems are concerned about is whether the order book should be available to potential traders and if so, how much of it.

The trend seems to be toward displaying at least part of the order book. The idea is that the order book gives potential traders information about the depth and liquidity of the market. Systems such as GLOBEX and CORES display the order book. NASDAQ has a system in which only some traders have access to the book. AURORA and APT are currently being designed to operate much like the open outcry system, in which each broker holds a confidential personal order book. In many ways this issue is closely related to the issue of access. To the extent that there is limited access to trading screens, there will be limited access to the order book.

Global Competitive Pressures

From the foregoing discussion, it is clear that the world is entering the 1990s with a confusing and diverse array of trading systems. At the CME, contracts that are traded during the day through open outcry are traded off-hours on GLOBEX. The same equities that are traded using a floor and a specialist system at the NYSE and Amex are traded in more automated regional exchanges such as the Pacific Stock Exchange (PSE) and the Cincinnati Stock Exchange (CSE), as well as on the proprietary Instinet system and SEAQ in London. And, as we have seen, even automated futures trading systems have significant differences.

It seems highly unlikely that the financial markets will be willing to sustain this type of diversity for several reasons. First, after the trading world gains some experience with the systems, it will become clear which trading systems are the most efficient. While it may not be true that the same trading system will be the best for different types of instruments such as equities and futures, it is probably true that there is an ideal type of system within a type of financial instrument.

Second, electronic trading makes it very easy to add trading of a new instrument to an existing system, because it simply involves adding some software. Once it becomes clear that a given system best meets the needs of the financial community, the exchange with that system can try to lure trading from other exchanges. This type of switching can happen very quickly. In 1988, the London FOX began automated trading of a sugar futures contract that had been dominated by the Paris Futures Exchange (PFE) for years. Within one year, the FOX had become the primary market for the contract. While those exchanges that currently dominate trading in a given financial instrument will have an initial advantage in retaining trading volume, efficiency of trading will determine trading location over time.

Third, there is considerable value to the financial community to standardization. It is very expensive for the users of markets to maintain the hardware and software necessary to trade over several different trading systems. For example, institutional users of futures contracts very likely will trade both Treasury Bond futures at the CBOT and Eurodollar and Index futures at the CME. These same users objected vehemently when the CME and the CBOT presented specifications for radically different automated trading systems. As a result, the two exchanges are currently involved in discussions to standardize their electronic trading systems.

Impediments to Competing

In the competitive environment of the 1990s, each system that hopes to become dominant will face one or both of two important impediments: government regulation and groups determined to retain special access to the market. While most regulators of trading in financial instruments espouse support for automation, there is a prevalent fear of automation among the public. For example, there is widespread public suspicion that computerized trading of equities on Wall Street has led to increased volatility in U.S. stock markets. There is a similar feeling that is growing in Japan. This kind of feeling has in the past led to limits on the use of automated trading such as the "circuit breakers" installed after October of 1987.

Another type of regulation has no relation, at first glance, to automation. For example, the Securities and Exchange Commission (SEC) has recently proposed that stock index futures trading be regulated by the SEC and not the Commodity Futures Trading Commission (CFTC). One possible outcome would be that the SEC could impose the same kinds of margins on stock index futures trading that exist for trading of equities. In a world of electronic trading, however, this will simply drive trading to a Japanese or European system where the government does not impose such stringent regulations. Thus, the global links provided by the new automated trading systems make the likelihood of driving trading to a "flag of convenience" much higher; traders in New York can just as easily trade on a system sitting in Japan or Europe as in Chicago or New York. In fact, a large portion of trading in European equities is on SEAQ in London. There is an important precedent. Taxes and regulation of U.S. depository institutions created the Eurodollar market by driving U.S. dollar-denominated deposits to unregulated accounts, virtually overnight.

Besides the government, proponents of new electronic systems face constituencies that are greatly alarmed at the prospect of the trading public having direct access to the markets. The rhetoric of these constituencies is usually that unless a certain group gets a trading "edge" with special access to trading, there will be no one to provide liquidity. This argument is often made by those supporting the open outcry futures system and the specialist system for equities; those on the floor get an edge by observing the behavior of other traders. However, liquidity is ultimately determined by the trading public and that public will prefer to trade on systems where it will have the best possible access to the trading system. The Tokyo Stock Exchange's CORES supports extremely liquid markets in both equities and interest rate futures without giving any edge to a specified group of market makers. For example, the Yen-denominated long term government bond futures contracts trades a dollar volume well in excess of the highly successful U.S. Treasury Bond futures contract on the CBOT. Various parties make markets when profit opportunities arise. Interestingly, the Tokyo

Stock Exchange recently moved 100 high capitalization stocks from floor trading to CORES, with no apparent loss of liquidity.

Those creators of trading systems that possess the political skills to overcome these two impediments to competing will survive.

A Scenario for the Year 2000

The most likely scenario is that by the year 2000, financial instruments of the same type (i.e., futures or equities) from around the world will be traded over a single global network operating 24 hours a day. This network will either operate under regulations agreed upon by all of the major trading nations or will operate virtually free of regulation. The history of international regulatory cooperation favors the latter. There will be a limited role for brokers, because the bulk of trading will be done by institutional investors with direct access to the trading network. Clearing will be linked electronically, so that a trader's overall trading position will be monitored constantly by agencies guaranteeing performance of that trader. There will be no designated market-makers or other entities with special access to the market. Liquidity will be provided by a variety of traders, who will monitor bid-ask spreads on a real-time basis searching for profit opportunities. Finally, the costs of running these networks will continue to drop as communications and computing technologies become cheaper and more sophisticated. With falling costs, there will be a continual increase in trading volume and continual financial innovation.

The Intersection of Technology and Financial Services

Paul F. Glaser
Citicorp

Staggering changes in the financial services sector have been stimulated recently by changing technology. Along with the changes have come well-publicized problems attributed to the technically-driven aspects of finance. Financial markets in the 1990s appear to be riskier than the markets of the 1980s. So the ways in which market participants have dealt with these risks and what they have learned from the recent behavior of the markets is crucial to the future application of technology in all sectors of the economy. With proper foresight, market participants will be able to manage new risks by merging technology and financial theory in order to spawn innovation that meets real economic needs and that efficiently addresses regulatory problems.

Isaac Asimov has said, "It was only with the coming of the Industrial Revolution that the rate of change became fast enough to be visible in a single lifetime." Since the Industrial Revolution, of course, each wave of technological development has accelerated the pace. In the past, few arenas have experienced more accelerated change than finance. But because it took the financial world so long to enter the machine age, the pace of change in finance now seems exceptionally bewildering. It is true that on balance, technology is extremely beneficial, giving both consumers and corporate customers a broad range of new products and services at a reasonable cost. But because of this rapid acceleration, technology is often viewed as detrimental to the rational function of the marketplace.

For example, some market participants believe the advance of financial technology has bizarre social consequences. It was not until 1973 that women were allowed on the floor of the London Stock Exchange. That is remarkable in itself. What is even more remarkable is that they are not there anymore because the London Exchange now consists of a network of buyers and sellers who do business at computer terminals, much as with the NASDAQ system in the United States.

Other participants say the perceived influence of technology is much more disturbing. During the adjustment of October 19, 1987, the stock market lost about one-third of its value over a three-day period. Some market-watchers blame the derivative marketplace—technology-driven products like options and futures—for causing the market to plummet. Whatever the real cause, large numbers of customers abandoned the stock market because they lost confidence in the battle against the effectiveness of computers in the market: an effect and a result which continues.

On a given day, it may be possible to point to certain downside market events and single out technology as the culprit. Looking back, however, makes the underlying conditions generally clearer: if technology is a problem, it is because it reflects human failings in concept, design, execution, judgment or motive. Advances in technology may allow market participants to try new strategies, or to try old strategies on a scale and at a speed that seem to change the nature of the task. But when scale and speed are increased, so are the associated risks.

Technological Risk and Technological Solutions

One way to measure technological risk is to determine whether or not it plays a significant role in pivotal market events. Questions about Black Monday, for example, have arisen primarily over two issues: the underlying capability of the settlement, clearing, and depository infrastructure used by the world's banks and exchanges, and the stability of the technology-based products and services offered by brokerage houses.

Market participants and regulators learned that, for the most part, the systems did perform well despite problems. With 85 percent accuracy, the New York Stock Exchange traded 600 million shares on both October 19 and 20, three times the level normally considered high. In Tokyo and London, the results were better still.

Although Black Monday rocked the financial markets, the experience was put to good use. The NYSE has equipped itself for one-billion share days. Major international market participants have formed a Group of Thirty to consider ways to reduce systemic risk by negotiating new global standards for clearing and settlement.

Another perceived risk is the existence of products and services that have drawn the most fire: derivative instruments, such as options and futures, that make program trading and portfolio insurance possible. Here the question of the chicken or the egg arises: would derivative products have existed without the computer? Would a market adjustment have occurred without an options and futures market?

Now, new issues emerge. Will added capacity and the growing sophistication of trading programs combine to make the next adjustment more efficient than the last? Will it all be over in an hour?

A celebrated case that illustrates the market's underlying capacity was the failure of Bank of New York's government securities clearing operations on November 21, 1985. The bank installed a new software release that led to a breakdown of its connection to the Federal Reserve Board's (FRB) securities wire. The FRB continued to receive securities and to debit the bank's reserve account. However, Bank of New York was unable to deliver the securities and accept payment from customers who were buying them. It took a $23 billion overnight loan from the New York FRB to keep the system going. This incident was clearly a software problem that originated with human programmers.

However, just as technology has the capacity to expose underlying weakness in an instant, the very speed of exposure can lead to speedy correction. It was estimated when the breakdown occurred that a complete overhaul of 700 relevant programs would have taken approximately 16 hours. That may not sound like a lot, but in the financial market it is a lifetime. So the bank tried a temporary fix called a "patch," which didn't work. After the crisis, the program was fixed overnight.

It can be argued that the Bank of New York situation was not a serious financial problem because the FRB held securities equal to the value of the bank's cash deficit. But the crisis created fear in the hearts of bankers, brokers and regulators who tried to correct the underlying problems.

What would have happened if the bank had not solved the software problem for several more days? What if the database had been destroyed, unable to deliver offsetting instruments? What if a clearing and settlement bank had gone bankrupt in the middle of the crisis?

These questions are crucial not only to financial institutions but to all businesses—say an airline reservation system—that rely heavily on information technology. Solutions for these arcane problems remain a high priority for financial institutions and regulators, as well as for vendors and customers.

Technology and the Operation of Financial Markets

The technological revolution and its resultant crises have affected virtually every aspect of the finance market. Satellites have allowed New York financial institutions to move their back offices to out-of-the-way places like Ireland, South Dakota, and Hong Kong. It means the world has become a single global marketplace. Starting the day in Tokyo, picking up in London and finishing in New York, there is a continuous flow of information that can be translated instantly into financial values. Earthquakes, floods, war, peace, and late-breaking government economic policies all can be factored into prices in real time.

But the benefits of this increased capacity are distributed unevenly, of course. The fact that small investors were shut out of the market during the peak volume period on October 19 is unacceptable to those with a sense of fair market play. In finance, as in every other technological enterprise, those who can invest in the requisite systems utilize technology more effectively to gain market share, improve cost efficiency, and probably gain the first shot at the best deals. On balance, however, technology has been a great leveler, and its benefits seem to devolve eventually to small investors as evenly as to large investors.

While these examples show top-down technological progress, progress also ascends from the consumer level upward. Home computer users can invest in virtually any market or any instrument from their homes. Future generations of automatic teller machines will empower consumers with greater accuracy and efficiency than ever before.

That is important because the volume in today's markets is staggering. Visa did its first billion-dollar day in 1989. World capital flows every day are 30 to 50 times larger than the volume of world trade. Half a trillion dollars changes hands each day over automated systems. This volume would not have been possible if financial institutions depended on clerks instead of computers. If they had depended on clerks, the incidence of error probably would have invalidated the system, even at much lower volumes.

The real cost of processing and transmitting information has dropped more than 95 percent in the last 25 years, which means a vast quantity of data can be stored and accessed quickly and cheaply.

Computerized transmission has changed the marketplace too. The banking industry used to be the only sector that knew enough about American companies to lend them money. Now, investors can acquire that information with the push of a button and buy corporate commercial paper at rates lower than those at which banks can lend. This efficiency can save money for individual borrowers as well as for corporations: home mortgages have fallen 100 basis points in cost relative to Treasury bills since the advent of mortgage-backed securities.

Technology also has changed the way Americans save, a trend with which most bankers are, unfortunately, very familiar. Today, the leading 300 institutional money managers in the United States command over $2 trillion in pension and mutual funds, a sum equal to about two-thirds of the total assets of all 14,000 commercial banks in the United States. The economies that result from these changes are significant. Twenty people with a computer can manage a $10 billion fund; a $10 billion bank, on the other hand, may have to pay the salaries of a staff of 5,000 employees to do the same task.

Technology and the New Finance

Few would argue with the desirability of the productivity gained from technological progress. It is the wizardry of finance theory that unsettles both the public and the policy-makers. But technology and financial theory can be re-combined to transform not only the markets, but the regulations that govern them as well.

Technology has given birth to the development of "new finance," which means that advances in financial theory can be brought to market with the aid of computers. It is now possible to unbundle, or segregate, investments into various components according to the amount of risk they carry, and then sell them to investors with different needs and different appetites for risk.

So theoretically at least, it is possible to create a corporate bond that is almost as safe as a U.S. Treasury bond, free of foreign-exchange risk, credit risk, vulnerability to interest-rate fluctuations, and even liquidity risk. It happens through a combination of currency swaps, interest rate swaps, forward contracts, caps, and floors.

Technology also allows investors to spread these risks among many geographic areas, economic sectors, or financial instruments. A prudent investor might have stocks, bonds, and precious metals. He might also have part of a big bank's credit card receivables or its mortgage portfolio. These securities are part of an ever-increasing proliferation of products that are introduced this rapidly only with the speed made possible by technology.

Financial technology does not represent only finance any more than money management represents only green pieces of paper. Financial technology, ultimately, is about the things we make, eat, drive, live in, and do for one another. While we can price individual items—say a new car, or a chicken leg—the enterprises that supply these products are often so large and so diverse that pricing the enterprise in aggregate is a much more complex task. Or at least it was.

With new technology, it is far easier to set a price and attract buyers for the largest corporations in the world. Take big corporate takeovers, which are nothing new. J.P. Morgan bought out Andrew Carnegie in 1900, and then added six other steel companies to form U.S. Steel. He got a total price comparable in constant dollars to the buyout of R. J. Reynolds. But life was simpler then. Morgan asked Carnegie to name his price and he wrote it on a slip of paper: $480 million.

In today's economic environment, no one person can set a price on a public company with that kind of speed and simplicity. But with modern technological number-crunching it can be done quite expeditiously, and dozens of deals can be brought to market at the same time. Whether or not these deals are a good thing, at least some of the money invested has made American companies more competitive and has created more economic value.

While most leveraged buyouts probably are founded on good economics, the fact that they take advantage of by-now widely publicized flaws in the tax code has not gone unnoticed. It is risky to pass judgment on these deals, but it is safe to say their financiers are motivated by the chance to make a profit and every regulatory mechanism—taxation, capital requirement, or any impediment to the efficient functioning of a market—creates an incentive for circumvention. The new technology gives financiers the tools. They can be dishonest like Ivan Boesky or they can be merely adventurous like the wizards at Shearson Lehman Hutton who announced the Unbundled Stock Unit (USU) in 1988. It shows clearly how advances in financial theory, powered by technology, can be brought to bear on both regulatory and market forces.

The USU is structured to help companies avoid being bought out, thereby increasing share prices and capturing some of the value created by disparities in the tax code. This instrument divides common equity into components that function variously like bonds, to pay interest at the current dividend rate; preferred stock, to capture any rise in the dividend; and warrants, wherein value appreciates like common stock. These units are sold in combination with one another, or separately, to investors with different needs and appetites for risk. The issuing companies benefit as well: the USU reduces their susceptibility to takeover while redressing the inequities of the tax code.

The USU example contains one of the most compelling implications emerging from the new technology. Technology allows practitioners of the financial arts to translate theory into action with great speed. Inevitably glitches appear. Volumes overwhelm systems. There are software problems or operational problems. But to date at least, these problems have been resolved with relative ease and without long-term damage to the economy.

The financial industry in one sense is the purest market that ever existed, and it is because of technology. When an innovation like mortgage-backed securities appears, specialist teams are quickly staffed and equipped at any bank that wants to get into the market. New hardware is deployed and software is written to support the instrument within months. Compare that to the speed of innovation at General Motors, for example. It will take seven years to bring its Saturn automobile to market; so much change can occur in seven years that the Saturn may not seem very new by the product rollout date.

Technology and Competition

There are other implications inherent in financial technology. Innovation leads to competition, competition leads to saturation, and this in turn leads to greater innovation. Some firms forge ahead, leaving to others the saturated lower-margin businesses. This market churning inevitably happens much faster in finance than in other sectors, and this rate will continue in the future. That is because it remains true that manufacturing ideas with the help of computers is easier than shaping thousands of pounds of steel and plastic into an automobile.

No one can really tell from which direction the next breakthrough innovation will come. When the transcontinental railroads were built, they opened up the American continent. Ultimately, however, the railroad rights of way may have been just as valuable for another reason: they were used to string telegraph lines as well. In our speedier technological age, we are finding dualities that are just as interesting, and we are finding them sooner and much more often.

For example, many countries distinguish between telegraph and telephone transmission. But the distinction between what constitutes a voice transmission and what constitutes a telegraph transmission is in serious question because voice now is digitized and transmitted by means that are considered telegraphic.

Technology and Regulation

Advances like these give headaches to industrial regulators. Their task now has to be the determination of effective regulation when innovation runs so far ahead of public policy that the product being regulated can not be defined. Regulators are being forced to make some tough calls on the nature of the products: is it defined by the medium, such as telegraph or telephone? Or is it defined by the content of the message? The stream of electrons pouring across international boundaries can be what we think of as money, which is subject to control in most of the world, or it can be information that leads to better use of money.

For example, when Soviet premier Mikhail Gorbachev came to New York and announced plans to demobilize a significant portion of the Soviet forces in Eastern Europe, the markets rallied. One theory was that lowering Soviet troop strength would reduce military pressure on the West and eventually lead to smaller U.S. budget deficits.

This may have been wishful thinking, and the markets returned to reality in short order; but money was made in the initial flurry, as it often is. The question is, what should happen to a hard-working reporter who comes up with an advance copy of Gorbachev's speech and calls his broker instead of his editor? What should happen if an international news-gathering organization forms a trading arm and requires that all legitimate news be filtered through traders before being released on the wire?

So there is no doubt that information is money. That is why there are no pay telephones at race tracks, at least until the arrival of the portable cellular phone. But we have reached a point in history when the issue of a free press has a place in the discussion of fair and orderly markets. If the issue is corruption, it seems that automated systems make people more accountable, not less. The recent scandal that hit the Chicago commodities exchanges is a case in point. If there had been less shouting and more automation on the trading floor, the resulting audit trail might have turned up the abuses much sooner. Regulators can work with the financial sector in the same way internal auditors function in technologically advanced corporations. With information available in real time, expert systems can monitor transactions and flag those that appear problematic.

The real challenge is defining and regulating what is legal. Today, savings accounts are masquerading as insurance policies, checking accounts masquerade as mutual funds, and commercial loans are packaged as securities. Regulators, meanwhile, must regulate institutions by financial sector, not by function, leaving jurisdictions muddled. Each new regulation is a challenge to be overcome, with great profit to the wizard who comes up with a way to do it. The time has come to step back, look at the new financial world that technology has created, and take a much broader view of the markets.

Implications for U.S. Competitiveness

How the nation plans for the inevitable market transformation will have crucial implications for the competitiveness of U.S. financial institutions, both nationally and internationally. For example, securitization of asset-backed loans could come to rival balance-sheet lending and traditional debt securities in the next five to ten years, at levels four to five times higher. This places extremely heavy burdens on the technology-supported operating bases of banks, on top of the support necessary for their conventional loans. Unless banks expand their operational capabilities to handle this growing market, they will end up as secondary players.

Competition is no less global in finance than in anything else. If the United States refuses to innovate, whether because of regulation or because financial institutions fail to invest in the future, the markets will go on evolving without us. In fact, the United States has not begun to approach the theoretical limits of technology in finance because those limits are a moving target. Even without some unforeseen breakthrough, computer technology will progress at a rate greater than the factor of two every four years that has been demonstrated over the past 25 years. Thus, we can expect profound advances in other technologies which, in turn, will have profound effects on financial services.

Technology and Meeting Customer Needs

Much of the technology available today is limited by the fact that Americans do not really like to use machines. They want to communicate with machines in very ordinary ways, to speak or write or wave their arms. By the turn of the century, devices that have the ability to do this in some fashion will be in everyday use. Everyone will be computer literate.

Computers will be able to discuss finance with customers and staff. This can be particularly useful when it comes to handling complaints, because the computer will be programmed to respond only to the substance of the complaint and not to the colorful language that sometimes goes with it. These same computers will be able to read and perform natural-language processing within limited domains, obviating the need for human intervention.

The extensive power of the computer also will support expert systems capable of monitoring external events, allowing them to seize marketing, sales, investment, and trading opportunities in real time. The systems supported by advanced optimization and approximation techniques will generate significant improvements in the prediction of customer behavior, the detection of fraudulent transactions, and the selection of profitable investment strategies. Such systems will be capable of supporting all financial market participants by evolving into expert advisors who do not sleep or take coffee breaks.

But we will continue to encounter problems: periodically we may be constrained by our capacity to absorb available technology; market conditions may reveal weaknesses, whether in capacity, in the Bank of New York example, or in the conception of what customers want, in the example of Shearson Lehman's Unbundled Stock Unit.

The issue of whether reliance on machines will place the market beyond anyone's control also will become a larger issue. There seem to be no systems in operation today that are beyond the control of intelligent humans on a macro scale. On a micro scale, however, there are programs which, when set in motion, do not allow for intervention without seriously affecting the outcome. Because of the diversity of the financial markets and the uncertainty of the effects of external events, those who rely completely on machines will be subject to considerable risk. Understanding the market and the capability of machines will lead the human decision maker to define the limits of unattended activity, which optimizes man/machine performance.

Relative to the markets, most Americans have reasonable fears about new ways of doing things that can be dispelled over time. The unfamiliar becomes commonplace. Technologists are in a continuous race to keep up with financial theorists and bring new systems on-line to support new markets. Ultimately, however, technology only reflects what is happening in the financial markets, bearing both glad tidings and bad news, each more efficiently. To those who are inclined to blame the messenger, the market makes no more sense now than it ever did. From a customer point of view, whether consumer or corporation, they now have more direct, on-line control over their finances and they will have still more in the future.

Conclusion

Certainly newspaper headlines, as well as the balance sheets and annual reports of many organizations, periodically reflect the application of technology gone wrong. The successes may not feature technology quite so prominently. Whether the news is good or bad, however, technology is only part of the story. It cannot succeed if it is applied for its own sake. The real test lies in whether or not customer needs are met, with or without technology, in innovative, cost-effective ways. Technology may be part of the problem, but it also is part of the solution.

An Overview of Automation of Information Dissemination and Trading in U.S. Securities Markets

David S. Ruder
U.S. Securities and Exchange Commission

Alden S. Adkins
U.S. Securities and Exchange Commission[*]

Information Dissemination Systems[1]

NASD

The National Association of Securities Dealers, Inc. (NASD) inaugurated NASDAQ, Inc., the automated quotation dissemination system in 1971 as a subsidiary.[2] While NASDAQ has changed during the years since its introduction,[3] it currently consists of three basic services.[4] Level I, which is disseminated through independent vendors to registered representatives and the general public, provides the best bid and ask quotation for each security quoted in the system. Level II provides a complete display of all market maker quotations. Level III

---

[*] The views expressed are those of David Ruder and Alden Adkins and do not necessarily represent those of the Securities and Exchange Commission, Commissioners, or Commission's staff.

disseminates the same quotation information as Level II, and permits the entry and updating of quotations.

NASDAQ, Inc. maintains the facilities that collect the quotations that are electronically entered by brokers from computer terminals in their offices, and then disseminated to vendors, market makers, and other subscribers for display on their video screens. In addition to establishing rules regarding quotation practices, NASDAQ prescribes the types of companies that can sell stocks on the NASDAQ system and determines by rule various financial, volume, and price criteria for those securities.[5] The NASD has proposed to allow real-time electronic dissemination through its system of information concerning NASDAQ securities that do not meet NASDAQ listing standards.[6]

The largest and most actively traded of these NASDAQ companies are designated as NASDAQ/National Market System securities.[7] For these securities, the NASD, in addition to quotation dissemination, provides dissemination of real-time last sale reports,[8] which are transmitted to NASDAQ by market makers. In this process, the market maker enters a price determined by subtracting or adding the markup or markdown implicit in the actual trade price. Trade reports must be submitted within 90 seconds of execution, and then are collected by the NASD and disseminated to vendors and to NASDAQ subscribers.[9]

Consolidated Transaction Reporting and Quotation Systems

The Consolidated Transaction Reporting System and the Consolidated Quotation System were established in 1974 and 1978[10] to provide electronic collection and dissemination of real-time trade and quotation reports in NYSE and Amex securities, as well as in certain regional securities. These systems are governed by plans developed jointly by participating markets and submitted for approval to the Securities and Exchange Commission (SEC).[11] Any changes to the plan over time also are submitted to the SEC for its review and approval under Rules 11Aa3-1 and 3-2. Participating markets include the NYSE, Amex, Boston (BSE), Cincinnati (CSE), Midwest (MSE), Philadelphia (Phlx), and Pacific (PSE) Stock Exchanges, and the NASD.[12] Their plans identify the securities for which trade and quotation reporting is provided, as well as describe procedures for the governance of these systems.

Under these plans, quotations and trade reports are submitted by participating markets electronically from the floors to a central processor, which is the Securities Industry Automation Corporation (SIAC) located in New York City. SIAC receives reports electronically. In the case of trade reports, it then transmits them in sequence electronically through high-speed and low-speed lines. The high-speed line is the instantaneous retransmission of trade reports to vendors and direct subscribers. This data can be accessed security-by-security via interrogation of a computer terminal. The low-speed line, or ticker, is the retransmission of the same price information at a speed readable by human eyes; the ticker is displayed on screens as a moving display of prices.[13] There are separate high- and low-speed lines for NYSE securities (Network A) and the Amex, and eligible regional securities (Network B). In the case of quotation information, SIAC collects the quotations from each market; calculates the best bid and offer based on price, size, and time of entry; and retransmits the information to vendors.

OPRA

All of the options exchanges are participants in the national market system plan for the collection and dissemination of quotation and last sale information for options.[14] The plan is administered by the Options Price Reporting Authority (OPRA), an organization composed of representatives from various options exchanges. Each exchange collects[15] and transmits to the OPRA system bids and offers at stated prices or limits with respect to options in which it provides a market. These are sufficient in number and timeliness to reflect the current state of the market of such options. OPRA, in turn, makes its quotation information available to securities vendors electronically and instantaneously. Changes to the plan are governed by Rule 11Aa3-2.

Order Routing and Execution

Exchanges

Regional exchanges have been leaders in developing automated small-order execution systems, for the most part because automated service is a good way to compete with primary markets. Four of the regional exchanges—BSE, Phlx, MSE and PSE—offer similar, but slightly different systems.[16]

The PSE was the first market to introduce an automated trading system. Its Comex system, now called SCOREX, was opened in 1969.[17] The SCOREX system automatically executes up to 1099 shares at the Intermarket Trading System (ITS) best bid or offer.[18] Brokers can route orders electronically to the PSE specialist through the system. When the order reaches the specialist, it is displayed to provide the specialist a 15-second opportunity to execute the order at a price better than the best ITS bid or offer. If the specialist fails to do so, the system automatically executes the order for the account of the specialist at the best ITS bid, if the order is a sell order, or the best offer, if the order is a buy order.[19] The system generates trade reports to the specialist, the broker, and the consolidated tape, providing a locked-in trade comparison. Specialists and individual brokers also can, and often do, agree to process orders larger than 1099 shares through the system.

The Phlx's system, or PACE,[20] automatically executes the best ITS bid or offer for orders of 599 shares or less. PACE also can be used to route orders of up to 1,099 shares, and to route even larger orders by agreement between the specialist and the broker. The PACE system, unlike SCOREX,[21] has no exposure time, so the system automatically executes the order without providing the specialist an opportunity to improve on the best ITS bid or offer—even if a superior price is available on the Phlx trading floor at the time the order is received.[22]

The MSE's system, MAX,[23] was introduced in 1981 and is similar to SCOREX. Guaranteed execution size at the best ITS bid or offer is 1099 shares, and there is a 15-second exposure period.[24] Specialists can agree to larger execution guarantees on an individual basis.

In 1988, the BSE instituted an automated order routing and execution system called BEACON,[25] which is similar to SCOREX and MAX. Execution size guarantees are 1299 for ITS stocks and 599 for certain other securities, and exposure time is 15 seconds.[26]

NYSE and Amex

In 1976, the NYSE instituted the Designated Order Turnaround System (DOT), another automated order routing system. Now called "SUPERDOT," this system routes orders electronically from brokers off the exchange to the specialist, and it allows member firms to route market and marketable limit orders[27] of up to 30,099 shares.

Today, SUPERDOT has been expanded beyond a simple order routing system to handle additional applications. Its Opening Automated Report Service (OARS) allows orders of up to 30,099 shares to be sent to a specialist prior to the opening. OARS stores these orders, then automatically and continuously pairs buy and sell orders, presenting the imbalance to each specialist up to the time he opens the stock for trading. After the specialist determines the opening price, in part based on any OARS imbalance, OARS automatically distributes within seconds execution reports to brokers for each order stored in OARS.

SUPERDOT also has execution capabilities. The specialist is expected to execute orders of up to 2,099 shares within two minutes. If he has not executed the order within three minutes, the system generates an execution for the specialist account at the NYSE quotation at the time the order was received by the system.[28] For orders of between 2,099 and 30,099 shares, no such execution capability is available currently.[29]

However, stocks that have an electronic order book no longer receive automated executions. This is because the electronic order book system usually results in executions in much less than three minutes. Electronic order display books now have been installed for most active NYSE stocks. Market orders electronically routed through SUPERDOT are displayed on a screen, either stored or executed, and reported back to the firm, all electronically.[30] One of the corollary benefits of the electronic display book is that it frees up NYSE printers for ITS commitments, so that queuing and delay problems associated with heavy traffic on NYSE printers are reduced.[31]

SUPERDOT has proven to be a very positive technological improvement for the NYSE. It has contributed to the trading efficiency of that market, and has permitted the exchange to handle greatly-increased volume. On an average day, SUPERDOT handles over 70 percent of NYSE trading. Since the October 1987 market break, the system has been enhanced to handle volumes of 600 million shares per day.

The Amex began operating its Post Execution Reporting (PER) System in 1977. The system generally is similar to SUPERDOT; but unlike the SUPER-DOT system, PER has no automatic execution capability. PER electronically routes market and limit orders of up to 2,000 shares from brokers off the floor to an Amex specialist. The specialist executes each trade, and the system then automatically routes execution reports back to the initiating broker.[32]

Program Trading/LIST Application of DOT

One of the more widely publicized automated routing applications in recent years has been the program trading application of the SUPERDOT system called LIST.[33] To facilitate the increasing use of portfolio trading by the institutional customers of its members and by its members,[34] the exchange adapted the SUPERDOT system to permit the entry from a brokerage firm office of simultaneous orders of up to 3,000 shares in over 450 different stocks. Now a broker off the floor can—electronically and almost instantaneously—transmit at the push of a button orders of up to 3,000 shares in over 450 stocks to separate specialist posts on the NYSE floor. These orders go to each specialist in the stock, and are executed individually in the NYSE's normal auction process.

In response to the problems encountered with program trading, the NYSE in October 1988 instituted preferential order routing for small orders and "side-car" procedures that use SUPERDOT capabilities.[35] The small order procedures provide preferential routing of orders numbering 2,099 shares or less after a 25-point Dow Jones Industrial Average (DJIA) move. The side-car procedure withholds program trade orders from the market for five minutes after a 12-point movement in the Standard & Poor's (S&P) 500 Index.[36] The orders are held aside by the specialist who, after five minutes, determines with the help of SUPERDOT whether or not imbalances exist and whether or not orders can be executed in an orderly way. If they cannot, the specialist halts trading in the stock, disseminates the imbalances and indications of interest,[37] and reopens the stock.[38]

The National Securities Trading System

The National Securities Trading System (NSTS) was put into operation by the CSE in 1978. It is the only wholly-automated exchange in the United States. NSTS permits CSE members to enter agency or principal orders electronically into the system where orders are stored, queued, and executed by the system's computer according to price and time priority.[39] The markets reflected in the system are updated and displayed instantaneously with the entry of new or revised orders, cancellations, or executions. It employs competitive market makers, although each security traded in the system has an assigned "designated dealer." This dealer is responsible for automatic execution of public agency market orders and marketable limit orders of up to 2,099 shares (the order size at which a guaranteed price exists), at the ITS best bid and offer. The designated dealer also must guarantee executions of public agency limit orders when the limit order price is penetrated by a transaction on another ITS market.[40]

NASD

SOES

When the NASD instituted NASDAQ, executions still were completed by telephone. In 1982, a surge in trading volume underscored the need for greater automation of the order execution process in the over-the-counter market.[41] With the increase in trading volume, the handling of routine small orders became an even bigger burden for market makers. So in 1985, the NASD introduced SOES, or the Small Order Execution System.[42] SOES, which provides automatic execution of certain trade sizes for retail customers at the best available NASDAQ quotation,[43] is restricted to orders entered by a broker on behalf of a non-broker customer ("agency orders").[44] In response to the difficulties customers experienced getting orders executed during the October 1987 market break, participation in SOES was made mandatory for market makers in NASDAQ/NMS securities.[45] If a market maker withdraws from SOES without an excuse—by failing to change quotations after its order exposure has been exhausted, for example—he is not allowed to act as a market maker in the security for 20 days. Participation in SOES is voluntary for market makers in other NASDAQ securities.

Executions for SOES orders that do not specify the market maker to whom the execution should be assigned ("preferred orders") are assigned to market makers at the best bid or offer on a rotating basis.[46] In addition to executing the orders, SOES automatically reports trade data to the clearing corporation.[47]

Limit Order File

In 1989, the NASD further automated trading with a centralized limit order file. This file stores all limit orders that are not executable immediately in SOES because they are not priced at the NASDAQ best bid or offer. It then executes them automatically based on time of entry if the best NASDAQ bid or offer reaches the limit order price. Like SOES, the system rotates executions among market makers at the best bid or offer (unless an order is preferenced), and also sends trade reports to the clearing corporation.[48]

Order Confirmation Transactions

The NASD also introduced a system called the Order Confirmation Transaction (OCT) System.[49] This system permits the negotiation through screen terminals of all-size trades between market makers and brokers as well as the automated, locked-in comparison of those trades once agreed on. For example, market makers can send orders to one another at their displayed quotations in NASDAQ. The system automatically permits the receiving market maker to accept or reject that order through a keyboard response. In effect, this system replaces negotiation by telephone with negotiation by computer links and screens. If the order is accepted, the system then generates locked-in comparison reports as well as trade reports for public dissemination.[50]

ITS

The Intermarket Trading System (ITS) introduced in 1978 is perhaps the most visible by-product of the 1975 Congressional mandate to establish an NMS.[51] ITS is a communications system that facilitates trading among competing markets by providing each market with order routing capabilities based on current quotation information. ITS links the exchanges and the NASD,[52] providing procedures for: 1.) display of composite quotation information at each of the participant markets so that brokers can determine more readily the best bid and offer available from any ITS market for a multiple-trade security; 2.) efficient routing of orders and administrative messages; 3.) measures to coordinate the opening of trading on ITS markets; 4.) trade-through protections of price priority for all orders entered in ITS markets;[53] and 5.) procedures for the governance of the system.[54]

Options

CBOE's Retail Automatic Execution System (RAES) opened in 1985 and provides automatic execution of trades of 10 contracts or less in index and stock options. Similarly, the Amex's Auto-Ex system, which was put into operation in

1985,[55, 56] also allows automated executions for orders of 10 contracts or less in index and stock options. Orders routed through RAES are executed at the displayed best bid or ask against market makers who elect voluntarily to participate as contra-brokers to RAES orders. Orders sent through Auto-Ex are executed at the displayed quotation against either the specialist or a registered options trader (ROT) in the crowd.[57]

Both CBOE and Amex impose certain obligations on participating market makers in order to ensure that executions are completed on a continuous basis. CBOE requires that market makers who sign onto RAES in groups participate in the system on a continuous basis for the duration of the week in which they sign on, and throughout the following expiration week. The Amex imposes somewhat less stringent obligations, requiring registered options traders to remain in the trading crowd for the majority of any business day in which they sign onto the system, and on the following expiration if the ROT has participated in Auto-Ex on any day of that week.

Because of substantial decreases in market maker participation in these systems during the October 1987 market break,[58] Amex and CBOE toughened their participation rules. Among other things, CBOE now may require market makers who are members of a trading crowd to sign onto RAES anytime there is inadequate RAES participation, absent a reasonable excuse.[59] Amex now requires the specialist to participate in Auto-Ex whenever the system is in use. It also requires market makers 1.) to remain in the trading crowd for an option once they have signed onto RAES and 2.) to sign off and back onto RAES only once during a trading day.[60]

PORTAL and SITUS

The Amex and the NASD also are working on automated systems that accommodate the institutional secondary trading of certain securities. These systems, called SITUS and PORTAL,[61] anticipate the SEC's rulemaking initiatives to permit the active resale of unregistered securities among institutions.[62] These systems are quotation dissemination systems combined with captive clearing operations to keep securities traded through the system in institutional hands only. As currently designed, however, these systems would not offer automated execution.

Proprietary Trading Systems

In addition to the automated systems run by self-regulatory organizations, non-SROs have developed proprietary trading systems in the U.S. The most notable is Instinet, which was developed in 1969 as an information system to permit trade negotiation among institutions. Since inception, Instinet has grown and developed more elaborate automated execution functions. Currently it is a network of computer terminals that permits the entry of trading interest indications by institutions or broker/dealers, as well as the execution against those indications by other Instinet subscribers automatically through a computerized system. Instinet operates internationally with terminals in several foreign countries.[63]

In addition to facilitating trading among Instinet subscribers, the system can be used by subscribers to trade against established exchange and NASDAQ quotations. This function initially was automated for smaller orders. But after the October 1987 market break, Instinet discontinued automated, small-order executions against exchange and NASDAQ dealers.

Instinet has a Crossing Network for basket trading by institutions.[64] Through this system, institutions electronically enter stock portfolio orders. The system pairs off buy and sell orders against each other, and then sends any unmatched orders to an exchange for execution or executes the residue against Instinet as principal. Jefferies and Company operates a similar system called POSIT.[65]

In the 1980s there has been increasing growth in a great variety of proprietary trading systems. Some of these systems primarily automate the execution function of two or more brokers. A municipal securities system has been designed, but it never was made operational. More recently, the SEC has considered a system called the Delta Options system to trade options on government securities. The Delta Options system offers electronic collection and dissemination of quotations, and the clearance and settlement of trades. Delta Options is largely a blind brokering system which allows systems users 1.) to input quotes on an anonymous basis through an intermediary or so-called blind broker, 2.) to see the quotes of other users of the system and 3.) to execute against those quotes through the blind broker. The system also allows system users to negotiate trades directly. It does not offer automated or computer-generated executions.[66]

Futures Markets

The recent automation development introduced by the CME GLOBEX system has an impact on the futures market that is well worth noting. The futures markets traditionally have been physically centralized, using an open outcry system in which brokers and dealers, called locals, congregate in a pit and effect trades directly by voice. The futures markets have developed some automated routing capabilities, but not automated execution systems.

The CME has worked with Reuters Information Systems to develop an electronic automated futures trading system that operates during the hours when the CME open outcry market is not available. The system operates internationally, and relies on office computer terminals in which traders enter orders. The system collects orders, calculates and disseminates a best bid and offer, and executes orders against each other based on time and price priority. With these capacities, the system has a future: the Matif (France), the New York Mercantile Exchange, and the Sydney Futures Exchange intend to participate,[67] and the Board of Trade of the City of Chicago has decided to establish its own after-hours trading system.[68]

Foreign Markets

Several significant foreign developments in automation and computerization should be considered by the U.S. In 1986, the United Kingdom adopted a NASDAQ-like screen-based quotation and trading system called the SEAQ (Stock Exchange Automation Quotation) System. The system entirely supplanted the physical exchange almost immediately after its introduction. Although the SEAQ system began with the dissemination of large quotation sizes (as much as 100,000 shares),[69] the quotation sizes were reduced substantially because market makers did not want to trade with other market makers at these displayed sizes. SEAQ also has eliminated the real-time reporting of large trades.[70]

The International Stock Exchange (ISE) recently supplemented its SEAQ system with an automated execution capability for small orders called Stock Exchange Automated Facility (SAEF). SAEF provides automated execution of up to 1,000 shares at the best SEAQ bid or offer. Executions are assigned to participating SEAQ market makers on a rotating basis. SAEF competes with the automated private systems of two U.K. broker-dealers, Kleinwort Benson and Barclays de Zoete. These systems, called Best and Trade, offer automated executions by their sponsors at the best SEAQ quotations of up to 5,000 shares.[71]

One of the more notable foreign automated execution systems was instituted in Canada at the Toronto Stock Exchange (TSE) in 1977. The CATS, or Computer Assisted Trading System, is an automated trading system with a public central limit order book for the 800 stocks that are traded. Approximately 20 percent of total TSE share volume is effected in CATS. This system operates in addition to the more traditional, physically-centralized auction market at the TSE. Stocks trading on CATS are not traded on the floor, but the system guarantees the price and time priority of orders absolutely. CATS uses market makers acting as both agents and principals instead of specialists.

In addition to automated information dissemination, automated execution and limit order protection also are offered by CATS. Its closest analog in the U.S. is the NSTS system used by the Cincinnati Stock Exchange. Foreign markets have bought or licensed the system for use on the Paris, Belgium, Madrid, and São Paulo Stock Exchanges.[72]

The Computer Assisted Order Routing and Execution System (CORES) of the Tokyo Stock Exchange is another important foreign automated system. Instituted in 1982, this system operates in tandem with a physically centralized and traditional auction market like CATS in Toronto. Stocks that trade in CORES do not trade on the floor.[73]

Orders for customer or member accounts are fed from terminals located in member offices. In Tokyo, the CORES system relies on Saitori members, who are the intermediaries on the Tokyo Stock Exchange. Saitori act solely as middlemen in transactions between exchange members effected on the exchange. The intermediary function of the Saitori in CORES is accomplished by matching orders put into the system by brokers through keyboard operation. Where the market situation and the trading pattern of a stock seem to assure a stable price formation, Saitori instruct the system to match buy and sell orders automatically within a pre-determined price range. The system has an order book function, which operates on a time and price priority basis, and can be seen in member offices. The system provides automated trade comparison as well as reporting to the market information system of the Tokyo Stock Exchange.[74]

Foreign derivative markets also tend to be highly automated. The Tokyo Stock Exchange's yen bond futures and stock index futures markets are automated.[75] In 1988, Switzerland instituted an automated options and futures market called SOFFEX (Swiss Options and Financial Futures Exchange), which has proven to be very successful,[76] and the London Futures and Options Exchange and the New Zealand Futures Exchange are automated.[77]

A recent and intriguing automated trading development in prospect abroad is a London International Financial Futures Exchange (LIFFE) system. Called the Automated Pit Trading (APT) System, it replicates electronically the open outcry trading that occurs in the pit. The system involves a video display screen that displays a pit split in half with buyers on one side and sellers on another. Traders are marked as boxes on the screen with identifying numbers and with numbers of contracts of traders bidding for or offering. The best bid and offer is displayed in the middle of the screen, as well as the number of contracts offered at that price. Bids or offers entered into this system are good only for five seconds, much like bids and offers made in a pit on a trading floor, which are good only if accepted immediately. In the industry, the quote is good only as long as "the breath is warm." To execute trades, the trader moves a mouse to the bottom of the computer screen to an area designating price, and then punches in the number of desired purchase or sale contracts.[78]

The Eurobond markets also are advancing toward increased automation. The Association of International Bond Dealers (AIBD), a self-regulatory organization for Eurobond markets, recently has developed the TRAX (Automated Transaction Exchange) System, an automated trade comparison process that facilitates the trading process in the Eurobond market. Through TRAX, all Eurobond dealers regardless of geographic location enter transaction information electronically. The system performs trade comparisons within minutes, plus end-of-day transaction reports to the Securities and Investment Board in the United Kingdom.[79]

International Links

Starting with a trading link between the Montreal Stock Exchange and the Boston Stock Exchange,[80] U.S. markets have developed several international electronic trading and quotation links since 1984. In addition to the Montreal-Boston link, trading linkages between the American and Toronto Stock Exchanges, and the Midwest and Toronto Stock Exchanges, were established in 1985 and 1986,[81] although the Toronto links were disconnected in 1988 due to lack of use.

Also, there are quotation links between NASDAQ and SEAQ and between NASDAQ and Singapore's automated quotation dissemination system. And there is a joint listing agreement and mutual offset arrangement for the Major Market Index Options between the Amex and the European Options Exchange in Amsterdam.[82]

The concept behind trading links is simple. Orders in individually listed securities are routed electronically among the floors of the linked markets. Best bids and offers in linked securities on each market are displayed on the floors of the other linked market. Orders are executed in the receiving market's auction process, therefore trading is not automated. Some best-execution protection also exists. For example, orders typically are guaranteed a price at the best quotation up to a specified number of shares.

Quotation links are the exchange of quotations from linked markets. For example, NASDAQ sends to ISE quotations in approximately 300 NASDAQ stocks for limited distribution to SEAQ market makers active in the securities. ISE sends to NASDAQ quotations for approximately 300 SEAQ stocks, again for limited distribution to NASDAQ market makers active in those stocks or in American Depository Receipts (ADRs) on those stocks.[83]

The Amex/EOE licensing arrangement permits the EOE to list and trade XMI options that are fungible with Amex options, which means a contract acquired in the Amex can be closed out on the EOE, but there is no direct quotation or trading link between the markets.[84]

Endnotes

[1]   A comprehensive overview of U.S. and Canadian securities information dissemination systems is contained in "The Creation and Distribution of Securities-Related Information in North America," Information Industry Association (1988).

2   *See* Special Study of Securities Markets, Report of the Special Study of the Securities and Exchange Commission (1963), reprinted in H.R. Doc. No. 95, 88th Cong., 1st Sess. (1063), Pt. 2, at 678.

3   For a good history of NASDAQ, *see* M. Simon and R.L.D. Colby, "The National Market System for Over-The-Counter Stocks," 55 *George Washington Law Review* at 17 (1986).

4   For a complete description of NASDAQ, *see* The NASDAQ Handbook (NASDAQ 1987).

5   *See* Schedule D of NASD's By-Laws, CCH 1754.

6   *See* Securities Exchange Act Release Nos. 25949 and 26545 (August 2, 1988 and February 14, 1989). The NASD currently requires end-of-day volume and price reports for non-NASDAQ securities. *See* Securities Exchange Act Release No. 25637 (May 2, 1988).

7   *See* Rule 11Aa2-1 and Schedule D of NASD By-Laws, 1754.

8   The Securities and Exchange Commission by rule requires such trade reporting. *See* Securities Exchange Act Release No. 17549 (February 17, 1981) (adopting Rule 11Aa2-1).

9   Schedule D of NASD By-Laws.

10 *See* Securities Exchange Act Release Nos. 10787 (May 10, 1974) (approving the Consolidated Tape Plan) and 14415 (adopting Rule 11Ac1-1).

11 *See* Restatement and Amendment of Plan submitted to the Securities and Exchange Commission pursuant to Rule 17a-15 under the Securities Exchange Act of 1934 (on file at the Commission); and Plan submitted to the Securities and Exchange Commission for the purpose of implementing Rule 11Ac1-1 under the Securities Exchange Act of 1934 (on file at the Commission.)

12 Instinet, although not a participant in the Plan, submits trade reports directly to the CTA.

13 There was some confusion concerning the operation of these systems during the October 1987 market break. During this time, the high-speed lines experienced only two brief outages so that, with these two exceptions, current trade reports could be obtained at all times. Due to volume, the low-speed

line was running several hours late. *See* "The October 1987 Market Break," a report by the Division of Market Regulation, U.S. Securities and Exchange Commission (February, 1988) (SEC Staff Report), at 7-4 – 7-5.

[14] *See* Plan for Reporting of Consolidated Options Reports and Quotation Information (on file at the Commission).

[15] The mechanics of this process differ according to whether the exchange uses a specialist system or a competing market maker system. Markets using the specialist system rely on the specialists for establishing quotations. Markets using competing market makers rely on an exchange employee who is responsible for monitoring and publishing quotations as they are made from among competing market makers, floor brokers, and the order book official.

[16] CSE is treated separately below.

[17] SCOREX is the acronym for Securities Communication Order Routing and Execution.

[18] The ITS is an intermarket communications system through which the exchanges and the NASD communicate orders (called "commitments to trade") in eligible stocks to one another. Separately each market disseminates through the Consolidated Quotation System (CQS) its best bid and offer in securities it trades, including securities eligible for trading through ITS. Thus, the best ITS bid or offer is the best bid or offer in an ITS eligible security disseminated by a participant in CQS.

[19] This is a simplified example of the execution of a market order in SCOREX. Non-ITS stocks also can be routed and executed through SCOREX, as can limit orders, i.e., orders to buy or sell at specified prices, or better. The PSE specialist has discretion whether to accept limit orders, although his evaluation by the Exchange depends in part on what percentage of limit orders he accepts. The limit orders accepted by a specialist not priced at the market (i.e., at current quotations) are stored and executed automatically when a transaction takes place in the primary market (generally the NYSE) at or through the limit order price.

[20] This system was introduced in 1976 as the Centralmarket System. PACE stands for Philadelphia Stock Exchange Automated Communication and Execution.

21 PACE also differs from SCOREX in its treatment of limit orders. PACE only requires the execution of 500 shares for every 1,000 shares that trade at or through the limit price on the primary market.

22 The SEC has expressed concern about this aspect of the PACE system. *See* Securities Exchange Act Release No. 19858 (June 9, 1983).

23 MAX stands for Midwest Automatic Execution.

24 Limit orders can be routed through MAX but execution is manual. The specialist is required to execute 300 shares of a limit order for every 500 shares that trade at or through the limit on the primary market.

25 BEACON stands for Boston Stock Exchange Automated Communications Order-Routing Network.

26 For a complete description, *see* Securities Exchange Act Release No. 25918 (August 25, 1988).

27 A limit order is marketable if it is priced at the current quotation. For example, a limit order to buy at 20 is marketable if the current offer in the market is 20.

28 Although few orders are executed automatically in this manner because the specialist rarely fails to act within the requisite three minutes, the SEC has expressed concern about the NYSE using the NYSE quotation instead of the ITS quotation for pricing these executions. *See* Securities Exchange Act Release No. 22498 (October 2, 1985).

29 The SUPERDOT system also can be used to route non-marketable limit orders, and to route and automatically execute at the NYSE quotation market odd-lot orders. Additional applications of SUPERDOT are available for program trades.

30 Although the execution is electronic, it is not machine generated. Thus, the specialist must affirmatively act, for example by touching the screen to enter the execution price to generate an execution.

31 In its report on the October market break, the Division of Market Regulation recommended increased use of electronic display books to avoid the substantial delays and cancellations experienced in ITS during the market break due to printer queues. *See* SEC Staff Report, supra note 13, at 7-48.

[32] The Amex also has instituted the AUTOPER System to facilitate the execution of orders by use of touch screen terminals through which the specialist can enter execution data. Id. at 7-24 – 7-25.

[33] LIST stands for List Order Processing.

[34] For a discussion of portfolio trading, see SEC Staff Report, supra, note 13, at Chapter Three.

[35] See Securities Exchange Act Release No. 26198 (October 19, 1988). Prior to this program, in April 1988, the NYSE had a six-month pilot that prohibited use of DOT to send index arbitrage orders after a 50-point DJIA move. See Securities Exchange Act Release No. 25599 (April 19, 1988). This pilot expired on October 19, 1988.

[36] A 12-point S&P 500 Index movement is approximately equal to a 96-point DJIA movement.

[37] An indication of interest is a range of prices within which a specialist may open trading in a stock.

[38] The NYSE previously has implemented procedures to address volatility problems associated with program trading on expiration Fridays. On these days, order imbalances, both pre-opening and pre-closing, are collected (largely through SUPERDOT), and publicly disseminated. The dissemination of these imbalances together with other procedures has helped reduce volatility formerly associated with expiration Fridays. See Securities Exchange Act Release Nos. 25804 (June 15, 1988) and 26408 (December 29, 1988).

[39] Public agency orders have priority over other orders at the same price, regardless of time of entry.

[40] For a more complete description, see Securities Exchange Act Release No. 19315 (December 9, 1982).

[41] See M. Simon and R.L.D. Colby, supra note 3, at 74.

[42] In 1984, the NASD had implemented the Computer Assisted Execution Service (CAES) principally to facilitate the link between the OTC market for listed securities and ITS. CAES, which also can be used to trade non-listed, National Market System securities, allows firms to route market orders or limit orders to specific market makers quoting the best bid or offer. Market

orders are executed automatically at the best bid or offer, and limit orders are printed and stored as day limit orders. CAES has not been used greatly, either to route ITS orders to other markets or to execute OTC orders. *See* Simon and Colby, supra note 3, at 52 and 73-74.

[43] There currently are three order-size limits for SOES—1,000, 500 and 250—which vary per stock depending on its average daily non-block volume, bid price, and number of market makers. In addition to limits on the size of orders that can be entered into the system, the NASD establishes an exposure limit which requires that market makers commit to execute a certain number of the maximum-sized orders if the market maker is quoting the best bid (or offer) or if an order specifies (preferences) a particular market maker for execution. The exposure limit currently is one: a market maker is required to execute only one maximum-sized order. Also, a market maker is free to elect higher exposure limits. The exposure limit had been increased to five in response to execution difficulties experienced during the 1987 market break, but was lowered for a six-month pilot starting October 1988 in response to concerted efforts by so-called professional traders to use SOES to hit the quotations of market makers who had not had time to change their quotations in response to news announcements. *See* Securities Exchange Act Release No. 25291 (June 9, 1988) for a description of the post market break reforms to SOES, and Securities Exchange Act Release No. 26361 (December 15, 1989) for subsequent modifications.

[44] Agency orders include orders entered into SOES on a riskless principal basis by a broker that is not a market maker in the security.

[45] NMS securities are the securities of the largest and generally the most actively traded OTC companies for which real-time, last sale reporting is required. In addition to mandatory participation for NMS securities, the NASD modified SOES in response to the market break to allow executions against locked or crossed quotations. *See* Securities Exchange Act Release No. 25291 (June 9, 1988). A locked market exists when the bid price of one market maker equals the asked price of another market maker. A crossed market occurs when one market maker's bid exceeds another market maker's ask. Prior to this modification, SOES executions would cease whenever quotes were crossed or locked, a situation which occurred frequently during the market break.

[46] Approximately 40 percent of SOES orders are preferenced.

[47] Another significant aspect of the treatment of small customer orders in the OTC market is the in-house systems most large integrated (i.e., acting as

both broker and market maker) broker-dealers developed to automate their executions of customer orders. Indeed, these systems account for a far greater percentage of executions of small orders in the OTC market than does SOES. However, unlike SOES as modified after the October 1987 market break, these systems cease to operate when quotations are locked or crossed. These systems are described in the SEC Staff Report, supra note 13, at 7-8 − 7-10.

[48] For a description of this system, *see* Securities Exchange Act Release No. 26476 (January 19, 1989). As currently designed, this system does not allow customer orders to be executed against each other between the current best bid and offer. So if the best bid and offer is 10-11 and two customers separately sent in limit orders to buy and sell, respectively, at 10 1/2, they would not be executed against each other. They would be filed to be executed against a market maker if the inside market moved to that price. The SEC has expressed concern about this aspect of the system. Id.

[49] *See* Securities Exchange Act Release No. 25263 (January 11, 1988).

[50] The NASD also is developing a complementary system, called Automated Confirmation Transaction (ACT), that facilitates the automated clearing of pre-negotiated trades.

[51] *See* Securities Exchange Act Release No. 14661 (April 14, 1978) (approving temporarily the Plan for the purpose of creating and operating an Intermarket Communications Linkage pursuant to Section 11A(a) (3) (B) of the Securities Exchange Act of 1934) (the Plan is available on file at the SEC). After a series of temporary approvals, the ITS plan was permanently approved in 1983. *See* Securities Exchange Act Release No. 19456 (January 27, 1983).

[52] The link with the NASD operates with respect to so-called "19-c-3 securities," listed on an exchange after April 26, 1979, that exchange members may also trade over-the-counter pursuant to Rule 19-c-3 under the Act.

[53] For example, if a customer leaves a limit order with the PSE specialist to buy at 20, the PSE specialist displays a bid of at least 20. If 20 is the best ITS bid, an ITS market generally does not execute trades at a price superior to 20 without satisfying the limit order left with the PSE specialist. The system does not provide time priority so that a limit order at 20 entered on the PSE at 10:00 AM has no priority over a limit order at 20 entered on the NYSE at 10:05 AM.

54   The ITS plan, supra note 51, sets forth these rules and procedures.

55   The PSE and NYSE do not have automated systems for options order routing or execution. In April 1989, the Phlx implemented an automated options order routing system called AUTOM, for Automated Options Market,
that it expects to expand to provide for automated executions. *See* Securities Exchange Act Release No. 26354 (December 13, 1988).

56   Prior to the implementation of their automated execution systems, both
Amex and CBOE had automated options order routing systems.

57   Limit orders on the book at the same price as incoming system orders are
guaranteed executions at the same price as system orders in all options in
which Auto-Ex is available, and in all equity options except IBM, in which
RAES operates. RAES does not protect public customer limit orders on the
CBOE 100 index options book, or in IBM options.

58   *See* SEC Staff Report, supra note 13 at 8-8 – 8-10.

59   *See* Securities Exchange Act Release Nos. 25995 (August 15, 1988) and
26373 (December 20, 1988).

60   *See* Securities Exchange Act Release No. 25996 (August 15, 1988).

61   SITUS stands for System for Institutional Trading of Unregistered Securities. PORTAL stands for Private Offerings, Resales, and Trading Through
Automated Linkages.

62   *See* e.g., Proposed Rule 144A, Securities Act Release No. 6806 (November
11, 1988).

63   For a more detailed description of Instinet, *see* letter from Richard G.
Ketchum, Director, Division of Market Regulation, Securities and Ex-
change Commission to Daniel T. Brooks, Cadwalader, Wickersham and
Taft, (August 8, 1986).

64   Broker-dealers currently cannot participate in this aspect of Instinet.

65   POSIT is described in a letter from Brandon Becker, Associate Director,
Division of Market Regulation, Securities and Exchange Commission, to
Lloyd Feller, Morgan, Lewis & Bockius, (July 28, 1987).

[66] For a more complete description, *see* letter from Richard G. Ketchum, Director, Division of Market Regulation, Securities and Exchange Commission, to Robert A. McTamaney, Esq., Carter, Ledyard & Milburn, (January 12, 1989). In response to the proliferation of these systems, the SEC voted to propose Rule 15c2-10.

[67] *See* "Electronic Futures Trading Cleared," *New York Times*, (February 3, 1989) at D-6. While GLOBEX is the first automated trading system proposed by a major U.S. futures exchange, the Intex Futures Exchange was a fully automated electronic futures trading system based in Bermuda with terminals located in the U.S. The system never proved successful and went out of business. For a description of Intex, *see* Securities Exchange Act Release No. 23795 (1986).

[68] "Chicago Board Discussing Link with London," *New York Times*, (February 21, 1989) at D-6.

[69] By way of comparison, in the U.S. the displayed size of most NASDAQ quotations is only 100 shares.

[70] *See* "Stickier Wickets," *The Economist*, (January 14, 1989) at 74.

[71] *See* "Electronic Stock Market Takes a Leap Nearer," *Financial Times*, (February 13, 1989) at 8.

[72] For a good description and discussion of CATS, *see* "The Toronto Stock Exchange," D. Unruh, Vice-President, International Markets, Toronto Stock Exchange, paper submitted to the SEC for SEC's February 1987 Roundtable on Internationalization of Securities Markets.

[73] The first section of Tokyo is the marketplace for stocks of larger, more actively-traded companies; the second section is for smaller, newly-listed companies. About 1,530 of the stocks listed on the Tokyo Stock Exchange trade in CORES and 150 trade on the floor. In 1988, 74% of total Tokyo Stock Exchange share volume was accounted for by the 150 stocks traded on the floor. *See* Tokyo Stock Exchange 1988 Fact Book, at 36.

[74] Japan's over-the-counter market also intends to introduce by 1992 a computerized system based on NASDAQ technology. *See* NASDAQ Notes, (February 1989).

[75] *See* "Japan, Derivative Financial Products Markets," 7 *International Finance Law Review*, (December, 1988) at 27. Interestingly, in response to volatility

experienced on the days stock index futures expire due to index arbitrage activity, the Japanese markets have instituted expiration day procedures similar to those in use on the NYSE. *See* supra, note 37, and "Japanese Regulators Want To Hold Down Volatility Caused by Stock Index Futures," *Wall Street Journal*, (January 26, 1989) at C-13.

[76] *See* "Swiss Options and Futures via Computer May Offer Glimpse of Future in Chicago," *Wall Street Journal*, (January 25, 1989) at C-15; and "Trades on Swiss Options Exchange Soar Beyond Sponsors' Initial Expectations," *American Banker*, (July 11, 1988). The German Exchanges expect to use the SOFFEX system in introducing financial futures and options to German markets. *See* "Germany Exchange's Cost Set To Top Dollars, 32M," *Financial Times*, (September 8, 1988) at 36.

[77] *See* "London Could Fox Them All," *The Economist*, (December 3, 1988). The Swedish Option Market launched in 1985 was the first completely electric options marketplace. *See* "Founder of Stockholder Options Exchange Pushes to Expand Operations in Europe," *Wall Street Journal*, (November 18, 1988) at A-18.

[78] *See* "LIFFE Plans to Put Open Outcry Pits on the Screen," *Financial Times*, (February 2, 1989) at 23.

[79] For a good description of TRAX, *see* TRAX brochure, available from AIBD. At one point, the AIBD considered the creation of a NASDAQ-style real-time trade and quotation dissemination system, in part in anticipation of the time when the U.K. securities market regulator, the Securities and Investments Board (SIB), would require such a system as a condition to registration of the AIBD under the Financial Services Act of 1986. *See* "Dealers' Group Taming Eurobond Market," *Wall Street Journal*, (May 22, 1986) at 24. Due to member resistance, the AIBD moved to the TRAX system instead, and SIB approved the AIBD's registration in April 1988. *See* "Bond Dealers Association Gains Designated Stock Exchange Status," *Financial Times*, (April 15, 1988) at 113.

[80] *See* Securities Exchange Act Release No. 21449 (November 1, 1984).

[81] *See* Securities Exchange Act Release Nos. 22442 (September 20, 1985) and 23075 (March 28, 1986).

[82] For a good description of these links, *see* Internationalization of the Securities Markets, Report of the Staff of the U.S. Securities and Exchange Com-

mission to the Senate Committee on Banking, Housing and Urban Affairs and the House Committee on Energy and Commerce (1987), V 49-56.

[83] For a more complete description *see* Securities Exchange Act Release No. 24979 (October 2, 1987) (approving the link as a two-year pilot). The NASDAQ/Singapore link currently is limited to an exchange of end-of-day quotations. *See* Securities Exchange Act Release No. 25457 (March 14, 1988).

[84] In 1984, the CME established a similar mutual offset arrangement for currency futures with the Singapore International Monetary Exchange markets. *See* B. Becker, 6 *International Tax & Business Lawyer*, at 242 (1988).

THE ECONOMICS OF THE IMPACT OF TECHNOLOGY ON FINANCIAL MARKETS

Trading Technology and Financial Market Stability

Sanford Grossman
The Wharton School

Introduction

An understanding of the role and functions of financial markets is a necessary precursor to understanding the effects of advances in trading technology. Markets serve the function of enabling parties to engage in trade. However this is not the only function of markets. Markets serve a price discovery function: providing and aggregating information across both active and inactive market participants. Financial market stability will be enhanced by changes in trading technology which improve the price discovery function.

Markets as Trade Enablers

A trading technology or a market place enables parties to trade. I will explain below how this is intimately related to the price discovery function. However, it is useful to begin with a brief summary of the more elementary function of bringing trading partners together.

For illustrative purposes, divide the potential market participants into three groups: brokers, market makers and final customers. Brokers, by definition, never desire a position in the security. Market makers, by definition, take a position only for short term trading profits, i.e., the average return from a position held for the long run will not reward them for the risk of capital committed over the long run relative to other uses they have for their capital. Final customers, by definition, are willing to accept the average returns for the risk of their positions over the long run, and are *trading* perhaps with great current immediacy to achieve that *position*. This division of actors is obviously artificial, but it will help to explain some important concepts.

Final Customers

The final customer could be a pension or mutual fund which wants to increase its equity holdings because of a change in its risk preferences regarding equity or because of an inflow of cash from clients of the fund. In this case it is buying equity to achieve a new (relatively) long run position. It could also be a bond dealer who sells bond futures to hedge a portfolio of bonds in its inventory.

Market Makers

The market maker could be a dealer buying at a price from which it expects high abnormal returns. The market maker buys the instrument in situations when the price is temporarily low, while the final customer buys the instrument because the long run average return is high relative to its risk. More precisely, the market maker takes positions because of the *variability* in the expected return, while the final customer takes positions based upon the long run average expected return. Many trading institutions who are usually final customers in the above definition, will function as market makers when there are clear variations in expected returns. For example an S&P 500 Index Fund may substitute futures for stock when futures are trading at a discount relative to stock. The fund is taking a position in the spread because it has a high (risk-adjusted) expected return.

To better understand the role of market makers, consider the following example. For reasons unrelated to information about future payoffs, a group of equity holders desires to sell a substantial block of equity. Assume that a negligible price fall would be required to induce the rest of the economy to increase its equity holding by the amount that is to be sold. That is, if final buyers could be matched with final sellers, then there would be no price impact of the trade. However, the potential final buyers are dispersed throughout the economy (if not the world), and are not in constant communication with the market. A market maker will buy the offered stock into his inventory to bridge the time interval between the arrival of the sellers and buyers. He bears risk while the stock is in his inventory, and hence must, on average enjoy a reward.

A market maker (or final customer, behaving like a market maker) buys when expected returns are high (relative to the normal risk-adjusted return for the asset), and sells when expected returns are low. A large unanticipated flow of sell orders which occurs in the absence of information about future payoffs, will lower price and raise expected returns (in the absence of market maker intervention). It is the fall in price, in the absence of news, which signals to the market makers (and eventually the final buyers) that their intervention is necessary. The price move is a crucial signal for allocating resources. The buying activity of market makers trying to take advantage of the high expected returns will diminish the size of the price fall, and thus tend to stabilize the market. Final customers would be made better off if a communications technology for firm bids and offers between themselves could be developed so that market makers are not needed. Unfortunately such a system is unlikely to be workable because of the risks inherent in leaving firm bids and offers on a screen in a volatile market. Further, most customers cannot plan all of their trades and reflect these plans in simple limit orders.

Brokers

In the artificial division of market participants, brokers are agents who do not take positions on their own account. They use their information acquisition network to match buyers and sellers. Brokers must know where to find buyers who are willing to buy from the broker's selling clients at the highest prices. Brokers will look to an organized market to find these buyers, and also use their sales force to find sellers who are not signalling their intentions through active participation in an organized market.

The existence of brokers who actively search for contra-parties to a trade is evidence of the importance of information flows for the smooth and efficient functioning of securities markets.

Markets as Information Conveyors

The ideal market would be one in which everyone in the economy could costlessly, effortlessly, and continuously participate. In such an ideal market there would be no brokers (and they surely would disagree with this definition of ideal), because there would be no search for contra-parties. There would also be no market makers, since no one is needed to bridge the gap in time between the arrival of buyers and sellers at the market; all potential buyers and sellers are always costlessly and effortlessly present. Unfortunately, discussions of ideal markets can be sterile, as I feel are discussions about ideal worlds without wars, earthquakes, bad weather, or government regulators.

A major factor which causes markets to deviate from the ideal is the fact that continuous participation and information retrieval and evaluation is neither effortless nor costless. If one party wants to sell, this information is not costlessly disseminated to, and processed by all potential buyers. More importantly no single person is being made aware of the collective demand and supply schedules of the rest of the market. The fact that we are not all part of this fantastic telepathic network creates the need for information to be provided by markets and brokers, as well as the need for market makers.

We can understand the role of technology by analyzing the extent to which it makes markets closer to the ideal. It is useful to divide technology into three broad classes:

1. General news, price, and quote delivery systems;
2. Order routing and delivery systems;
3. Order execution systems.

General News, Price, and Quote Delivery Systems

The revolution in news transmittal over the last 10 years has received little attention relative to innovations in order handling. Nevertheless, it has been extremely important. There has been a revolution in the extent to which large databases on companies and general economic conditions can be quickly and cheaply combined with current information. Ten years ago, there were no services which provided on-line, real-time, calculations of the current value of market indices (like the S&P 500), or the current bid and offer on the (cash side) of the indices. Since, there were no futures markets in stock indices, there was no real-time calculation of the basis.

The interest in real-time calculation of market indices is to some extent a reflection of the growth of index options and futures markets. However, the growth in those markets is in turn a reflection of the growth of the institutional market's focus on trading large diversified portfolios. This has been associated with a change in the way institutional trades are routed and executed.

Order Routing and Delivery Systems

The NYSE originally created the Designated Order Turnaround (DOT) system to handle small retail orders. It allowed a retail broker to, essentially, transmit a market order directly to the specialist's post, and electronically receive a confirmation, usually in less than two minutes. The broker is able to receive a market order from his customer, and often give the customer a confirmation, all in one short telephone call. At its inception, it was not anticipated that the DOT system would be used for large institutional orders. I believe, that at its inception, it was not contemplated that the DOT system would significantly impact on market prices or volatility. Brokers viewed it as a cheaper means of delivering and confirming orders. Market makers viewed it as an enhancement to the lucrative flow of retail market orders.

The trading of large orders through DOT (now SUPERDOT) was not anticipated because institutional orders were traded in a manner quite different from retail orders. In particular, an institution desiring to trade a block of shares in a single stock, would call an institutional broker who in turn would try to find the other side of the trade by telephoning other institutional clients. The brokerage firm might also take part of the trade for its own account. The trade would then be crossed on the NYSE between the parties that agreed to the trade off the floor. Alternatively, if a cross could not be arranged, a floor broker would be given the order with instructions to "work it"—but only very rarely to trade it immediately as a market order.

The market impact of a trade clearly depends on how the trade is executed. There are two reasons for this. First, orders which demand immediate execution convey information to other participants. Market participants know that one reason that a trader demands immediate execution is that he has information; they thus offer to trade at adverse prices with the trader who demands immediacy. Of course, immediacy may be demanded for other reasons, such as a liquidity or hedging need. The weight put on the information motivation for the trade will determine the size of the market impact of the trade. The market impact of a trade depends on the method by which it is executed for a second reason: if immediacy is demanded, and a cross cannot be effected, then someone must earn a return from taking the other side of the order into inventory. This return is to cover the risks and other costs of maintaining an inventory, and the market maker earns this return by taking the other side of the trade at an adverse price to the customer. This adverse price move is the market impact of the trade.

In the decade beginning in 1970, institutions became increasingly interested in trading large diversified portfolios. The rise in S&P 500 index funds is one example of this phenomenon. Futures markets provide a convenient method by which the equity risk present in a large basket can be transferred. Futures markets can accomplish in a single trade that which would require trading in many different individual stocks on the Stock Exchange. Of course, the stock and futures markets represent one unified market in which equity risk can be traded. Thus the stock market must reflect the same information about equity valuation which is being expressed in the futures market.

The stock and the futures markets are kept in equilibrium by two forces. First, if the S&P 500 can be bought more cheaply in one market rather than the other, then all buyers that are authorized to trade on either market will go to the cheaper market tending to raise price there, and all sellers who are authorized to trade on either market will go to the more expensive market causing prices there to fall. Not all institutions can freely choose where to trade. Hence there is another force which keeps the market in equilibrium, namely index arbitrage, where the instrument(s) in the cheap market are bought, and (almost) simultaneously the instrument(s) in the expensive market are sold.

In accomplishing index arbitrage or a large diversified portfolio trade where execution delays create great risk, the trader is forced to use a very fast order delivery and execution system. Thus the DOT delivered orders arrive and express great immediacy to the marketplace. For reasons given above, this demand for immediacy will create a price impact. My measurements of this price impact indicate that it is quite small, on the order of half of the size of the bid-ask spread on the cash S&P 500, namely about .2% for the typical program order. These measurements are summarized on Exhibits 1 - 3.

Exhibit 1 presents summary statistics on 15 minute observations of program trading and S&P 500 price volatility in the two months prior to the 1987 crash. The average share of 15 minute volume represented by program trading was 4.21% in that period. At its most intense, program trading represented 26.5% of volume. Exhibit 2 presents regression results relating program intensity to price volatility. As can be seen from the regression results, it is possible to estimate this relationship very accurately: If program trading represented 100% of volume, then this would be associated with a 2.5% price move in a 15 minute period. For the typical program order which represents 4% of volume, the associated price move was (4)(.025%) = .1%. Exhibit 3 considers the relationship between the net program buy intensity and the related price move. Unlike Exhibit 2 which focused on the *size* of the price move and the *size* of the program orders, Exhibit 3 focuses on the direction of each through a comparison of net program buying with the price change. Again, the data permit a very accurate measurement of the relationship. The regression presented in the Exhibit indicates that a 1.63% price increase would be associated with a situation where program buying represented 100% of the NYSE orders. As Exhibit 1 shows, the typical net program buy intensity (i.e., a 1 standard deviation move) represented 9.32% of volume. Hence the typical program buy was associated with a price increase of (.025)(9.32%) = .233%. This is smaller than the typical bid-ask spread exhibited on the NYSE for the purchase of the (index weighted) components of the S&P 500 stocks.

The technological improvements inherent in the DOT system interact with the informational function of markets in a complex manner. As a pure routing system for small orders, there is very little informational impact. However, as a routing system for large basket orders, the system begins to interact with the informational function of the market. The arrival of baskets, which are not arbitrage related, poses a particular informational problem. Namely, at the instant at which the order is offered at the specialist post, how do the traders know that the trade is part of a basket trade? The specialist will often know that the order came from a DOT terminal which usually sends baskets, but no one contemplat-

Exhibit 1   15 Minute Program Trading and Price Change Statistics

15 minute periods (8/24/87–10/16/87)

	Net Program Buy Intensity	15 Minute S&P 500 Percentage Price Change	Program Order Intensity	Intra-minute Volatility: 15 minute S&P 500 (High-low/low%)
Mean	-2.64%	-0.02%	4.21%	0.18%
Std. Deviation	9.32	0.23	4.01	0.17
Minimum	-43.99	-1.23	0.07	0.02
Maximum	33.18	1.31	26.50	1.33

$$\text{Net program buy intensity} = \frac{\text{Program buy shares} - \text{Program sell shares}}{\text{Total NYSE Volume}}$$

where each quantity is an aggregate over a 15 minute period.

$$\text{Program order intensity} = \frac{\text{Program buy shares} + \text{Program sell shares}}{2 \times \text{Total NYSE Volume}}$$

Source: New York Stock Exchange.

ing taking the other side of the trade in the individual stock knows what was the whole basket of which the stock is a single component. This piece of information is very relevant because, under the assumption that the basket was not arbitrage related (i.e., futures are at their theoretical value), it "should" have a smaller market impact on the each individual stock if it could be identified as part of a large basket trade. Its impact should be smaller because the party contemplating the other side of the trade does not have to worry about it being a trade initiated by someone who is informed about the stock. Unfortunately, the institution which uses the DOT machine to send a basket market order to express (and achieve) immediacy about the *basket as a whole* must bear the market impact cost which is the sum of a demand for immediacy in each of the stocks in the components of the basket. The latter market impact cost can be larger than the former because 1.) the probability that the order initiator is informed about the stock is higher than that he is informed about the whole market, and 2.) it is sometimes easier for a market maker to hedge an inventory of a diversified basket of stocks than it is to hedge a single stock.

The above remarks indicate that there are benefits to be derived from developing a technology to cross basket orders that are currently being sent through DOT. Of course, part of the "technology" is already in place, namely

Exhibit 2   15 Minute Volatility versus Program Intensity

15 minute periods (8/24/87–10/16/87)

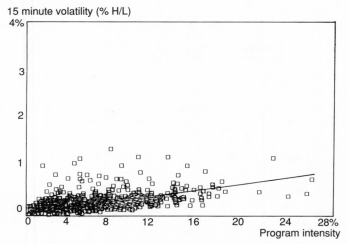

$\%$ intra-minute volatility $= 0.0250\%$ net program buy intensity
                                    (0.0011)

$R^2 = 0.35$ Number of observations $= 1,014$

Source: New York Stock Exchange.

S&P baskets and MMI baskets can be traded directly on futures markets as baskets.[1]

The above remarks concerned non-index arbitrage basket trades. Index arbitrage related DOT orders, by themselves do not put any informational burden on the trading system. Quite the contrary, the absence of DOT delivered index arbitrage orders would put a burden on the system. Index arbitrage occurs because trading on one market is expressing a demand for the services of the other market. For example, if institutions as a group sell futures in an attempt to reduce their equity exposure, then buyers must be found for equities. If the buyers are other institutions or individuals who have access only to the stock market, then someone must transmit the selling pressure from the institutions expressing that pressure in the futures markets to the people who are the buyers in the stock market. Index arbitrageurs are the messengers which bring the orders from one market to the other. In the case of net selling of futures, index arbitrageurs buy the futures, and then sell the stock on the stock market where there are willing buyers. The information that there are more willing buyers on the stock market than the futures market is provided by the event which initiated the arbitrage in

Exhibit 3   Net Program Buy Intensity versus Price Change

15 minute periods (8/24/87–10/16/87)

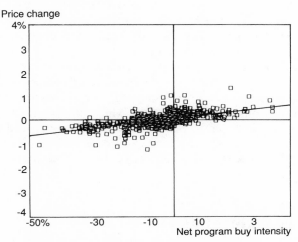

% price change = 0.0163% net program buy intensity
                        (0.0006)

R^2 = 0.45   Number of observations = 1,014

Source: New York Stock Exchange.

the first place, namely the fact that futures are at a discount relative to their cash equivalent theoretical value. The information needed to bring the correct buyers and sellers together is provided by market prices, namely the spread between futures and stocks. This is an example of a situation where technology is extremely important. The ability to accurately compute the buy price on the cash market and then transmit orders electronically makes the market function more effectively. Intermarket demand and supply is reflected by the prices and this brings forth the appropriate response.

Elsewhere, I have argued that the information provided by the price of the futures or cash instrument only reveals current demand and supply conditions.[2] It is of course useful to know that at the price of the last trade, demand is different that supply. However it would be more useful if this was known in advance so brokers could search for the other side of the trade. I have argued that the implied volatility in option prices is one useful signal regarding the future order flow at prices away from the current market price. Unfortunately current position limit regulations limit significant institutional participation in the options market.

Alternative technologies should be explored for conveying information regarding future order flows at prices away from the current price. This could be accomplished by making public an aggregate statement of what is in the limit order book. A facility could also be developed for the acceptance and dissemination of basket limit orders on the DOT system. Presumably the system could net out the demand and supply of baskets at the same price and send to the specialist post only the excess of demand over supply.

An exploration needs to be made regarding automated order routing for futures markets. This is clearly a very different issue than automated routing for the stock market. First, each Exchange has only one or two pits in which equity futures are traded, unlike the stock market where orders have to be routed to many physically separated posts. Second, there is no specialist to whom orders could be electronically routed for execution. For these reasons order routing innovations are likely to be less important for futures markets than they have been for stock markets.

Order Execution Innovations

Thus far we have discussed order routing, but only touched upon the issue of order execution. The area in which execution technology needs the most improvement is in multiple instrument and/or multiple security trades. By this, I mean not only basket trades, but also intermarket futures, options, and stock trades. We cannot have a single physical market in which all *intermarket* trading takes place. As long as there are distinct physical markets, some form of electronic, off-the-floor intermarket trading will be demanded by customers. A customer who wants to simultaneously trade Yen futures, IBM stock, US T-bond futures, and Japanese T-bond futures, presently must either put one leg of the trade on at a time, or call various brokerage houses to get bids on the overall trade. The latter, in effect, gives the customer a search market, rather than an organized (low search cost) market. An alternative to the current system is the development of a computerized market in intermarket portfolios. In such a "market," trades could display bids and offers for intermarket portfolios. I am not sanguine about the liquidity of such a market, and conjecture that it will simply turn into a telephone market where traders look at the screen and then make telephone calls to find out what are the "real" offers.

Technology cannot solve a fundamental problem faced by market makers or customers who are searching for the best prices. This problem is that a deep liquid market requires firm bids and offers for large sizes. But, anyone giving such firm bids and offers for large size is giving the market a free option to hit his bid. The potential losses associated with bids left on the screen can cause a computer market to be thin and lead customers to telephone in order to find out the true bids. The screen is used to advertise interest, rather than as a mechanism for revealing true bids and offers when markets are volatile. I believe that the prices of completed trades provide the best signal about the markets willingness to trade at that price. Advertisement of the fact that someone has been willing to trade at a particular price is often the best mechanism for attracting the buy or sell interest which is necessary for market stabilization and efficiency.

Endnotes

1   Under CFTC regulations, futures contracts cannot be crossed, and any sort of prearranged trade can be interpreted as a violation of CFTC regulations. Of course, since baskets can be traded directly, the market impact cost (even without a cross) will be much smaller than the spot transaction since the two problems mentioned above will not exit. Indeed, the bid-ask spread on S&P 500 futures is often one tenth that of the bid-ask spread on the basket of S&P 500 stocks. *See* Grossman (1988a,b).

2   *See* Grossman (1988c).

Additional References

Grossman, S. "Program Trading and Stock and Futures Price Volatility," 8 *Journal of Futures Markets*, (August, 1988a) pp. 413-419.

Grossman, S. "Program Trading and Market Volatility: A Report on Interday Relationships," *Financial Analysts Journal*, (July-August, 1988b) pp. 18-28.

Grossman, S. "An Analysis of the Implications for Stock and Futures Price Volatility of Program Trading and Dynamic Hedging Strategies," 61 *The Journal of Business*, (July, 1988c) pp.275-298.

Before and After October 19: Structural Changes in U.S. Financial Markets

Louis Margolis
Salomon Brothers

Much of the responsibility for the events of October 1987 has been ascribed to changes in technology: not only electronic technology, but also what the Japanese refer to as "zaitech." Zaitech translates roughly as financial technology or financial engineering. In the broad sense, zaitech includes the creation of new financial structures, new instruments, and new techniques.

The association of technology with innovation, change, and instability is natural in American society. Our understanding that growth and change bring instability was shaped by Joseph Schumpeter, who demonstrated that the process of innovation in a capitalist society is inherently destabilizing. Schumpeter called this process "creative destruction." Although he emphasized the creative aspects of the process, changes which are constructive for most elements of society often create personal disaster for others. The asymmetric allocation of technological benefits and costs is a complex policy issue, but most of the problems seem understandable and manageable.

Although technological change affects the stability of financial markets in many ways, there seem to be three features of technology that are of particular concern to the American public. Foremost among the three is the myriad techniques and activities that have been called computerized trading or program trading. The second related issue is the growing trend in world markets toward replacing exchange floors, specialists, and open-outcry trading systems with electronic order matching and limit order books, which eliminate the need for personal contact between the parties to a transaction. These electronic markets generally reduce overheads and headcounts. They also leave many investors with the nagging fear that when they need to trade, there will be no one there to provide liquidity. The third area in which technology affects market stability is information distribution. The impact of the information revolution on market stability has received relatively little attention. The increase in the quantity of information and the speed with which it is disseminated leads to rapid, simultaneous, and often unanimous decision-making.

These three aspects of technology have important effects on the way markets function and on stability. But the primary cause of instability seems not to be technology. Recent instability comes from a complex interaction of technology, economics, and unyielding social and legal structures. This same kind of interaction frequently has played a major role in the painful side of the process of innovation. Certain implications for change are obvious in the following analysis.

The Significance of October 19th

October 19, 1987 has become the most completely dissected and analyzed day in the history of world financial markets. But a thorough understanding of what happened that day includes a look at changes in the stock market that were evolving for some time previous—rather than just a pinpointed look at a particular trigger point. A long look backward uncovers a proliferation of options and futures. The movement to alternative trading strategies had accelerated. Indexation, portfolio trading, and electronic trading systems all were trying to tell us something about the structure of the market.

On October 15, 1987 at an evening speech to 70 pension plan sponsors, Dr. Henry Kaufman spoke about the potential for "lurches" in the equities markets, fixed-income markets, and currency markets. By lurches he meant substantial movements to different price levels, with very little trading activity. This timely warning foreshadowed a principal concern about the equity market of 1987—that it dropped so abruptly, not that it went down. Secondary to this is why the market went so high. These events were a manifestation of an incomplete transition to a new equity market structure.

The year 1987 marked the end of a 13-year bull market and the end of a unique period in American history. In 1987, the market approached its private-market value: the S&P 500 was trading at three times book value. Yet over the past 80 years, it had generally traded in a range of one to two times book value. The price/earnings ratio on trailing earnings in 1987 peaked for the post-World

War II period. Dividend yields reached their lowest levels in 60 years, or since the third quarter of 1929.

To understand why things changed so abruptly, it is helpful to look back a few years. In the 1960s, most pension fund assets were managed in balanced accounts. With the help of pension plan consultants, sponsors began to select specialized active managers for their equity assets and, eventually, for fixed-income assets as well. In the early 1970s, the pension officer emerged as an investment manager or at least as an asset allocator; he was no longer simply an administrator. Equity assets were concentrated in fewer hands, creating a structure that was relatively slow to respond to dramatic changes in price.

Changes in Asset Allocation

As the traditional role of investment managers changed from full-spectrum investment advisors to equity specialists or fixed-income specialists, investment horizons shortened. Now managers must react to short-term developments because their performance is evaluated at least quarterly. These short-term reactions are selection decisions, not market timing decisions. Most active equity managers avoid market timing: their stated policy is to stay as fully-invested as possible. This approach is dictated by their employers, the plan sponsors, because pension plan sponsors want to control asset allocations. Under normal circumstances these asset allocations change slowly.

The transfer of asset allocation decisions to plan sponsors has reduced flexibility. A few years ago, plan sponsors discovered residual, unwanted cash in their accounts because each manager kept some cash reserves. These unintended cash balances naturally interfered with the plan's asset allocation objective. The plan administrators conducted a survey and found that they always ran about eight percent extra cash. One multi-billion dollar pension plan now allocates 105 percent of its normal commitment to equities as one way of dealing with residual cash. The plan simply hired another manager to invest the residual cash that was already allocated to other managers. Another development was the creation of sweep funds by banks, which swept unintended cash into a separate fund that used stock index futures to equitize that cash. Instead of the short-term money market return, the plan received an equity market return. This approach let funds be more fully invested at all times. It also reduced their ability, willingness, and need to respond to marginal changes in value.

Meanwhile, other changes were occurring to undermine this deceptively stable structure. The speed of electronic communication accelerated the exchange of information. Declining telephone costs and modems to connect computers made telex and telegrams obsolete. Federal Express and, subsequently, facsimile transmission sped the delivery of documents. As the time needed to transmit information has dropped, the traditional swings between optimism and pessimism—between buys and sells—has been compressed into very short periods. Globalization facilitated by electronic linkages between markets transmits changes in valuation from one market to another around the world.

But innovation was not confined to communication or even to electronics. The money management industry was developing new products during this period in response to the changing needs of their clients. Tactical asset allocation was a stabilizing product. At great risk of oversimplification, tactical asset allocators tend to buy when stocks decline and sell when stocks rise. They are natural providers of liquidity. Tactical asset allocation programs accounted for an estimated one to two percent of total pension fund assets in early 1987. The four largest asset allocators were all more than 90 percent in bonds in the summer of 1987. Asset allocators bought more than $7 billion in stock during and after the break, but this was not enough to make a difference.

Another "high tech" money management innovation grew by leaps and bounds in the mid-1980s: portfolio insurance, as an offspring of option theory. Its practitioners created synthetic options by trading in the futures markets. This technique assumes that markets are continuous. This assumption did not hold on October 19. The role of portfolio insurance in the market break highlights a failure of the structure to adapt to new technology. Exchange traded options had existed since 1973. Portfolio insurers were natural users of options. If they had bought puts rather than count on a continuous futures market, they would not have had to trade during the break and they would have avoided the opprobrium heaped on them. Portfolio insurance did not use the options markets for two key reasons. First, the exchanges had no long term option contracts until it was too late. Ironically, the first listed options with a life of more than one year began trading at the opening of the market on October 19. Second, the SEC unwisely had imposed position limits that prevented large investors from taking large option positions. These position limits have not received their share of the blame for market instability, although the importance of a liquid put market as an alternative to dynamic hedging in futures markets and as an antidote to instability has been analyzed.

The portfolio insurers had a planned response to market decline. It had the vulnerability of any stop-loss strategy, but it was a clearly defined plan; unfortunately, the buyers had no countervailing plan. In fact, the policy of investing as much as 105 percent of desired amounts in equities to utilize cash balances left most would-be buyers without a strategic reserve. During the week of October 19, very sizeable buying occurred, but not by active managers because they had no cash. They were fully invested by mandate or could not respond for other reasons. So much for the new financial technologies and the active managers. What about other participants?

The Decline in Liquidity

The traditional providers of marketplace liquidity have been specialists and block traders. They suffered during the 1974-87 period from a dramatic diminution of their margins because of the contemporaneous decline in commissions. But these firms gradually have shifted assets, both capital and human, away from block trading. The ad hoc joint venture between the block trading houses and the specialists that evolved from 1965 to roughly 1985 is now being disbanded. The reduced profitability of the secondary trading of stocks, as distinguished from the new issuance of shares, is unique in Wall Street history. This shrinking profitability is causing the marketplace to seek alternative structures to find the liquidity needed by an increasingly concentrated group of shareholders. The policy that forced negotiated rates and encouraged the use of commissions to buy goods and services from nontraditional sources other than the securities houses now is having a dramatic effect on the structure and composition of the resources dedicated to facilitating this secondary trading of stocks. The result is that some participants have the flexibility and resources to adjust to these new equity market structures, others do not.

There may be unintended consequences of moving to a deregulated commission environment, where large financial entities are causing basic structural changes in the way securities are traded in the United States. These changes were never intended by the Congress, the SEC, or the U.S. Department of Labor, which regulates pension accounts. Furthermore, the volatility of the markets and the events of October 1987 are manifestations of this incomplete restructuring process. The market is trying to substitute alternative methods of trading within the traditional framework of the exchanges. The proliferation of alternatives—options, futures, electronic systems, portfolio trading, one-price auctions, and excessive volatility during periods of stress—should be viewed from this perspective.

The Decline of Commissions

After a number of modest changes in commission rates which began about 20 years ago, fully negotiated commission rates were implemented in 1975. A transaction that would have brought a brokerage firm $0.40 a share in the 1960s might bring in less than $0.04 a share today. The fixed commissions of two decades ago were used to pay for the traditional services of the securities houses. Today, an investment manager can use commissions almost like cash to buy nearly anything he needs to run his business. In fact, approximately one-third of institutional commissions are committed to soft dollar purchases of goods and services other than traditional brokerage firm research and the ongoing commitment of capital for liquidity when needed. At least one major institution uses 70 percent of its commissions for the purchase of goods and services from alternative sources. These commissions are never "recycled" through the block trading mechanism, and they are not available to provide liquidity when it is needed.

The decline in commission rates was accompanied by a dramatic surge in volume, which has temporarily obscured substantial changes in the traditional methods of trading equity and providing liquidity. This is understandable. As the cost of trading declined, investors and investment managers became more willing to trade in response to modest shifts in company or industry prospects. The increase in volume, combined with declining revenue per unit and the inexorable growth of expenses, led to dramatic changes. Twenty years ago, the commission brokerage business was profitable; today, secondary trading of equities is not a source of profits for any major securities firm. For years, the dominant source of earnings for brokerage firms dealing with retail investors was profits from interest charges or credit balances in margin accounts; but institutional firms lack this cushion. Currently, most institutional firms use equity sales, research, and trading to support other businesses. The deteriorating profitability of the basic brokerage business explains the redeployment of resources away from secondary trading and block trading to new security issues, mergers and acquisitions, and leveraged buyouts. These new activities, together with specialized securities services such as asset management, arbitrage, and derivative trading, have become the new major profit sources.

Higher commissions in the past may have discouraged trading activity, but they also provided a kind of insurance. Block traders and exchange specialists had incentives to make bids and offers that would stabilize the market. At old commission levels, they could afford to provide liquidity during periods of stress, even if it meant losing money on a specific trade. They relied on the financial incentives of an historic and future flow of commissions at a profitable level. At current levels of commissions, however, the financial incentive is insufficient to cover the risks of significant block positions. A block trader cannot afford to lose money on even a few trades. And the specialist has seen a sharp drop in his floor brokerage. In the early 1970s, about two-thirds of the typical specialist's income came from floor brokerage and the balance from trading. In 1983, the relationship was reversed, with two-thirds of income from trading. Although more recent figures are not available, this trend probably has become even more pronounced.

During past market breaks, the public has expected Wall Street to come to the rescue. In 1987, announcements of corporate stock buybacks were the functional equivalent because reduced profitability rendered general market support from brokers impractical. Salomon Brothers and other firms offered to stand with the specialists on difficult openings and reopenings, but the impact of this effort was limited. New York Stock Exchange specialists in the aggregate had approximately $1 billion dollars in capital on October 19. While their historic return on capital had been excellent, this capital was not a meaningful contribution to liquidity on a day when nearly $25 billion in stock was changing hands. At low commission levels, block traders and specialists could not accumulate a cushion to provide the liquidity that was essential for smoothly functioning equity markets during periods of stress.

It is interesting to contrast the ability of the U.S. securities industry to respond to the demand for liquidity with the corresponding response in Japan. Japanese brokers were a major stabilizing factor that October, partly because high fixed commissions had been retained in the system. Although Japanese broker profits had come from sources as diverse as in the United States, the secondary trading of Japanese equities also was highly profitable. Average commission levels on large trades were between five and ten times U.S. levels. Nomura Securities, the largest Japanese broker, had a market value larger than that of any U.S. company other than IBM and Exxon, and larger than all the U.S. brokers combined. Nomura has resources to outlast any adversity it deems temporary, but it dramatically cut its New York equity research and trading staff by effectively withdrawing from the institutional equity business in this country.

It is tempting to use the Japanese experience to illustrate another issue: the impact of volatility on the corporate cost of capital. U.S. price/earnings multiples or capital costs probably would not approach Japanese levels even if volatility disappeared completely; but there are clear theoretical and empirical relationships between volatility and cost of capital. Lack of liquidity and consequent volatility reduce the effectiveness and raise the cost of the capital-raising mechanism. The United States does not necessarily need regulations or legislation to restore profitability or fixed rates. This is simply the reality of a powerful trend.

New Providers of Liquidity

As Adam Smith might have predicted, new providers of liquidity are springing up. For one, the locals or floor traders in the futures pits make an important contribution to liquidity. Fortunately, economic incentives have attracted other traders, including firms that perform option and futures arbitrage both domestically and internationally. And asset allocation strategies have increased in popularity because they performed better in 1987 and because investors see an opportunity in them to profit by providing liquidity. Structural changes are expanding access to markets and increasing access to information on the size and flow of orders. GLOBEX, SOFFEX, INTEX, and screen-based trading in Japan are alternatives to the exchange floor system. Clearly these systems will not reduce access to the market by providers of liquidity—they will improve access.

It is also clear that electronic systems should not be blamed if regulatory and competitive forces have combined to reduce the incentive for any providers to enhance liquidity.

Portfolio Trading

Just as asset allocation strategies of various kinds have grown in popularity, major institutional investors of all stripes have changed trading policies. They have responded to the changes in market structure, to the changes in transaction costs, and to the fact that investors who have focused on individual stock selection have not been conspicuously successful in recent years. One such shift is toward indexing, which in various guises has become increasingly popular. Indexing is fund creation designed to track one of the popular stock market indices, most commonly the S&P 500. The growth of indexing and asset allocation, and the relative decline of stock selection, have led to a shift in emphasis among institutional managers from block trading to portfolio trading. The ad hoc joint venture between the block positioning firms and the exchange specialists that worked well during the past two decades in handling block trades can not meet the need for portfolio trading in the present environment. That is because exchange rules are designed to prohibit member firms from crossing portfolios as portfolios during normal market hours.

Consequently, either trades are executed in individual stocks or portfolio risk is adjusted in the futures markets. Portfolio trades do occur offshore, outside normal U.S. market hours. Again, as Adam Smith might have predicted, if a market structure will not adapt, a new market structure will be created. Exchange rules not only have forced portfolio trading into the futures markets and offshore, they have encouraged a massive reallocation of personnel and capital in response to changing market structures.

More and more U.S. equity trading is taking place away from the NYSE floor, with some going to the third market or other exchanges and some going outside the United States. The success of the U.S. stock index futures markets is, in substantial measure, due to the demand to trade portfolios or portfolio risk packages combined with the reluctance of the older market places to meet the need. Barring dramatic rule changes, the trend away from the NYSE is inexorable, and the securities industry probably cannot stop it. The marketplace is adjusting to the incomplete transition away from the traditional providers of transaction liquidity and moving toward a new structure. And U.S. regulators cannot stop it. Although the interest equalization tax was the proximate cause of the development of the Eurodollar markets, a substantial contributing cause was the inflexibility of U.S. securities regulation. When offshore security markets were undeveloped and unsophisticated, U.S. regulators could make rules that applied worldwide. They no longer have that luxury. October 19, 1987 illustrated the impact of an unrealistic demand for liquidity on a market structure that had not evolved to the point where new providers of liquidity were in a position to offer sufficient liquidity and stability.

Program Trading

No treatment of the impact of technology on market stability is complete without a look at computerized or program trading. In the early days of portfolio trading, the usual procedure was for a client to read the names and quantities of the stocks to be purchased or sold in a portfolio or basket transaction to a Salomon representative over the telephone. When a small number of securities was involved, it was easy enough to make sure that Loews Companies was not sold when the seller expected to sell Loews Corporation. If several hundred stocks were involved in a portfolio trade, the opportunities for misunderstanding in a telephone conversation obviously multiplied.

Then arrangements were made to transmit lists of stocks from clients to the Salomon Brothers trading desk using computer terminals and modems. The client's list of stocks was printed at Salomon's terminal and distributed to the equity traders who handled the transaction. Modems operated a good deal more slowly than they do today, and significant time elapsed between initiation of the portfolio list transmission and receipt of the final items on the list of securities. A common question around the trading room was, "Is the program done yet?" meaning, "has the computer program transferring the list of portfolio securities from the customer finished printing?" Perhaps because "program" has fewer syllables than "portfolio," portfolio trades came to be known as program trades. This misleading, high-tech terminology would not have created problems had it not been for a very high-profile misunderstanding of what a program trade is.

Stock Index Arbitrage

Stock index futures and options were introduced in the early 1980s. Their introduction was partly a response to demand from institutional portfolio managers to trade portfolios rather than individual stocks and partly a way of reducing transaction costs in the implementation of asset allocation and market timing decisions. Long stock index futures positions in combination with short-term fixed income securities are an almost perfect substitute for an appropriately weighted stock portfolio constructed to replicate the underlying index. Conversely, selling futures contracts against a portfolio of stocks is a low-cost way to reduce a portfolio's market exposure. Futures contracts and the cash market for stocks must sell in a close and predictable relationship to one another if futures are to be an adequate substitute for a portfolio trade. Investors with relatively low transaction costs found a profitable niche performing stock index arbitrage to exploit and correct any price discrepancies between the cash and futures markets.

Business Week and the Multi-Billion-Dollar Misunderstanding

Partly because the Levine and Boesky scandals focused public attention on risk arbitrage (a similarly named but dramatically different technique) and partly because index arbitrage made use of moderately sophisticated computer models, stock index arbitrage began to catch the fancy of the press and the public. Perhaps because portfolio trading and index arbitrage both used computer programs or perhaps because taking a position in a basket, or portfolio of stocks, was integral to the index arbitrage technique, a writer for *Business Week* confused index arbitrage and portfolio trading and produced a classic cover story in which he christened "index arbitrage" with the name "program trading," a reference that did not exist before.

Conscientious efforts by many securities industry professionals, academics, and other reporters have not succeeded in overcoming the confusion created by this article. A few securities industry executives and press pundits have deliberately or ignorantly added fuel to the fire. Portfolio trading became confused or commingled with index arbitrage, with computerized trading (whatever that is), and eventually with portfolio insurance.

For reasons probably best explained by a linguist, "program trading" became the preferred term to encompass all of these phenomena. Confusion over terminology colored public policy debates on stock market volatility, market structure, causes of the crash of 1987, and steps to be taken to restore investor confidence. Some securities industry professionals who should have known what was happening advocated regulatory or structural changes that would reduce market efficiency, would increase market volatility, and would improve their own firm's industry position or image.

The best way to work through the confusion is to examine the way portfolio trading and index arbitrage affect market prices. Portfolio trading, like any other trading, affects the price level of securities. Obviously, a small portfolio trade is unlikely to have a measurable effect. A very large portfolio trade clearly has market impact. Usually a portfolio trade has much less impact on an individual stock than a trade in a block of that specific stock. Because the portfolio trade involves a large number of issues, a portfolio trade implemented through the SUPERDOT network to the specialist system can have the effect of pushing a large number of stocks quickly to the specialists' bid (for a sell program) or offer (for a buy program).

Portfolio trades entered over the SUPERDOT network have accounted for some sizeable point moves in the averages. Although these moves were relatively small in percentage terms, they attracted a great deal of attention. Some of the often alleged but statistically immeasurable intraday volatility of 1986 and early 1987 is probably attributable to portfolio trades moving through a system that was not designed to handle them.

Index arbitrage is frequently undertaken in response to a portfolio trade. Just as the capital commitment and distribution capability of the block trading firm is instrumental in mitigating the impact of a large transaction in a single stock, index arbitrage helps spread the impact of a portfolio trade over the stock and futures markets to dampen the impact of the transaction. To the extent that a portfolio sale pushes the prices of stocks down, an index arbitrageur is a buyer of stocks and a seller of stock index futures. The capital committed to index arbitrage and to the stock index futures market making activities reduces the impact of portfolio trading. Index arbitrage spreads a movement in one market over several markets and reduces the impact in any single location.

Obviously this description does not tally with the perception that the stock index futures markets "force" the stock market down. In fact, the futures markets often move up or down slightly ahead of the underlying stock market. An investor who decides that the equity exposure of his portfolio is too high or too low can most quickly and most economically change that exposure in the stock index futures market. To the extent that the futures price drops below the appropriate relationship with the cash market, index arbitrageurs buy futures contracts and sell stock either long or short in the cash market to exploit and eliminate any pricing discrepancy. Markets are the anvil on which investment decisions are hammered out. Investors and the health of the capital markets are best served if markets are free to reach equilibrium without artificial constraints.[1]

The Policy Implications

Despite the Brady Commission's more narrow focus on October 19, its recommendations generally are appropriate, though occasionally committed to slowing down inevitable changes. If this view of what is happening in the marketplace is correct, the United States is in the middle of a massive market-driven restructuring of the financial markets. The creative destruction of the capitalist system which Schumpeter described is building a new structure to meet needs that were not envisioned as recently as 10 years ago. The regulatory and policy implications seem clear. The concept of deregulation in the United States has restored vitality and initiative to corporate America. Yet, it is an open question whether or not a highly regulated industry can go from fixed prices to open competition without concurrent deregulation in other areas. These are tough political issues for which no support for slowing or reversing the trend is seen.

Turning back the clock on negotiated commissions is politically difficult. The only feasible choice is to remove regulatory obstacles to the development of a new market structure. Specifically, the key Brady Commission recommendations should be implemented; investors should be free to trade non-standard portfolios during normal trading hours; and option position limits should be eliminated. In short, regulatory policy should permit new market structures, new products, and new technologies unless there is inadequate risk disclosure, opportunity for fraud, or clear danger to the financial structure. The evidence of recent years is that structural and regulatory rigidity in the face of inexorable forces of economics and technology have been the greatest obstacles to innovation. As long as these obstacles delay the still incomplete restructuring process, volatility will be a problem.

Endnotes

[1] One of the confusing issues frequently raised in late 1987 was the notion that index arbitrageurs were somehow exempt from the uptick rule on short sales of common stock. Such an exemption did not and does not exist. The confusion arose from a particular and unusual circumstance in which an index arbitrager might hold a long stock position in a related account and thus be entitled to make a long sale on a down tick. Because the sale was not a short sale but a conventional long sale, no uptick was necessary. Many index funds liquidate long stock positions in the cash market and replace the market exposure with long futures positions. Other index arbitrageurs close out long stock, or short futures positions when the valuation spread that originally attracted them reverses. The key point is that index arbitrage involving the sale of stocks can occur in a declining market without short sales. Index arbitrageurs who sell short are subject to the same rules as everyone else, and should be.

Market Making in the Electronic Age

Junius W. Peake
Peake/Ryerson Consulting Group, Inc.

In the next decade, and even more into the next century, automation will have an increasingly important impact on the trade execution process of the world's financial markets. Automation also will affect how market makers keep and build market share. This chapter explores the structural elements that highly-automated, rapidly-moving global financial markets will need for market makers to continue profitable and efficient operations during the 1990s and beyond.

Until now, the process of technological change in financial markets has led to an era of confusion. A typical headline reads: "Wall Street Runs Scared."[1] And it seems that way: brokerage earnings are down; costs are up. Many institutional investors, now passionate disciples of modern portfolio theory, invest ever more gargantuan sums of money into indexed "baskets" of equities traded at home and around the world. Individual investors seem to have fled the market almost entirely.

In partial answer to the institutional deluge, electronic markets are blooming like dandelions around the world, primarily in Europe, but also in North America, South America, and Asia. "Spanish Bourses Come On Line";[2] and "Outlook Bullish for the Electronic Market: Computer Systems are Taking Over the World's Leading Bourses,"[3] read press accounts of the market.

To add to this trend, there has been a recent movement by international information vendors to stake out roles in the trading process for financial instruments. Their pioneer is Reuters, the British company which is the world's largest distributor of financial information. Reuters has linked up with the Chicago Mercantile Exchange to trade financial futures when the trading floors on these exchanges are closed.[4] And Reuters is modifying the same GLOBEX system to trade equities and options by their own subsidiary, Instinet, the Cincinnati Stock Exchange, and the Chicago Board Options Exchange. Telerate, another information company, is also building automated financial trading systems.

About 15 years ago, U.S. President Gerald Ford signed the Securities Reform Act of 1975 as landmark legislation for the securities industry. Despite the passage of many years, America's equities markets still do not have the national market system called for in the law. The United States is still slipping behind in the race for the technology already being implemented by other countries, including those in a soon-to-be-unified Europe and in America's major Asian competitor, Japan.

The Current Market Structure and Its Problems

In the past two decades, the combination of new derivative financial products (especially fungible options on securities and indices, and futures on financial instruments and indices) together with the growth of institutional investing and the development of index strategies in portfolio management, have combined to form a market structure which set the stage for the near-catastrophe of October 1987.

In the wake of that disaster came reforms instituted voluntarily, and by rule or regulation. Most of these reforms have not addressed the structural market defects nor have they helped the market making and liquidity requirements of the market environment for the 1990s and beyond. Some of the regulatory medicine instigated by exchanges even exacerbated the potential for future market shocks.[5]

One such misguided regulatory effort was to mandate that market makers reserve substantially more capital in the mistaken belief that making more capital available will, by itself, reduce volatility.[6] Requiring more capital to perform any function increases the total return required. Instead of needing, say, $1 million to be a market maker, $2 million now is required. As a result, these investors will expect a return on investment that is twice as large. To meet this objective, the market maker must therefore enlarge the spread in the securities he trades, trade twice as often as before, take positions double the earlier amount, or engage in some combination of these three strategies.

In normal transactions, a market maker buys a client's position or sells a new position to the client because he believes he can trade out of the position at a profit. Having taken on risk, the market maker becomes an eager seller of the position, usually an even more eager seller than was the client. Market makers then aggressively seek buyers for their positions so they can make another—

hopefully profitable—trade. There is one of two results: either the position is sold to the ultimate investor or an unhedged position remains open, or unsold, by a market maker. The latter case sets the stage for market volatility. In fact, the more market makers trade unhedged, the more market volatility increases. This is true because market makers, whether over-the-counter or specialist, are not investors. They are traders who would like to finish each day even and riskless.[7]

Ultimately, there are only two ways a market maker can eliminate position risk: the position itself can be sold or a second position can be acquired, which eliminates the original position's market risk. This is a hedging strategy frequently executed by the use of derivative instruments.[8] A hedged position is not, however, a closed position. Having traded away market risk by buying another instrument, both transactions must eventually be unwound. The long position has to be sold; the short position covered. These transactions themselves carry a new risk, that the prices at which the positions are unwound will be at significant variance from true value. In the event of unusual market conditions, it may cost the holder of the position far more than logic would dictate for one leg of the position to be lifted.[9]

Market makers also carry the risk that one leg of the position may not be executable after the first leg is lifted because of trading cessation in a market, or because one of the counterparties to a position may default and be unable to pay for or receive the financial instrument. However, these are relatively slight in relation to the risks taken by a market maker with an unhedged position.

Once a market maker puts on a hedge for a position acquired from a client, the urgency to remove that position is greatly reduced. True, there is a cost for carrying a hedged position; but if the hedge is made correctly, market risk is eliminated.

A hedged position also allows market makers to assume larger positions for a given amount of capital because they can hedge their position risk, either partially or fully. The better the hedge, the less the risk of loss due to adverse market movement. If cross-margining and a reduction in capital "haircuts" are allowed for hedged positions, the capital required is even less.[10] When a market maker is fully hedged, his only expenses while holding the positions are the carrying costs (margin and capital charges), if any, plus the cost of unwinding them at a later date. He is no longer under intense pressure to unwind the position. As a result, he is less likely when hedged to make bids, offers, or trades that increase pressure on the market price of any instrument involved in the hedge. Instead, he can wait for an optimal time to unwind both positions.

In addition, high volumes of trading, especially coupled with collapsing market prices, bring enormous operational pressures on non-automated execution systems, whether they are based on face-to-face shouting or on telephone calls. The following table shows uncompared sides for certain periods in 1987 at the

National Securities Clearing Corporation, which services the New York and American Stock Exchanges and the National Association of Securities Dealers:[11]

Table 1   NSCC Uncompared Sides[12]

	Jan - Sep (Average)	Oct. 15	Oct. 16	Oct. 19	Oct. 20	Oct. 21
NYSE	8,000	11,848	20,098	56,626	49,413	37,251
ASE	1,000	1,058	2,335	6,743	7,798	5,913
OTC	6,200	6,867	11,873	27,685	27,035	26,266
Totals:	15,200	19,773	34,306	91,054	84,246	69,430

The almost sixfold increase in the daily number of uncompared trades[13] from the January-September daily average to October 19 resulted in an almost overwhelming workload for the floor and office clerical staffs who dealt with these problem trades. If the exchanges had not almost immediately shortened their trading hours, the volume of uncompared trades could well have been the harbinger of an operational catastrophe. In addition to the operational burden, resolving the additional uncompared trades could have been very costly.

Other structural problems, far worse than a high uncompared rate, also exacerbated the 1987 crash. Because of the reality of a logically unified market trading in cash instruments (stocks), options, and futures (confirmed by the authors of the Brady Report), the cessation of trading in any component of an index made trading in related instruments extremely risky at best, or catastrophic at worst.

According to the Brady Report, the average opening delay on the NYSE for the 187 stocks that reported delayed openings was one hour and 35 minutes; the average delay of the 90 stocks that opened late the next day was one hour and 25 minutes.

With many underlying equities not priced or trading, there was no way for the options or futures on equity indices that contained these securities to be priced accurately. Traders had to "fly blind," as a pilot flies in clouds without instruments. In addition to delayed openings, there were 175 NYSE stocks in which trading was halted on October 20, and 10 in which trading did not occur at all.[14] The erratic price actions of related markets during 1987 illustrates how important it is to keep all markets open at all times. Any component of a trading system which shuts down because of heavy volume breeds fear and panic in times of stress.

Market making in NYSE stocks is limited by rule to members who are registered specialists.[15] These specialists operate within restrictions about how they may use derivative instruments to hedge their positions.[16] Few specialists have either the facilities or the experience to conduct hedging strategies as a means of reducing or eliminating market exposure from their positions in their specialty stocks. Specialists also are not permitted to reduce market risk by investing in a highly-diversified portfolio. They are limited to making markets in their assigned stocks.

Over-the-counter market makers not only operate without similar restrictions; they are free to work in an office environment to facilitate maximum use of modern technological tools to assist their trading. By contrast, thousands of people on an exchange floor work and trade elbow to elbow in cramped quarters, unable to use a desk or computers as the non-floor trading personnel do.

Features of an Ideal Trading System

Maximization of Capital Use; Minimization of Risk

Market makers prefer to perform search rather than dealer services for their clients; there is a very good reason for this: looking for the other side of a trade before it is made costs less money and is less risky than looking for the other side after a trade has been made. So market makers prefer to find the other side of an order without having to acquire a customer's unwanted position. However, if the only service they offered was to act as a broker, their clients would lose the advantage of immediacy.[17]

A market maker must commit his capital to buying unwanted client positions at almost any time. In fact without his capital commitment, the market maker's key role is not being activated. The time when immediacy is demanded most is when markets are most volatile. This is also when the risks generated by unhedged position-taking are also greatest. So if a market maker can hedge an unwanted position, he is much more willing to commit capital.

Within today's market structure, capital usage is not maximized and risk is not minimized. While options and futures sometimes can be used as a way to reduce market risk, the cash, futures, and options markets trade in a different milieu and at differing speeds. If a client wishes to buy a "basket" portfolio of stocks—i.e., the underlying securities for the Standard & Poor's (S&P) 500—the dealer who offers that basket cannot calculate instantly the exact total price at which those 500 securities can be bought. So the market maker is at risk in the market. Using present trading systems, it takes a considerable period of time to buy 500 different stocks. As a result, a market maker's bid price for a customer's basket position must have a built-in margin of safety.

For that reason, market makers need the ability to take and hedge positions instantly at known prices. This is only possible in an integrated, real-time automated quotation and execution system. Such a system permits the execution of orders at known prices.[18] It encompasses not only the cash market, but also the futures and the options markets. When execution is instant, simultaneous transactions in multiple instruments become possible.

Automated execution in the cash market means that basket portfolios in any combination can be traded in microseconds. This is a far better approach than trading cash baskets as single units. "The whole is equal to the sum of its parts," is a fundamental law of mathematics, and it is also true in basket trading. At this time there are fungible, exchange-traded synthetic baskets of equities, the prices for which track baskets of stocks comprising popular indices. But creating a synthetic cash basket does not resolve the trading of baskets, it only adds one more instrument to the trading process which must be arbitraged to keep its price in line. Arbitrage already exists among the cash, futures, and options markets. Adding an unnecessary synthetic cash basket instrument which must be arbitraged is costly and uneconomical, and further complicates the understanding of trading by an already befuddled public.

It is also true that hedging is never perfect. Sometimes it is necessary to use a cross-hedge. This strategy takes opposite positions in two different financial instruments that the cross-hedger anticipates will have future price movements in the same direction at known relative rates of speed. Cross-hedging is risky at best; but the use of an automated execution system reduces risk somewhat, because a direct logical (and analytic) connection can be made between the firm's internal computer systems and those of the markets on which the instruments are traded. This use of computers to monitor historical and current price movements accurately and in real time would permit a more efficient analysis as well as the management of complex and risky trading positions.

Anonymity

The costs and benefits of having anonymous bids and offers in a market system is seldom discussed in professional or public literature. Under all systems, financial or otherwise, there must be tradeoffs and this is true in market making as well. No single market maker has access to all customer order flow. If he did, he would have no one to whom he could sell an unwanted position. Market makers will always compete with other market intermediaries, including other market makers. Each competing market maker, of course, cannot set prices for his financial instruments to create a separate universe for his clients in which to trade. If a market maker were to try, an arbitrageur would be there to profit from the difference between the first market maker's prices and the other price.

So a single market maker cannot service the entire customer universe[19] or operate in a closed universe within which he alone sets prices. But there are alternatives, including systems that disclose some or all of the market makers' quotes to other market makers. But this type of trading system has a problem which has been the cause of some concern in London's Stock Exchange Automated Quotation (SEAQ) system, for example. In SEAQ, some dealers (unofficial market makers, some would say) take advantage of registered market makers who show the prices at which they are willing to trade.[20]

Another approach used by a number of debt and foreign exchange markets, is to satisfy the demand for anonymity by using the services of one or more intermediaries, known as inter-dealer brokers. For a fee, these brokers provide trading services to the market maker community. For some reason, this technique never has been successfully applied to most equities markets. Perhaps it has not been implemented because of cost, or because it makes trading more cumbersome. Whatever the reason, in both exchange and over-the-counter equities markets, there is little doubt about the identity of professional bidders and offerors. On exchange floors, specialists see the identities of almost all bidders and offerors; in over-the-counter markets such as NASDAQ, competing dealer quotations are posted for all other market makers to see.

Anonymity has value and people pay for it. The best and least costly way to assure anonymity, while at the same time guaranteeing that every market maker is exposed to all entered order flow, is to use a screen-based automated execution system. Under such a system, all entered bids and offers are queued by time of arrival within price, and the sum total of all bids and offers at each price is displayed. The first bid at the highest price has preference for execution at that price; also the first offer entered at the lowest price has similar rights. All market participants see the book of unexecuted bids and offers. However, no one except system officials sees the identities of those who entered them.

Under this system, the economic benefits to a market maker outweigh any drawbacks. Each market maker knows at all times what his own orders were, their location within the order queue, each trade showing time and volume, and the aggregated size of all declared bids and offers at each price.

As a result, each market maker is assured that his bids and offers are exposed to all buying or selling interest every time he enters an order, which maximizes liquidity. In addition, a market maker still attracts his own order flow from customers on the basis of his quotes, expertise, and service. He solicits bids or offers from investors offering to act as broker, executing orders through the system against bids and offers on the electronic book, and providing immediacy services to his clients by buying or selling at a better price when it seems advantageous.

Following is an example of how an automated execution system works in the electronic marketplace with a hypothetical stock called "ABC":

Figure 1

| Close: 50.25 | * ABC * | High: 50.30 |
| Open: 50.20 | Last: 49.85 | Low: 49.80 |

BIDS	PRICE	OFFERS
	50.15	5,000
	50.10	1,000
	50.05	10,400
	50.00	600
	49.95	
	49.90	—————— 1,500
* *	49.85	* *
	49.80	
	49.75	
2,000 —————	**49.70**	
1,400	49.65	
11,000	49.60	
200	49.55	

The market is 49.70 bid for 2,000 shares; 1,500 shares are offered at 49.90, the last sale was 49.85. All bids and offers are aggregated at each price; no identities are disclosed. The bidder for 11,000 shares at 49.60 could be a single buyer; it also could be the aggregate of bids from a number of buyers.[21]

Assume a customer wishes to sell 10,000 shares at a price of 49.70 or higher. If the market maker is willing to buy this stock at 49.70, he first enters a sell order at 49.70 for the 10,000 shares and immediately enters a buy order at the same price for his own account for 8,000 shares. The first sell order executes 2,000 shares against the bid at that price; the 8,000 shares are crossed against the market maker's order.[22] However, if any other participant in the market entered an order that took price/time priority, the other participant is not excluded from the trade. The result of this trade is the immediacy provided by the market maker for his client. As he does today, the market maker still has an incentive for soliciting order flow from clients.

Having once taken a position, the market maker knows for a certainty that he can access the best possible available bids for that position in the market at all times. Since all bids and offers require clearance through the system, displacement by superior-priced orders is always accomplished.

Some professionals argue that "sunshine trading," the disclosure of bids and offers with size, will not work, and that an open order book will be an empty one. One leading academic warned that, ". . . anyone giving . . . firm bids and offers (in an electronic system) . . . is giving the market a free option . . ."[23] He goes on to imply that few people will enter orders into an open order book. But many experts do not agree, saying that orders will be entered into a properly-designed, fully-automated execution system.

It is the identity of the buyer or seller which more often than not provides more valuable information than the bid or offer prices. This is one of the reasons specialists achieve such a high rate of return on investment.[24] While it is true that bids and offers provide information to the market, prices alone are not enough. Bids provide more information than do offers; an investor may be selling his asset for a variety of reasons unrelated to his perception of the asset's future value.[25]

Bids and offers in a properly-designed electronic system are always subject to cancellation at any time before execution, and always disappear if they are executed. No one can predict when or whether a bid or offer will be canceled or executed. Therefore the time value of any option granted by a bid or offer's existence is of almost no value at best; the market information of greatest value to the marketplace continues to be reports of actual executions because executions are real—they cannot be withdrawn and money changes hands after each execution.

With the proliferation of index strategies in portfolio management, many bids and offers do not provide informational content about the future value of individual stocks. There is no informational value about a single stock's potential worth if the order for that stock is entered as part of an order to buy the S&P 500 index.

Under a properly-designed automated execution system, the informational content of all bids and offers is of unknown value to others because no person except the order initiator knows whether a specific order is based on an indexed trade.

An automated execution system requires that all bids and offers be entered, so the system can not be an empty one if any trading is to be done. To the contrary, there should be many anonymous bids and offers entered for varying periods of time and at different prices as market makers and investors learn to use the system to its maximum potential. Every bid and offer entered into an automated system is real and executable unless canceled. That fact will make attempts to manipulate prices foolish; the built-in audit trail that a computerized system generates enables regulators to detect price manipulation and thereby deter fraud.

More Efficient, Lower-Cost Operations

The Group of Thirty recently published a report offering nine recommendations for the improved settlement and clearance of financial transactions, including several badly-needed and long overdue suggestions for improved financial transaction processing. The Group of Thirty avoids commenting directly on automated execution systems, but says in the report: "In an ideal world, (trade) comparison would be instantaneous."[26] Instantaneous trade comparison is possible only within an automated execution system. But the "ideal world" referred to is do-able given today's technology and it is also the best solution. The issue is whether or not there is sufficient political will to pay the costs to implement automated execution for cash, futures, and options markets.

Market makers' volumes are variable; so market makers want their costs to be variable as well, to match transaction-based revenue streams. But today's financial markets are based on fixed costs and are expensive to operate. Here is just one example: The Securities Industry Automation Corporation (SIAC), as the technological arm for the NYSE and the Amex, provides services to the National Securities Clearing Corporation (NSCC), the Composite Tape Association, and the Consolidated Quotation System. SIAC spent almost $160 million in total expenses in 1987, the most recent year for which information is published.[27] NSCC's total expenses were more than $73 million the same year.[28] These sums do not take into account other monies spent by the NYSE, the Amex, the so-called regional exchanges, the NASD, the boards of trade for futures, the options exchanges, their clearing corporations, or their members and member organizations. While the totals are not readily determinable, the entire cost of executing and processing financial transactions soars to billions of dollars annually.

In contrast, a fully-automated execution system for financial trading costs only a small fraction of these amounts. Whether operated by financial information companies, exchanges, vendors, or some combination, the probability is that charges for these automated execution facilities will be based largely on transaction volumes.[29] That means market makers and other financial intermediaries will be in better control of their costs, and are not subject—as they have been—to the combination risk of high fixed costs and variable revenues.

More Efficient Use of Margin

In a real time trading system, keeping track of risk is much simpler than in non-automated systems. In a real time system, there is inherent capability to perform instant cross-margining of positions in cash, options and futures, and in markets of different countries, and in different currencies. By contrast, today's market makers are required to allocate capital far in excess of that which is required if all positions across markets, countries, and currencies are netted.[30]

Also in today's environment, many market makers do not or are unable to take full advantage of risk-reducing techniques. Some market makers, such as stock exchange specialists, do not because of restrictive rules and lack of appropriate technology, partly as a result of cramped working conditions. Others do not make full use of hedging techniques because of high transaction costs, and the complications and time involved in the execution process.

Centralized Order Flow

For the financial world of the 1990s, market makers say they would like to see the order flow of each financial instrument centralized. In an electronic system, it is easy to funnel all buy and sell orders into a central book of bids and offers for each instrument. The benefits of such a system would be great. First, with a single, centralized order flow, each participant always would have access to all bids and offers, not just to a subset. This maximizes liquidity. Second, market makers no longer would have to commit capital by making markets in securities which did not require market making capital at that time, or in securities in which they did not wish to make markets. Since all bids and offers would be accessible, market makers could insert bids, offers, or both in any security whenever they believed the spread was too wide, or when they wished to trade a position for their own account or for a client. They could maximize market making capital by supplying market making services in any financial instrument, no longer saddled with the requirement to make "continuous markets" in certain instruments, whether or not these instruments needed their participation. Finally, whatever their own position in an instrument, under an automated system a market maker would be assured of access to the maximum amount of liquidity available, because all order flow would be accessible. This would reduce risk and lower costs.

Elimination of the Short Sale Rule

Another salient factor is the short sale rule,[31] which is counterproductive to market efficiency. First, increasing liquidity requires that more buyers compete for the asset. A short seller, by definition, must be a future buyer of that asset or its equivalent. All other buyers must have the freedom to buy or not to buy any asset; the short seller must at some point buy the asset he is short. The second reason the rule should be lifted is that cross-instrument hedging and trading strategies require simultaneous execution of trades in more than one instrument, including the short selling of listed stocks on occasion. A short sale restriction can inhibit the use of the strategy entirely, or make its implementation far more costly.

To make appropriate use of hedging strategies, it is sometimes necessary to short the cash instrument while going long the futures or option. If there is a regulatory impediment to this strategy, there will be less position-taking by market makers. As noted earlier, a short seller always becomes a buyer at some future time; and when he buys he becomes a provider of liquidity. This stored buying power, much like the energy stored in a battery, can be used later to help stop price declines in a collapsing market.

Improved Techniques for Basket Trading

The most important hedging instruments created during the past two decades are fungible, exchange-traded options and financial futures. Options and futures on specific financial instruments can create almost perfect hedges for market makers who trade the underlying cash instruments.[32] With the move by many investors toward indexation of portions of their portfolios, options and futures on financial indices are now among the most important hedging vehicles. The SEC has approved trading in index participation instruments on the American and Philadelphia stock exchanges. Although not considered baskets of stocks, futures, or options, they are their synthetic equivalents, which clone popular indices such as the S&P 500.[33] Whether index participation instruments will become a commercial success has not yet been determined.

Before the introduction of these new alternative products, investors wishing to sell or buy portfolios containing the exact underlying stocks in the precise amounts as represented by a popular index, such as the S&P 500, were required to enter orders for each of the 500 different securities. This is a costly and time-consuming process using today's trading mechanisms. So to obviate the need for metering and executing all those orders, some large dealer firms become de facto market makers in these baskets, rather than trading the individual stocks, by quoting a market to their customers for predetermined dollar amounts of these baskets of securities. They do so, in part, because they can hedge their risks somewhat by trading in the futures and/or options markets or because they are confident they can move the acquired position at a profit. The price differences at any moment in time among the cash, futures, and options markets create inter-market arbitrage profit opportunities: the arbitrageur buys the cheap instrument and sells the dear one, profiting from their price difference.

Most of the securities comprising the S&P 500 are listed on the NYSE. Under the NYSE's rules, only registered specialists are permitted to make markets on the floor in listed stocks. Each specialist is allocated certain stocks in which he becomes the assigned market maker. No specialist makes markets, for example, on all the NYSE-listed stocks which are components of the S&P 500. As a result, no single specialist presently can to trade the S&P 500 basket.

The current mechanism for trading a basket is an electronic order delivery system called SUPERDOT, which delivers orders to buy or sell NYSE-listed stocks from the offices of members to the specialist posts on the floor of the exchange. The SUPERDOT process takes time and there is no assurance that the price paid or received for any individual stock was the one quoted when the order was placed.

Because of their nature, options and futures contracts must represent standardized baskets of financial assets.[34] In these markets, too, automated execution systems lend themselves to improved market making services. In a market with instantaneous execution, basket trading becomes simple and less risky. A market maker or customer can buy or sell any combination of securities in the cash market to create a basket transaction. He can do so by entering a preprogrammed order to buy or sell the underlying securities. His computer will be able to show him the cost or proceeds of such a transaction in total; no longer will he have to wait minutes or even (under crisis conditions) hours to see his trade executed.

Many of the larger financial institutions, until now reluctant to engage in market making in a physical pit environment, should welcome the opportunity to commit capital to that function in futures and options from a trading room screen that enhances the power of their in-house analytical and trading systems to provide trader support.

Improved Trading Strategies

With an integrated, automated execution system encompassing cash, futures, and options markets, the full power of computers can be employed in support of market making and other trading operations. Under this system, traders can make larger trades using the same amount of capital needed today for non-automated systems. This benefit results from measuring total exposure at all times, and in real time. In non-automated systems, this is not possible; investment and commercial banks must build in cushions to accommodate the risks that imperfect information implies. With a combination of real time information, a locked-in trade, cheap and variable transaction costs, instant execution, and a functional integration of markets, the entire business of trading is revolutionized.

Conclusion

Under an automated execution system, market making enters a new era, and market liquidity is maximized. This is because not only do professional intermediaries—market makers—supply immediacy to the markets, but because investors, too, can add their buying power to the larger intra-day liquidity pool. Some large institutional investors already function as de facto market makers; under a fully-automated execution system, that trend will accelerate. This reality should not, however, be of concern to existing dealers because the presence of investors as market makers only increases market liquidity. This, in turn, reduces risk for professional market makers. That is vitally important because reduced risk should narrow spreads and increase market depth—and greater depth implies less unnecessary volatility. With less volatility attracting more investors to the arena, more business and profits will emerge for market makers and brokers.

Whether or not this trend matures depends on the existence of an automated execution system that features the appropriate elements:

- automated execution systems for cash, futures, and options markets that can merge into a synchronous whole;

- anonymity of participants within the system;

- a best price/first-come, first-served rule (price/time priority);

- centralized order flow;

- regulations and systems that permit maximization of a market maker's use of capital by harmonizing and shortening the settlement periods for all financial instruments and by creating the capability of netting offsetting positions for margin purposes;

- improved trading strategies;

- elimination of the short sale rule.

Wall Street; LaSalle Street; Main Street: none can afford to continue paying the costs of existing trading systems. In addition to their costs in dollars, they are too inefficient and slow to meet the needs of market makers or investors, whose needs the financial markets exist to serve.

Endnotes

[1]   Douglas Harbrecht and Richard Fly, *Business Week*, (May 1, 1989) at 24-26.

[2]   Peter Bruce, *Financial Times*, (April 25, 1989) at 18.

[3]   Alan Cane, *Financial Times*, (May 2, 1989) at 11.

[4]   This system, called GLOBEX, is scheduled to begin operations in late 1990.

[5]   *See* J. Peake, M. Mendelson and R.T. Williams, Jr., "Black Monday, Market Structure and Market Making," in *The Challenge of Information Technolo-*

gies for the Securities Markets: Liquidity, Volatility, and Global Trading, Henry C. Lucas, Jr. and Robert A. Schwartz, ed., (Dow Jones-Irwin, Homewood, IL, 1989) for a further discussion of these points.

[6] The term "market maker" here encompasses stock exchange specialists, over-the-counter market makers, and any other professional trader who regularly buys and sells for his own account hoping to profit from small changes in market price.

[7] J. Peake, "Where is the Investors' Market?" *Investment Management Review*, (July/August, 1988) at 30-34.

[8] Derivative securities—i.e., options or futures—are derived from their underlying financial assets.

[9] During the October 1987 market break, there were many occasions when futures, options and cash markets traded at wide disparities. In addition, a short squeeze also can create situations in which there are wide variances between true values and actual market prices among related instruments.

[10] Cross margining permits offsetting related positions against each other to determine the amount of true market risk borne by a market maker at any moment in time. For example, a market maker who owns 100 shares of ABC stock at a cost of $40 per share, who also owns a put option on 100 shares of ABC at a strike price of $40 is fully hedged because he can exercise the put at any time prior to its expiration date. He also can deliver the 100 shares at $40 per share even if the stock is selling at a lower price. In such a case, the margin and capital requirements would be less than if the market maker did not own the put option.

[11] A side is half of a trade. A buyer is one side of a trade, the seller the other side. Under existing comparison systems such as that operated by the NSCC, the member representing the buyer submits his version of the details of a trade made on an exchange or over-the-counter to the clearing corporation; the seller's representative does likewise. If the details of the trade agree, the trade is considered a match; otherwise it is uncompared and must be resolved later.

[12] *Report of the Presidential Task Force on Market Mechanisms* (The Brady Report) (January, 1988) Table B-19, at VI-48.

[13] An uncompared trade must be resolved manually by the clerical and trading staffs of the firms involved.

[14] Ibid, at VI-33.

[15] NYSE, Rule 390.

[16] NYSE, Rule 105.

[17] Immediacy refers to the provision of client execution services immediately rather than after another counter order arrives in the marketplace.

[18] To be sure, it is possible that another order can arrive in the market ahead of the one being entered. However, in almost all cases, being able to hit a price on the screen with a single keystroke has a higher probability than sending an order to a physical location for execution.

[19] For example, the NYSE specialist is a monopolist who operates in a limited world. There are over-the-counter market makers, specialists on other exchanges, institution to institution crossing networks, and other methods for trading which avoid his location. The last thing a market maker would like is to reveal his actions to competitors.

[20] SEAQ, like NASDAQ, is not an automated execution system. It is an electronic billboard on which registered market makers alone are allowed to enter bids and offers in their registered securities. Neither bids nor offers entered by any other broker or dealer, or by any customer, can be placed on these billboards.

[21] A price differential of five cents is used. In an electronic system, trading in this smaller differential or even in a one-cent difference is a trivial task; it seems archaic to keep the traditional 12 1/2-cent minimum price differential when the commission can be a small fraction of the present minimum price spread.

[22] Note that the marketplace does not know the identity of the buyer or seller, nor for whom the order was executed, unless either the market maker or client chooses to disclose that information. Anonymity has served a useful purpose; and when the market maker wishes to dispose of his new 8,000 share position, he can do so with the assurance that he will be able to expose it to all outstanding offers in the market without having the market know for certain that he is the seller.

[23] S. Grossman, "Trading Technology and Financial Market Stability," presented at the Rodney L. White Center for Financial Research at the Wharton School, (May, 1989) at 15.

[24] In 1987, for example, the average rate of return on NYSE specialists' capital approximated 38 percent.

[25] For example, an individual may sell a stock to raise money for taxes, education, or vacation. A pension fund may sell stock to provide funds for pensioners. However, a buyer is making his decision from an unlimited universe of choices (except when covering a short sale). Buyers and sellers of index funds do not convey the same type of information when they enter an order.

[26] Group of Thirty, *Clearance and Settlement Systems in the World's Securities Markets*, (March, 1989) at 23.

[27] Annual Report of the Securities Industry Automation Corporation (1987).

[28] Annual Report 1987, National Securities Clearing Corporation. There is some inter-company expense between SIAC and NSCC which has not been eliminated. NSCC is the organization which handles comparison, clearing, and settlement functions for the NYSE, the ASE, the NASD, and a number of other over-the-counter markets.

[29] GLOBEX's management has said the bulk of its fees will be based on transactions.

[30] In futures markets and on sellers of options, there is no margin deposited in the usual sense. The monies required by futures commissions merchants and brokers are actually good-faith deposits to assure performance of the obligations.

[31] The short sale rule requires that short sales of listed securities, or selling securities not already owned by the seller, must not be made unless the previous price change of a transaction was an up tick.

[32] Financial futures contracts on specific securities, such as those on U.S. Treasury bonds, are not perfect hedges, because the instrument on which the contract is based is not a specific issue in existence at that moment.

[33] For a description of the first Index Participation proposal, read "More Tips on CIPs: News on Cash Index Participations from the Philadelphia Stock Exchange," (September 26, 1988).

[34] Exchange-traded futures and options work only because the contracts traded are fungible instruments. The guarantor and issuer of the option or futures contract is the exchange's clearinghouse.

How Automated Trade Execution Systems Affect Trading, Price Discovery and Quantity Determination

Ian Domowitz
Northwestern University

Wayne Gardner
Loyola University

Price discovery and quantity determination constitute the two basic functions of any market mechanism. The potential for efficiently carrying out these fundamental tasks via automated systems in the financial markets has been formally recognized since 1963.[1] Automated systems that contribute to the price and quantity determination process now include price information dissemination services, automatic order routing, clearance and settlement procedures, and computerized trade execution systems. The last class of automated procedures is the focus of this chapter. Although other aspects of automated markets contribute to the price determination process, there is relatively little controversy surrounding their desirability in today's fast moving, high volume markets. These functions are largely clerical and accounting operations. Computerized trading floors, on the other hand, represent a step beyond the facilitation of existing activities in the market. They may, if given the time and opportunity to develop, revolutionize exchange operations and radically change securities trading as we know it today.

Unlike such functions as automated order routing, automated trade execution has generated a great deal of controversy. One aspect of the controversy is that the same set of desirable market characteristics is claimed by both sides of the debate. It is undeniably true, for example, that the availability of information is a critical issue in financial markets. Proponents of computerized trading argue that a computerized system improves the flow of information, allowing a greater amount of and more complete information about current prices, volume, bids, and offers to be displayed to a wider range of market participants than is currently feasible.[2] Those who argue against such developments believe that the information flow on an exchange floor cannot in any way be replicated by computerized information. They emphasize special aspects of floor trading as primary stimuli for the development of opinions and ideas that contribute in an essential way to the price discovery process and the generation of liquidity in the market.[3]

Liquidity itself is a key ingredient of market viability. It can be argued that an automated system should generate continuous prices with a large number of bids and offers available at any one time, reducing market thinness. Proponents of floor trading not only disagree with such a statement, but say that only the physical trading floor can produce the atmosphere and incentive structure needed to promote actions taken by local market makers, that, in turn, contribute to liquidity.[4]

There are many more examples. But with both sides of the debate claiming property rights to the issues that have a "mom and apple pie" ring to them, a rehash of the debate seems fruitless. In fact, both the professional and academic literatures on this topic consist exclusively of such debates on the one hand, and of proposals for the design of automated execution systems on the other hand. Instead, this chapter analyzes existing systems, either under recent regulatory review or in operation, relative to the price discovery and quantity determination processes. The analysis is partly motivated by the lack of substantive information in debates about automation of trading; most arguments are not grounded in the actual process that generates prices and quantities via computer. They merely speculate about the results of any such computerized process. Similarly, some professionals who do not trade on an exchange floor misunderstand how price and quantity determination works there, even how it might compare to what happens on a computerized floor.

There is further motivation in the current view of the SEC that "identifies the Commission's obligation to see that technological change introduced into the market is functionally sound and workable."[5] An understanding of how the computer is expected to set prices and quantities is essential to any such evaluation. The algorithms by which different systems operate are not easily available in print. What is needed is a clear statement of the computerized trading rules for a representative subset of automatic trade execution systems.

Following is an examination of the price discovery and quantity determination process within the context of floor trading via the open outcry method. Once the method of analysis is established and a set of benchmarks achieved, trading by computer is similarly examined for the cases of futures, options, and stocks. A clear statement of the computer algorithm is given for each case: GLOBEX for futures, RAES for options, and NASDAQ's SOES for stocks.

Price and Quantity Determination in Open Outcry Auctions

Futures, options, and, to some extent, stocks are traded in open outcry auction markets.[6] This method of competitive auction in the financial industry dates back at least to the beginning of organized futures markets over 135 years ago.[7] Today, trades are executed as soon as bids and offers match; but at a given point in time, only a fraction of the trading crowd trades at the continuous market clearing price determined by a subset of the market's supply and demand curves.

These double auction markets operate without an auctioneer to oversee and coordinate the price discovery process, and recontracting is not possible. So the basic rules of trading are quite simple. Once a trader calls out a bid or offer, any subsequent bid or offer must be higher, or respectively lower, than the standing order in the market. A contract is traded when the outstanding bid or offer is accepted. If more than one trader attempts to accept the bid, there are rules of thumb on trading floors that determine how such orders are split on average.[8]

This process differs from the classical competitive benchmark of the Walrasian auction, which uses an auctioneer to call out tentative prices in reaction to demand and supply pressures in the market. Trades are executed only when a price is found at which the total supply of an asset equals the total demand. All trades are carried out at this price, and the market clears. Consider the simple supply and demand schedules in Figure 1, for example. At a price of three, supply exceeds demand; a price of one elicits excess demand for contracts. Convergence to a price of two, with a concurrent quantity of two, is based on the essential idea that the price must increase or decrease as demand is greater than or less than supply. The Walrasian or competitive price and quantity is found at the intersection of supply and demand, as intuition would suggest. This is the classic example of an optimal call market. The continuous market clearing of the outcry auction is replaced by periodic clearing, but with a theoretical benefit: the Walrasian batch market is more likely to encompass the entire available supply and demand schedule, leading to better price discovery and quantity determination.

As in Monroe (1988), there are simplifying assumptions that can be used to analyze the floor trading process. Continuous floor trading is broken into small

Figure 1

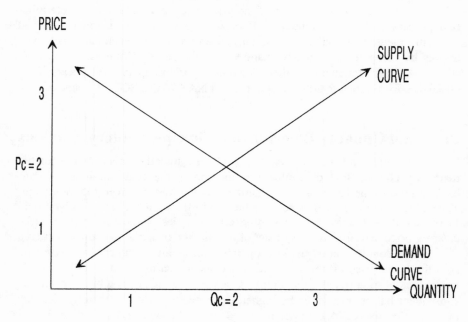

discrete periods and is limited to six players. Individual trades are for a single contract. Demand curves are assumed to slope downward in the short run, an assumption that has both empirical and theoretical support in these markets.[9] Each trader has a limit price and, for the sake of simplicity, it is assumed that it is possible for each trader to call out his limit price, permitting "stepped" supply and demand curves. It is unlikely that any trader would actually do so for strategic reasons, and the analysis below allows for contracting away from limit prices. This ignores strategic bidding, however. Changes in trader expectations that shift supply and demand schedules are not permitted in the very short run, i.e., during the period of contracting in these examples. These conditions permit calculations of both the continuous market clearing prices(s) and the Walrasian price, quantity, and buyer/seller surplus for any given trading scenario.

Consider the situation depicted in Figure 2.[10] Three supply-side traders with limit prices of 1, 2, and 3 (labeled Sa, Sb, and Sc) stand ready to transact with three demand-side traders with limit prices of 3, 2, and 1 (Di, Dj, and Dk).

Figure 2

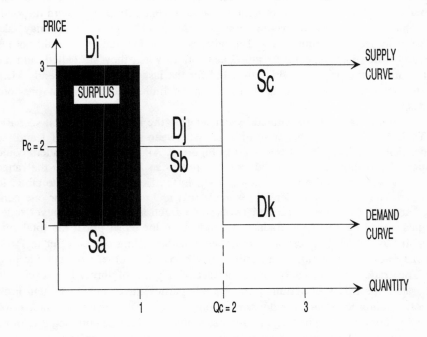

In a Walrasian auction, all transactions (Qc units) occur at the clearing price (Pc) and the total buyer/seller surplus is equal to the shaded area, split equally between Sa and Di in this case. As in the example of Figure 1, a Walrasian auctioneer calls out tentative prices until the quantity demanded equals the quantity supplied. In Figure 2, the competitive clearing price of two again is located at the intersection of supply and demand. The auctioneer uses this price to execute Sa and Sb requests to sell against the Di and Dj buy orders, yielding a final quantity of two contracts transacted. The combined buyer/seller surplus of two is generated by Di buying one contract one dollar below Di's limit price, and by Sa selling a contract for a dollar above limit. For the purpose of comparing actual trading outcomes to this competitive benchmark, define a Walrasian or competitive outcome as the Walrasian quantity, total Walrasian buyer/seller surplus (regardless of how it is split among traders), and a marginal, or final, price equal to Pc. The Walrasian outcome for all examples is then a quantity of two, a surplus of two, and a final price of two.

Scenarios are constructed in the following way. One of the three supply-side traders calls out an offer at or above the corresponding limit price. The demand-side traders may all respond, but assume that only one of them responds first, and that the trader arriving first gets the order.[11] Transactions may take place away from the limit prices. The other demand-side traders who did not get the order then may respond to subsequent offers when they are called, and are not bound to the prices at which they bid for the last offer. A period ends when no further trades are possible, given the price limits and pattern of previous trades.

The process is demonstrated by considering the results of the first scenario in Table 1. Trader Sa calls out an offer at or between the limit price of 1 and the upper demand-side price of trader Dj in Figure 1. All demand-side traders could respond by making a counter bid, and the price can fall anywhere in the range (1-2), shown next to the first match (Sa-Dj) in the first example in the table. In this particular scenario, trader Dj responds first and a trade occurs for one contract at a price between one and two. Some fraction of the total buyer/seller surplus goes to each of the traders, depending on the exact price; the total surplus so far is one. The scenario continues with Sc calling out an offer at P= 3. Di makes the counter bid, because this price exceeds all other demand-side limits. The trade takes place for one contract at a price of three. No surplus is generated for this transaction because both parties have traded at their limit prices. Trading then ends for the period; only Sb and Dk remain and their price limits do not overlap. The tally: two transactions each for one contract, one price in the interval (1-2), and a final or marginal price of three; the total consumer surplus is one.

The competitive outcome, however, is not achieved in this scenario. Trader Di was unaware that Sb had a lower limit price, obviating the possibility of a buyer/seller surplus of two, in particular. But the example does demonstrate that the open outcry method may not always lead to the most competitive price discovery and quantity determination. In fact, for this example, the market did not even converge to the competitive price.

All possible unique outcomes of scenarios in which the supply-side starts the auction in Table 1 have been documented. The three sections each consist of scenarios in which a different supply-side trader calls out first. The price column shows the range of possible prices for each match, while the transaction row shows the total quantity traded, assuming one contract per trade. The surplus column contains the total buyer/seller surplus. All cases are listed but some are less likely than others. For example, trading sequences that begin with the supply-side trader calling out a limit price are unlikely in practice; scenarios #4 and #5 have this characteristic, among others.

The competitive outcome occurs in four of 14 cases, including three cases in which the interval of final trade prices includes the Walrasian price. For com-

Table 1 Outcomes for the Floor Trading Example

Assuming that Sa calls out his offer first

	(1)		(2)		(3)		(4)		(5)		(6)	
	Match	Price	Match	Price	Match	Price	Match	Price	Match	Price	Match	Price
	Sa-Dj	1-2	Sa-Di	1-3	Sa-Dj	1-2	Sa-Dk	1	Sa-Dk	1	Sa-Dk	1
	-	-	Sb-Dj	2	Sb-Di	2-3	Sb-Di	2-3	Sb-Dj	2	Sc-Di	3
	Sc-Di	3	-	-	-	-	-	-	Sc-Di	3	Sb-Dj	2
Q	2		2		2		2		3		3	
S	1		2		2		1		0		0	

Assuming that Sb calls out his offer first

	(7)		(8)		(9)		(10)		(11)	
	Match	Price	Match	Price	Match	Price	Match	Price	Match	Price
	Sb-Di	2-3	Sb-Dj	2	Sb-Di	2-3	Sb-Dj	2	Sb-Dj	2
	Sa-Dj	1-2	Sa-Di	1-3	Sa-Dk	1	Sc-Di	3	Sa-Dk	1
	-	-	-	-	-	-	Sa-Dk	1	Sc-Di	3
Q	2		2		2		3		3	
S	2		2		1		0		0	

Assuming that Sc calls out his first offer

	(12)		(13)		(14)	
	Match	Price	Match	Price	Match	Price
	Sc-Di	3	Sc-Di	3	Sc-Di	3
	Sa-Dj	1-2	Sb-Dj	2	Sa-Dk	1
	-	-	Sa-Dk	1	Sb-Dj	2
Q	2		3		3	
S	1		0		0	

Q = Number of transactions and quantities transacted

S = Buyer and seller surplus

plete price determinacy, i.e., convergence to the Walrasian equilibrium price of two, only one of 14 qualifies. Both notions of the Walrasian process may be useful; the latter is a severe benchmark, but corresponds more precisely to the ideal. The four competitive outcomes above produce the largest surplus with the least number of trades, as does the Walrasian call auction.

Two additional observations relate to the competitiveness of the open outcry process. First, it is clear from the results in Table 1 that resources may be misdirected in such a market when it clears a quantity in excess of two contracts. This situation also was noted by Monroe (1988), but instances in which such an outcome occurs are unlikely; all such cases correspond to the initial offer being at a trader's limit price. Second, trades made to the right of the intersection in Figure 2 can cause an otherwise eligible order at the margin to go unfilled. This happens in scenario #4.

Futures Trading: The GLOBEX System

The CME submitted the basic organization, rules, and amendments to existing rules concerning the GLOBEX trading system to the CFTC in a series of letters beginning May 11, 1988.[12] GLOBEX is an automated system for trading CME futures and options outside regular floor trading hours in Chicago. Although the rules currently before the CFTC pertain solely to a subset of current CME contracts, it is envisioned that all CME contracts, as well as other domestic and even foreign exchange contracts, eventually will be traded on the system.

GLOBEX provides a variety of trade reporting and quotation information in addition to trade execution functions. GLOBEX screens display the best bid/offer price and quantity for each contract, last sale, daily high-low, and volume of contracts traded. Only "good-until-cancelled" limit orders and simple spread transactions are now accepted, eliminating the idea of market orders, and the display gives the appearance of a closed book, both of which might be considered unacceptable from the regulatory point of view.[13] Plans include the expansion of the order types, however, and the screens eventually will be able to display a list indicating the volume of open bids and offers at prices other than the best for the 10 best bids and offers, with associated size.

Following are rules governing the automatic trade execution system:[14]

1. Order Eligibility
   A new order is eligible to be matched with a standing order, and a trade will result whenever the following conditions occur:
   1.1   One order is a buy and the other is a sell order.
   1.2   The two orders apply to the same contract.

1.3   The price of the buy order is greater than or equal to the price of the sell order.

2. Trade Price
   If an order match is possible according to the criteria of Rule 1, then the trade will take place at the price of the standing order.

3. Trade Quantity
   If an order match is possible according to Rule 1, then the trade will take place for a quantity equal to the smaller of the:

   3.1   remaining quantity of the new order;

   3.2   remaining quantity of the standing order.

4. Maximization of Total Trade Size
   If there are multiple standing orders eligible for matching against a new order, matching will be considered in priority sequence until one of the following conditions is attained:

   4.1   the new order is completely filled;

   4.2   all eligible standing orders have been considered.

5. Standing Order Priority
   The priority of a standing order, relative to other standing orders for the same contract, is based on the following:

   5.1   Price: for buy orders, higher price is higher priority; for sell orders, lower price is higher priority.

   5.2   Quantity: a standing order for "primary quantity" has higher priority than for "secondary quantity" if they are both at the same price.

   5.3   Time: Within the same price and quantity type, older orders have higher priority.

There also are special rules for setting an opening price in the GLOBEX system. Rule 5.2 requires some additional explanation. When entering an order, a trader can specify a primary quantity and a secondary quantity. The secondary quantity is excluded from the best bid and offer display, and is executed only after all shown quantities at a specific price are filled. The secondary is executed with the same priority as the displayed quantities. Once the displayed quantity of an order is fully executed, any unfilled secondary quantity is cancelled. In other words, a trader need not "show his hand" completely when entering a potentially large order.

These rules are illustrated with a simple example. Consider the following Display 1 for one specific contract.

Suppose that at 10:03 a buy order is entered at 35.67 for seven contracts. The order is first matched with the best offer on the book, which is 35.65. This

---

Display 1

Order	Time	Price	Primary Quantity	Secondary Quantity
sell	10:00	35.65	2	3
sell	10:01	35.65	2	4
sell	10:02	35.71	3	2

---

order first removes the primary quantity of two and then removes the secondary quantity of three of the 10:00 order, given the time priority rule. The remaining two are executed at 35.65 of the 10:01 order. The remaining four of secondary quantity are dropped from the system because secondary orders cannot stand alone. The new best standing offer now is 35.71 at 10:02.

Now turn to the analysis of the price discovery process in the context of trading scenarios analogous to those presented for floor trading. Consider the same setup as depicted in Figure 2, but with a different interpretation. Suppose traders Sa, Sb, and Sc have limit orders resting on the book at prices one, two, and three to sell one futures contract. The time of entry into the computer system is irrelevant here; the lowest offer has the highest priority. Traders Di, Dj, and Dk initially are sitting at their terminals but have no bids on the screen. Only the best offer is displayed on their screens. We assume that the three demand-side traders each bid at their limit price, rather than simply attempting to lift the available offer. Although calling out a limit price is not optimal on the floor, rules 1.3 and 5.3 create a situation that does not arise in the trading pit. If a broker matches the best bid or offer directly, there is a risk that other incoming orders will be entered ahead of the broker's order, which exhausts the quantity available and causes the failure of order execution. Regardless of the assumption, matches will be determined by their respective times of entry; GLOBEX does not allow ties with respect to time. Now further assume that brokers execute small orders against the GLOBEX book, rather than entering limit orders between the spread as would be the case with large orders. In other words, small orders are treated essentially as market orders. This is a natural assumption in context; small orders do not need to be "worked," and the broker is more assured of timely execution if contracts are purchased from the book.

Consider the set of circumstances culminating in the results of the first scenario in Table 2. In this example, trader Dj enters the system before the others. Dj is matched with trader Sa, and the trade is executed for one contract at a price of one. The surplus of one goes to Dj. The new best offer is now the contract offered at a price of two by Sb. This particular scenario continues by assuming that Di enters an order next, ahead of Dk. Di is paired with Sb at a

Table 2   Outcomes for Trading Scenarios on Globex

(1)		(2)		(3)		(4)	
Match	**Price**	**Match**	**Price**	**Match**	**Price**	**Match**	**Price**
Sa-Dj	1	Sa-Di	1	Sa-Dk	1	Sa-Dk	1
Sb-Di	2	Sb-Dj	2	Sb-Di	2	Sb-Dj	2
–	–	–	–	–	–	Sc-Di	3
Q	2		2		2		3
S	2		2		1		0

Q = Number of transactions and quantities transacted
S = Buyer and seller surplus

price of two; the surplus of one goes again to the demand-side trader. Trading ceases for the period. The remaining bid and offer do not overlap.

All distinct outcomes under this setup are summarized in Table 2. Only four distinct outcomes occur on the GLOBEX system—disregarding direct lifting of offers—compared to 14 floor outcomes under similar assumptions. GLOBEX produces a much higher ratio of Walrasian outcomes: 50 percent of the total. If the requirement that the Walrasian outcome include the competitive surplus of two is relaxed, and only price discovery and quantity determination are considered, a Walrasian outcome will occur 75 percent of the time.

The GLOBEX book collects bids and offers, and holds them at firm prices. The result is fewer trades to the right of the market clearing quantity. Although this result is a good feature of the system, the cause is potentially a weakness if the possibility of much larger orders is considered. The economics of the auction analysis is similar, if more complicated, because traders are reluctant to leave large orders on such a book at firm prices. Further analysis of the role of the secondary quantities in GLOBEX is required if this issue is to be settled in terms comparable to floor trading.

Options Trading: The RAE System

The Chicago Board of Options Exchange (CBOE) Retail Automated Exchange System (RAES) was approved as a pilot program in January, 1985 and first implemented on February 1, 1985.[15] The system has been approved as permanent and has been expanded from trading in a single index options contract to include additional index options, as well as options on 178 equities.[16] RAES is designed for small public customer orders and marketable limit orders for eligible series of options contracts; eligibility is defined by series that are expected to have the highest public customer volume. Only quantities of no more than 10 index options contracts in the first and second months and no more than five equity options contracts in the first month are allowed. Option price is a factor in determining eligibility as well; currently, series with a price over seven dollars in the indices and 10 dollars in equities cannot be traded through RAES. The system automatically executes market orders against market makers' bids and offers in the queue.

Unlike GLOBEX, RAES operates during regular floor trading hours, allowing the direct pricing of market orders. Once the routing system receives an order, it automatically assigns a price determined from the displayed crowd market quote at the time of order entry. A buy order pays the offer; a sell order sells at the bid. Market makers are assigned as contra-brokers on a rotational basis from an eligibility list.[17] Limit orders, which are processed subject to certain "reasonability checks,"[18] have priority over RAES orders and automatically are routed to the book when the book touches market.[19]

The rules behind the RAES algorithm are summarized below:[20]

1. Order Eligibility
   A new order is eligible to be matched with a standing order and a trade results whenever the following conditions occur:
   1.1 a market order is entered into RAES to buy or sell;
   1.2 at least one market maker is signed onto the system in the option class corresponding to the market order.

2. Trade Price
   If an order match is possible according to the criteria of Rule 1, then the trade takes place at the best floor market quote available.

3. Trade Quantity
   A market maker is responsible for providing up to 10 contracts on demand.

4. Maximization of Total Trade Size
   Every order is matched with only one market maker in the rotation.

5. Standing Order Priority
   The priority of a standing order, relative to other standing orders for the same contract is based on:
   5.1 Price: all incoming orders are executed at the best price currently posted in the system;
   5.2 Rotation: market makers are assigned incoming orders on a rotating basis without regard to the market maker's particular bid or offer.

The next example should help to illustrate these rules. Consider the following book for a specific contract:

Display 2

	Order	Trader	Assigned Rank	Price	Quantity
Period 1					
	Sell	A	First	3 3/8	10
	Sell	B	Second	3 1/8	10
	Sell	C	Third	3 3/8	10
	Sell	D	Fourth	3 1/4	10
Period 2					
	Sell	D	First	3 1/4	10
	Sell	E	Second	3 1/2	10
	Sell	F	Third	3 3/8	10

Suppose that three market orders to buy 10 contracts apiece are entered sequentially into the system. The offer ranked first in period #1 is hit at the lowest price currently in the system, 3 1/8. The second ranked offer in the rotation is then hit at 3 1/8. The third offer in the queue is now hit at 3 1/4, which is the lowest price in the system at this point; trading ends for this period. The price of 3 1/4 is held over to the following period, and trader D is now ranked first. Now suppose that three contra orders are entered in period #2 for 10 contracts apiece. The first order is matched with our fourth trader at 3 1/4. The last two orders then are given to the first and second traders in this rotation, and executed at a price of 3 3/8. Trading now ceases for the period.

Trading scenarios on RAES again are based on the setup in Figure 2. The interpretation of this diagram differs from that of the floor or GLOBEX, however. In the pit or on GLOBEX, trades occur among floor brokers who are buying and selling for customers or for their own account. RAES executes customer market orders against market makers' best bids and offers in the system in which these prices are given, pricing the market orders based on concurrent floor trading activity. The important point concerns the market maker's role and obligations in RAES. A market maker provides immediacy to both sides of the market by posting a bid and an ask simultaneously, and is required by the exchange to provide a constant source of bids and offers in RAES.[21] In order to avoid unnecessary confusion in the examples, ignore the demand side of the market maker spreads and concentrate on the supply side of the market. Assume that incoming orders to buy (Di, Dj, Dk) are customer orders and that the contra offers currently posted in the system are part of the supply side of the market makers' spreads (Sa, Sb, Sc).

Suppose that Sa, Sb, and Sc are quoting offers for a particular call option (same month, same strike price), and customer market orders have not been entered into the system prior to this period. Trading begins by some information, say, leading to the entry of Di, Dk, and Dj from off screen. They are randomly matched with the supply-side traders, who are ranked in a designated order in the system. Suppose Sb is hit and removed by Dk for a trade of one contract at a price of one. In this scenario, Sc is the next market maker in the rotation. If Di is matched with Sc, the trade for a contract is executed again at a price of one, leaving Sa to be removed from the system by Dj at the lowest price remaining in the system: one. Trading ends for this period. Three contracts have been traded, all at a price of one, and no surplus is obtained.[22]

The example above is scenario #9 in Table 3, where all outcomes possible in RAES are exhibited given the three feasible rank orderings of market makers under the rules of the system. Outcomes one to four are the same as those realized on the GLOBEX system displaying only the best bid and offer. These scenarios create a situation in which incoming orders are matched at the lowest price in the system, replicating the GLOBEX rules. This particular rotation (Sa, Sb, Sc) generates all Walrasian outcomes possible in the case of six traders. As the number of traders grows, such a "GLOBEX sequence" becomes progressively less likely. As it stands now, the Walrasian outcome is reached three out of 16 times, including a case in which the Walrasian surplus is not reached. The competitive benchmark is achieved only 1/8 of the time for a Walrasian surplus.

The assumption of equal likelihood for each of the RAES trading scenarios is realistic given the random rotation characteristic of the system. The rotations do generate outcomes that are impossible on the floor, however. Trades five through 13 cannot occur on the floor, because sellers do not call out offers lower than their respective limit prices. Trades can be executed at the lowest offer in the system (a price of one) against market makers with limit prices above one until the best offer is hit and removed from RAES.

Stock Trading: The SOES System

The National Association of Securities Dealers Automated Quotation system (NASDAQ) was developed to facilitate the trading of over-the-counter (OTC) stocks. The result has been an OTC market for stocks with no centralized trading floor, yet the volume traded on this market over terminals and telephones now rivals the volume of the NYSE itself. The surge in trading volume that

Table 3 Outcomes for the Market Order Example on RAES

Assuming that rank order is Sa, Sb, Sc

	(1)		(2)		(3)		(4)	
	Match	**Price**	**Match**	**Price**	**Match**	**Price**	**Match**	**Price**
	Sa-Di	1	Sa-Dj	1	Sa-Dk	1	Sa-Dk	1
	Sb-Dj	2	Sb-Di	2	Sb-Di	2	Sb-Dj	2
	-	-	-	-	-	-	Sc-Di	3
Q	2		2		2		3	
S	2		2		1		0	

Assuming that rank order is Sb, Sc, Sa

	(5)		(6)		(7)		(8)		(9)		(10)	
	Match	**Price**	**Match**	**Price**	**Match**	**Price**	**Match**	**Price**	**Match**	**Price**	**Match**	**Price**
	Sb-Di	1	Sb-Di	1	Sb-Dj	1	Sb-Dj	1	Sb-Dk	1	Sb-Dk	1
	Sc-Dj	1	Sc-Dk	1	Sc-Di	1	Sc-Dk	1	Sc-Di	1	Sc-Dj	1
	Sa-Dk	1	Sa-Dj	1	Sa-Dk	1	Sa-Di	1	Sa-Dj	1	Sa-Di	1
Q	3		3		3		3		3		3	
S	0		0		0		0		0		0	

Assuming that rank order is Sc, Sa, Sb

	(11)		(12)		(13)		(14)		(15)		(16)	
	Match	**Price**	**Match**	**Price**	**Match**	**Price**	**Match**	**Price**	**Match**	**Price**	**Match**	**Price**
	Sc-Di	1	Sc-Di	1	Sc-Dj	1	Sc-Dj	1	Sc-Dk	1	Sc-Dk	1
	Sa-Dj	1	Sa-Dj	1	Sa-Di	1	Sa-Dk	1	Sa-Di	1	Sa-Dj	1
	-	-	Sb-Dj	2	-	-	Sb-Di	2	Sb-Dj	2	Sb-Di	2
Q	2		3		2		3		3		3	
S	1		0		1		0		0		0	

Q = Number of transactions and quantities transacted

S = Buyer and seller surplus

began in the fall of 1982 motivated the need for greater automation of the order execution process in the OTC market;[23] the NASD filed a proposal for its Small Order Execution System (SOES) with the SEC in October, 1984. The system was speedily approved and began operation in January, 1985.[24] SOES now accounts for about 13 percent of all OTC transactions, providing automatic execution of limited sizes at the best available NASDAQ quotation.[25] The system works in tandem with NASDAQ: market makers enter bid and ask quotes into NASDAQ, which are reflected in SOES. Participation in SOES now is mandatory for all market makers in NASDAQ National Market System (NMS) securities. Market makers maintain two-sided quotations for a security in which they are registered in the system, under certain rules governing limits on minimum size of transactions.[26] Orders may be designated for routing to a particular market maker within SOES, a practice called "preferencing," which accounts for approximately 50 percent of all orders.

An automated centralized limit order book was established within SOES in February, 1989.[27] Prior to this development, only market orders were accepted, priced at the inside quote. The limit order operation also rotates executions among market makers unless an order is preferenced. Orders are executed when the inside price is equal to or better than the limit price on a first in, first out basis, but does not include "limit order protection." So it is possible that an execution may not occur for an eligible limit order. For example, suppose the file contains three orders to sell a security at six, and the inside quote reaches or goes beyond six. SOES attempts to execute all three orders at the inside. If, however, the inside falls to 5 3/4 and the system has executed only two of the three orders, SOES will not execute the last order. It remains in the book until the market again breaks the limit.

The SOES automatic execution algorithm is summarized as follows:[28]

1. Order Eligibility
   A new order is eligible to be matched with a standing order whenever the following conditions occur:
   1.1   a market or limit order is entered to buy or sell;
   1.2   at least one market maker is posting a bid and offer for the particular stock;
   1.3   the inside quote in the NASDAQ system is equal to or better than the price of a limit order.
   1.4   a trade is not executed whenever two limit orders which can be matched are entered between the best bid and offer.
2. Trade Price
   If an order match is possible according to the criteria of Rule 1, then the trade takes place at the best market maker quote in the system.

3. Trade Quantity

   Market makers are required to provide up to 100, 200, 500, or 1,000 shares per order, depending on the stock in question.

4. Total Trade Size

   Every incoming order is assigned to only one market maker.

5. Standing Order Priority

   The priority of a standing bid/offer, relative to other standing bids/offers for the same stock is based on the following:

   5.1 Price: for buy orders, higher price has higher priority; for sell orders, the lower price has higher priority.

   5.2 Rotation: the first market maker in the rotation with the highest/lowest bid/offer gets the first customer order, followed by the next market maker with the highest/lowest price in the rotation, subject to maximum execution limits.

   5.3 Prearrangement: any broker with a customer order may choose to execute the order with a particular market maker in the system if that person has agreed beforehand to meet the best quote in the system.

6. Incoming Order Priority

   All market or limit orders entered into SOES must conform to the following rules.

   6.1 Time priority: all executable orders must be executed on a first-in, first-out basis;

   6.2 Limit order types: allowable types include fill-or-kill, day orders, good-till-canceled, and good-till-date.

Rule 2 encompasses quotes made by any market maker in the NASDAQ system, not just within the automated system. SOES executes incoming orders at the best price within NASDAQ, but only against market makers in SOES who currently are posting prices. With respect to rule 5.2, it is interesting to note that in the pilot phase, the SOES rotation scheme was like RAES, i.e., execution occurred in the system on a rotational basis regardless of the bids and offers of the individual market makers in the rotation. The role of exposure limits is explored in Domowitz (1989).

Consider Display 3.

First, the 100 shares from the limit book at 5 1/4 is matched with the 5 1/8 offer entered at 10:00. The trade is at 5 1/8, by Rule 2. The 9:56 day order at 5 1/8 is matched with the 10:02 market maker's offer for 100 shares at that price. The fill-or-kill order is dropped from the system; it could not be matched with a limit order and there is no matching market maker order at this stage.

Display 3

	Market Markers' Quotes				Orders on the Book			
Time	Order	Price	Quantity	Time	Price	Order	Type	Quantity
10:00	offer	5 1/8	100	9:50	5 1/4	buy	GTC	100
10:01	offer	5 3/8	100	9:52	5 1/8	sell	FOK	100
10:02	offer	5 1/8	100	9:56	5 1/8	buy	DO	100

Proceeding to the analysis of price discovery and quantity determination, note that Rules 2, 3, and 6 are nearly identical to their counterparts on GLOBEX,[29] but there are two major differences that matter in conducting and analyzing the trading scenarios. Rule 5.3 allows for human intervention in the trading process. Such prearranged trading has an impact on market conditions in every period; as noted above, some 50 percent of trades are prearranged. Second, Rule 1.4 does not allow the crossing of customer limit orders entered between the best bid and offer. The scenarios are selected to focus on the first of these differences.

It is assumed that the demand-side traders all have made prearrangements to buy from each of the supply-side traders.[30] Outcomes are summarized in Table 4. Consider scenario #8 in this table. Here, Di and Sc have such an agreement. The best price in the system is one, and Di buys one share from Sc at that price. Suppose that Dj has a purchase arrangement with Sa; this arrangement also is completed at a price of one, which was still the best price available. Sb's offer of two is now the best price. Trading ceases, however, even if Dk and Sb had an agreement to transact, because a price of two is above Dk's limit price of one.

One unique feature of SOES is that it creates the greatest number of possible trading patterns. The prearrangements match orders below the supply-side limit offers, like a RAES rotation; unlike RAES, however, such trades need not follow a predesignated rotation, which creates more possibilities. Prearranged trading on SOES also produces the greatest number of non-Walrasian outcomes. Only two of 32 scenarios result in the Walrasian price, quantity, and surplus; a total of five yield the competitive price and quantity outcomes.

One comment on SOES Rule 1.4 prohibiting executions within the spread is needed here. Consider Figure 3, in which traders Sa and Sb have limit offers entered at prices of 2 and 3, respectively. Di and Dj enter limit bids at prices of 4 and 3, respectively. These orders are executed in GLOBEX in any time sequence, achieving a Walrasian outcome, but the same orders cannot be matched in SOES. To demonstrate the effects of this lack of execution, the scenario can

Table 4 Outcomes for the Prearranged Trading Example on SOES

	(1) Match	Price	(2) Match	Price	(3) Match	Price	(4) Match	Price	(5) Match	Price	(6) Match	Price
	Sa-Di	1	Sa-Di	1	Sb-Di	1	Sb-Di	1	Sb-Di	1	Sb-Di	1
	Sb-Dj	2	Sc-Dj	2	Sc-Dj	1	Sa-Dj	1	Sc-Dk	1	Sa-Dk	1
	-	-	-	-	Sa-Dk	1	-	-	Sa-Dj	-	-	-
Q	2		2		3		2		3		2	
S	2		1		0		2		0		1	

	(7) Match	Price	(8) Match	Price	(9) Match	Price	(10) Match	Price	(11) Match	Price	(12) Match	Price
	Sc-Di	1	Sc-Di	1	Sc-Di	1	Sc-Di	1	Sa-Dj	1	Sa-Dj	1
	Sb-Dj	1	Sa-Dj	1	Sb-Dk	1	Sa-Dk	1	Sc-Di	2	Sb-Di	2
	Sa-Dk	1	-	-	Sa-Dj	1	Sb-Dj	2	-	-	-	-
Q	3		2		3		3		2		2	
S	0		1		0		0		1		2	

	(13) Match	Price	(14) Match	Price	(15) Match	Price	(16) Match	Price	(17) Match	Price	(18) Match	Price
	Sb-Dj	1	Sb-Dj	1	Sb-Dj	1	Sd-Dj	1	Sc-Dj	1	Sc-Dj	1
	Sa-Di	1	Sa-Dk	1	Sc-Di	1	Sc-Dk	1	Sb-Di	1	Sb-Dk	1
	-	-	Sc-Di	3	Sa-Dk	1	Sa-Di	1	Sa-Dk	1	Sa-Di	1
Q	2		3		3		3		3		3	
S	2		0		0		0		0		0	

(Table continues)

Q = Number of transactions and quantities transacted

S = Buyer and seller surplus

Table 4 Outcomes for the Prearranged Trading Example on SOES (Continued)

(19) Match	Price	(20) Match	Price	(21) Match	Price	(22) Match	Price	(23) Match	Price	(24) Match	Price
Sc-Dj	1	Sc-Dj	1	Sa-Dk	1	Sa-Dk	1	Sa-Dk	1	Sa-Dk	1
Sa-Di	1	Sa-Dk	1	Sb-Di	2	Sb-Dj	2	Sc-Di	2	Sc-Dj	2
-	-	Sb-Di	2	-	-	Sc-Di	3	Sb-Dj	2	Sb-Di	2
Q	2		3		2		3		3		3
S	1		0		1		0		0		0

(25) Match	Price	(26) Match	Price	(27) Match	Price	(28) Match	Price	(29) Match	Price	(30) Match	Price
Sb-Dk	1	Sb-Dk	1	Sb-Dk	1	Sb-Dk	1	Sc-Dk	1	Sc-Dk	1
Sa-Di	1	Sa-Dj	1	Sc-Di	1	Sc-Dj	1	Sa-Di	1	Sa-Dj	1
-	1	Sc-Di	3	Sa-Dj	1	Sa-Di	1	Sb-Dj	2	Sb-Di	2
Q	2		3		3		3		3		3
S	1		0		0		0		0		0

(31) Match	Price	(32) Match	Price
Sc-Dk	1	Sc-Dk	1
Sb-Di	1	Sb-Dj	1
Sa-Dj	1	Sa-Di	1
Q	3		3
S	0		0

Q = Number of transactions and quantities transacted

S = Buyer and seller surplus

Figure 3

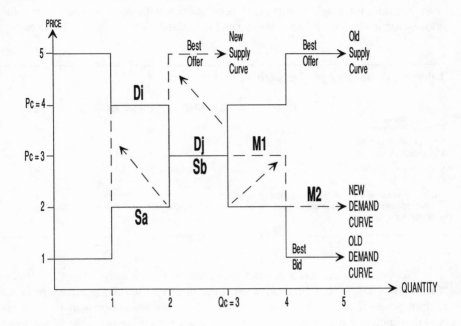

be expanded a bit. Assume that market makers M1 and M2 enter bids at prices of 3 and 2, which remove Sa and Sb from the system. The new clearing price moves to 4 from 3, leaving the orders of Di and Dj unexecuted for the period. On the other hand, if two more market makers submit offers that remove these demand-side traders from the system at this stage, the final quantity outcome is four with a surplus that depends critically on the overall pattern of the market makers' offers. Either way, the outcomes are substantially different from the Walrasian competitive outcome and from the outcome achievable on GLOBEX.

Rule 1.4 also raises the issue of timely execution in SOES. In the previous example, orders submitted by Di and Dj can go unexecuted and conceivably could remain so for some time as the market clearing price rises to four—unless the orders were of the fill-or-kill variety. The phenomenon of "chasing the market" is plausible. The extent of the problem as a practical matter is not known.

Conclusion

Floor trading and computerized execution mechanisms now can be evaluated with respect to a single competitive benchmark—with some caveats along the way, however. It is useful to create a final scorecard, summarized in Table 5.

Table 5   Frequency of Competitive Outcomes

	Floor*	GLOBEX	RAES	SOES
Competitive price	.14	.75	.44	.34
Competitive quantity	.86	.75	.31	.34
Competitive surplus	.43	.50	.13	.13
Competitive outcome**	.57	.75	.19	.16

* Unlikely scenarios were eliminated before computation; see text.
** Computations allow price indeterminacy on the floor and do not include the competitive surplus requirement; see text.

Floor trading achieved a strict Walrasian outcome only one of 14 times. "Strict" here refers to a final price outcome that equalled the competitive equilibrium price. If this requirement is relaxed to allow outcomes with price intervals that included the Walrasian equilibrium, a competitive outcome is achieved 31 percent of the time. Further, certain scenarios are unlikely, given that they require the outcry of limit prices to start the auction. If the probability of such scenarios is set at zero, the competitive outcome is realized 14 and 57 percent of the time, depending on the price outcome as above.

Price indeterminacy is not an issue in interpreting the outcomes of the various computer systems. Walrasian quantity outcomes are paired with competitive prices, or the price is determined not to be competitive. Automated systems achieved the competitive price and quantity without the associated Walrasian surplus in some cases. The competitive outcome is achieved 50 percent of the time in GLOBEX, including the surplus; the Walrasian price/quantity pair is realized 75 percent of the time in a system in which only the best bid and offer are displayed.[31] Options and stock systems conform far less to the competitive ideal: even without the competitive surplus requirement, RAES hit the benchmark only 19 percent of the time. The percentage drops to 13 if the surplus is included. Similarly, SOES achieves the Walrasian outcome 16 percent of the time without the surplus calculation and only six percent otherwise. It is virtually impossible to raise these percentages by cutting out improbable cases, as with floor trading, due to the random character of rotations and prearrangements.

Investigations of automated trading systems, as with any other economic mechanism or market, must be based on an acceptable set of benchmarks that allow cross-system comparisons, as well as on comparisons with regulatory phrases such as "open and competitive" or "least anticompetitive." The Walrasian paradigm is a classic competitive standard in market analysis, but it is not the only possibility. Other standards that are richer in terms of strategic behavior might be developed and applied, although the qualitative conclusions reached here may not be overturned. As mentioned in the introduction, the goal is not only to perform such analysis, but also to state the algorithm governing the price discovery and quantity determination process in a form amenable to the research of others as well. The constructive design of automated trading systems, or of any other automated market in the future, critically depends on the ability to understand precisely their properties in terms of prices and quantities.

Endnotes

[1] *See* Special Study of Securities Markets, Report of the Special Study of the SEC (1963), in H.R. Doc. No. 95, 88th Congress, 1st Session, pt. 2 at 358 and 678.

[2] *See*, for example, Powers (1977).

[3] Melamed (1977) contains a rather complete defense of organized floor trading. Domowitz (1990) presents a summary of the issues from the regulatory perspective.

[4] For example, a trader would be unwilling to place large resting limit orders on an "open book" in an automated system. The "atmosphere and incentive" aspect rests largely on the perceived desirability for human interaction in the trading process. We believe that "markets create themselves" in a sense independent of computers or people. The wheat futures market in Chicago circa 1970-71 is a good example. The market was languishing with respect to volume, but there were plenty of traders available to go into the pit. If there is no expected change in prices, as was the case at the time, there will be no trading by floor brokers or computer.

[5] *See* Ruder and Adkins (1990)

[6] The NYSE opens with a batch system, setting an initial call price, and trading is thenceforth by double auction, with one modification. A specialist keeps the limit orders, which are away from the current price.

[7]   *See* Melamed (1977).

[8]   There is little concern with "large order" scenarios in this chapter; the economic analysis is similar but substantially more complex. *See* Domowitz (1989).

[9]   Empirical support is contained in studies by Schleifer (1986) and Harris and Gurel (1986). Heterogeneous expectations concerning asset prices can motivate the assumption from a theoretical point of view; *see* Black (1971) for additional discussion.

[10]   Monroe (1988) also considers six traders with these corresponding limit prices. Our floor trading analysis is, therefore, directly comparable to hers.

[11]   Most trading pits contain many traders dealing in several contracts with different characteristics. It is possible for traders to initially miss a bid or offer called out on the other side of a large and noisy crowd. Responses also may not be simultaneous for similar reasons. Cases in which orders are large enough in size (number of contracts or shares) to be broken up among several traders can be analyzed similarly.

[12]   In the original submission, the system was called the PMT system, changing the name on June 20, 1988. The original proposal is published in 55 *Federal Register* 25528, (July 7, 1988). The system was approved in February, 1989.

[13]   *See* Domowitz (1990) for discussion of this issue.

[14]   These rules are summarized in CME Responses To Questions Contained In CFTC Letter dated October 6, 1988, Exhibit 1, Question no. 25 (January, 1989).

[15]   *See* SEC Release No. 21695 (January 28, 1985).

[16]   *See* SEC Release No. 25995 (August 19, 1988).

[17]   *See* SEC Release Nos. 25995 (August 19, 1988) and 26373 (December 28, 1988) for eligibility requirements for market makers on the system.

[18]   If the order's limit price is under $3, RAES will execute the order if the market quote is 1/2 point or less from the limit price. If the order's limit price is $3 or more, the order is executed if the market quote is $1 or less from the limit price.

[19] IBM and S&P 100 contracts are traded on the system even when the limit price on the book is greater/less than the current best offer/bid in RAES. These contracts are extremely liquid.

[20] Rules 1, 2, and 5 are contained in SEC Release No. 21695 (January 28, 1985). The remainder were obtained from John Shalvis, a RAES operations specialist at CBOE (May 4, 1989).

[21] Dealers on the floor or in Globex also may make markets in this way, but are not required to do so. During the October, 1987 market break, market makers pulled all bids and offers out of RAES. CBOE officials responded by making RAES participation essentially mandatory. *See* SEC Release No. 25995 (August 19, 1988).

[22] A surplus of zero can occur here as surpluses are "swapped" among buyers and sellers. To illustrate, consider example #9 in Table 3 again. Sb transacts with Dk at a price of one less than Sb's limit price for a quantity of one, yielding a "surplus" of -1. Dk trades at the limit price, yielding no surplus. Sc trades at a price of two below his limit price, resulting in a surplus of -2, while Di trades at a price of two below limit, yielding a surplus of 2. Dj also gains a surplus of one, and Sa transacts at limit for no surplus. The surplus total is zero.

[23] *See* Simon and Colby (1986).

[24] *See* letter from J.M. Cangiano, Secretary of the NASD, to M.J. Simon, SEC, (October 18, 1984), and the attached file SR-NASD-84-26. A description of the SOE system is contained therein. *See* also SEC Release No. 21743 (February 12, 1985).

[25] *See* SEC Release No. 26361 (December 22, 1988).

[26] The role of, and restrictions on, market makers were topics of post-1987 reforms following the market break. *See* SEC Release No. 25291 (June 9, 1988), and Release No. 26361 (December 22, 1988).

[27] *See* SEC Release No. 26476 (January 26, 1989) for a description of the limit order file.

[28] Rules 1.1, 1.2, 5.1, 5.2, and 5.3 are taken from the SOES Users Manual (revised June, 1989). Rules 1.3, 6.1, and 6.2 come from the SOES Limit Order User Guide (January, 1989). Rules 4 and 1.4 are found in SEC Act

File No. SR-NASD-84-26, (October 18, 1984), and Release No. 26476 (January 26, 1989), respectively.

[29] There are three differences between the two systems that do not affect our scenario analysis, but are worth a mention. First, in SOES all orders hit only a single market maker, while the GLOBEX system allows the quantity of an incoming order to be executed against multiple standing orders. SOES also must execute the orders at the best bid or offer in NASDAQ, a market outside the system but running in tandem. GLOBEX opens only when the floor is closed. Finally, SOES matches incoming orders with market makers on a rotational basis; GLOBEX assigns incoming orders to standing orders according to time priority.

[30] The purpose is to show how many combinations are possible. In these examples, every one of the demand-side traders has a prearrangement with every one of the supply-side traders in some combination. For the sake of simplicity, it is assumed that supply-side traders (market makers) exhaust their execution limits after any trade. *See* Domowitz (1989) for a relaxation of this assumption.

[31] As noted, GLOBEX eventually will move to an open book system displaying the 10 best bids and offers with associated size. Preliminary analysis of such an open book indicates that when there are no traders to the right of the intersection of supply and demand, outcomes are the same under open and closed book systems. If orders exist to be right of the intersection, an open book may generate suboptimal pricing and quantity determination, however. Such results depend on rather specialized assumptions and should be interpreted with caution. Further analysis of this situation is important from the regulatory perspective; *see* Domowitz (1990).

Additional References

Black, F., "Toward A Fully Automated Exchange," 27 *Financial Analysts Journal*, (July/August, 1971), pp. 29-35, and (November/December, 1971), pp. 25-28, 86-87.

Domowitz, I., "The Mechanics of Automated Trade Execution Systems," unpublished manuscript, Northwestern University (1989).

Domowitz, I., "When Is A Marketplace A Market? Automated Trade Execution In The Futures Market," this volume (1990).

Harris, L. and Gurel, E. (1986), "Price and Volume Effects Associated With Changes In The S&P 500 List: New Evidence For The Existence Of Price Pressures," 41 *Journal of Finance*, (1986), pp. 815-829.

Melamed, L., "The Mechanics Of A Commodity Futures Exchange: A Critique Of Automation Of The Transaction Process," 6 *Hofstra Law Review*, (1977), pp. 149-172.

Monroe, M., "Indeterminacy Of Price And Quantity In Futures Markets," 8 *Journal of Futures Markets*, (1988), pp. 575-588.

Powers, M., "Computerized Trading—A Framework For Analysis," *Proceedings Of The CFTC Conference On Automation In The Futures Industry*, on file at the Commodity Futures Trading Commission, (1977), pp. 55-93.

Ruder, D. and Adkins, A., "Automation Of Information Dissemination And Trading In The U.S. Securities Markets," this volume (1990).

Schleifer, A., "Do Demand Curves For Stocks Slope Down?" 41 *Journal of Finance*, (1986), pp. 579-590.

Simon, M. and Colby, R., "The National Market System For Over-The-Counter Stocks," 17 *George Washington Law Review*, (1986) pp. 34-38.

Order Routing: A Technological and Economic Perspective

Rajiv M. Dewan
Northwestern University

One of the basic functions of a market is to bring buyers and sellers together so they can trade. This is performed by the order routing system of the market mechanism. In addition to routing orders from investors to market makers, the order routing system also provides trade information to exchange data systems for clearance and consolidation, and to investors for trade confirmation. Most of these functions require data management and data communication systems—systems that have been revolutionized by changes in information technology.

The effect of technological change on order routing has not been confined to the automation of pre-existing order routing methods. Today, market participants and the economic games played by them have changed: new investors, like pension fund managers, and new market makers are trading in new ways.

As a result, markets with automated order routing systems differ sharply from those without automated systems. The following markets illustrate this point.

Order routing on the New York Stock Exchange in the late 1960s illustrates the common chronology of order routing in all of the early, and some of today's, financial markets. The investor called his local broker and placed an order. The broker then either called his own firm's trading desk—if his firm was a member of the exchange—or the trading desk of a member firm with whom he had a contract. The member firm transmitted the order by phone or by pneumatic tube to its booth on the exchange floor. A runner at the booth took the order and presented it to the specialist for execution. Trades were confirmed by using the reverse route.

The NYSE's automated order routing system, developed in 1976, is called the Super Designated Order Turnaround (SUPERDOT) system. With SUPER-DOT, the market and limit orders[1] are entered by a broker or large institutional investor into a terminal and then transmitted directly to the appropriate specialist. After the specialist executes the trade, the confirmation notice is routed back to the investor. Details of the transaction also are sent to the appropriate divisions for clearance, settlement, surveillance, and dissemination of trade information. As an indication of SUPERDOT's significance, 73 percent of the NYSE share volume was generated from SUPERDOT orders by September 1987.[2]

This description of the change in the way orders are processed understates the impact technology has on the financial markets. Add to it the impact of the change in market participants, and in the games they play. For example, the impact of increased immediacy that is made possible by automated systems permits the development of new trading strategies called program trading.[3] These new strategies include such risk management methodologies as portfolio insurance, which requires rapid change in portfolio position based on market movement. This means portfolio insurance is crucially reliant on the immediacy provided by automated order routing systems. The availability of risk management strategies, in turn, has permitted the entry of new players, such as pension fund investors, into the equity market. The net result of these changes is that today's market is vastly different from earlier markets.

This comparison of NYSE order routing before and after the development of an automated order routing system illustrates the importance of a joint economic/technological perspective when order routing systems are studied. While the technological perspective is sufficient to predict the effect of technology on immediacy, predictions about whole-market impact require an economic perspective. An overview of existing order routing systems in today's markets, the value of a joint perspective and the impact of current trends in information technology—on order routing systems in particular and markets in general—are assessed below.

Existing Order Routing Systems

In general, the order routing process has two components: investor order routing, from the investor to the broker, and broker order routing, from the broker to the market maker. It is instructive to make this distinction because the technology used to implement these two components is quite different.

Broker Order Routing

Broker order routing generally gets more attention than investor order routing because brokers concentrate orders from individual investors and, consequently, they can take advantage of scale economies of operation which arise from the technology and the economics of the markets. The setup cost for communication and other related equipment generates the large-scale advantages from technology. Other advantages arise from the economics of direct or indirect participation in clearance and exchange organizations. For this reason, broker order routing systems tend to be automated more often than investor order routing systems.

There are many kinds of broker order routing systems, including exchange-owned, nonretail firm-owned, or retail firm-owned. The nature of the ownership is important here because each system has different levels of access to the information systems of other market participants. For instance, exchange-owned systems are tied more closely to exchange data systems, among them SUPERDOT at NYSE, SOES at NASDAQ, and PER at Amex. Some broker systems are owned by firms that provide financial data communication services, including Instinet of Reuters Plc., and Data Network Service (DNS) and Message and Order Processing System (MOPS) of ADP Financial Information Services, Inc. These non-proprietary systems are not tied to a particular exchange or to a particular retail broker. As a result, they can serve a broad range of investors and route orders to additional exchanges. In fact, they often link with exchange-owned order routing systems. Some trading firms that participate in market making and brokerage, such as Shearson Lehman and Merrill Lynch, have in-house proprietary order routing systems that are linked to either non-proprietary or exchange-owned order routing systems. These systems are most closely tied to investor order routing systems.

The advantage of broker order routing systems is that they can serve many functions. Most commonly, they route market and limit orders for single stocks, either directly to a market maker or to a runner at the exchange floor.[4] In addition, these systems can disassemble basket orders into orders for individual stocks and route them to appropriate market makers. They also accept and route pre-opening orders to market makers. After the order is executed, the order routing system provides trade information to clearance, settlement, and surveillance systems.

Order routing systems also are responsible for providing input to the market making function. Consequently, automated broker systems are a support system for market making because they reduce manual handling of orders, help the market maker discover prices and, therefore, reduce transaction costs. In many cases, the efficiency of a broker system is augmented by an order execution system for small orders that is run at the behest of market makers, including such systems as the Small Order Executive System (SOES) at NASDAQ and SUPERDOT at NYSE. Although these systems are touted as automated market making systems, many do not run independent of the market makers. The market makers have the option to, in effect, exit from automated systems. Furthermore, automated market making plays a much smaller role than automated broker order routing. For instance only two percent of share volume, or 15 percent of trade volume, in NASDAQ is a result of automated execution. On the NYSE, only very small orders are automatically executed by SUPERDOT. This is in contrast to the significant role of order routing systems—more than half of all orders on NYSE are routed by SUPERDOT.[5]

Investor Order Routing

Investor order routing from investors to brokers, in contrast to broker order routing, typically takes place over the telephone. Investors who trade often substitute data communication for voice communication by accessing a broker system with a personal computer to place an order. Institutional investors commonly have direct-line access to broker trading floors and can participate in such trading networks as Autex.

Similar to broker order routing, investor order routing yields certain scale advantages. For example, many institutional buyers invest in special communication systems and other related trading resources to gain advantages. One common form of communication investment is to buy or lease a direct line to brokers or dealers. Leasing a direct communication line literally buys that investor an option or reserves communication capacity. In addition, many other order routing enhancements used by brokers also are available to institutional investors. For example, financial firms can use companies such as Automated Data Processing (ADP) to transmit their orders to the markets.[6]

By investing in broker communication systems with many more sophisticated options, institutional investors can profit from readier access to the markets. Most important, the probability that these investors can get through to the broker much more rapidly is sharply increased. This was demonstrated profoundly by the difference in market access between individual and institutional investors during the market break in October 1987. As reported in several surveys conducted by the SEC and by the Brady Commission, most institutional investors did not experience inordinate difficulty in getting through to the brokers' trading desks during that market break. Individual retail investors, however, did not fare as well; they reported large delays and more difficulty getting through to their brokers in October 1987.

The Importance of a Joint Perspective

Some basic issues that must be considered in the design of efficient order routing systems include the time it takes to route orders and trade confirmation notices, the content of the order message presented to market participants, the identification of market participants, and the locations of market participants who are supported by the system.[7] The descriptions below illustrate the importance of joining economic and technological perspectives in order to analyze these issues effectively.

Content of Order Message

Because order routing provides input for market making, one of the more important decisions in designing the system is how to decide the content of the message presented to market makers. One approach is to replicate the content of a manually-routed order message. This may seem simple at the outset, but it presents certain technological challenges. For instance, the physical activity on the exchange floor and among market participants conveys information to the market maker. This is most apparent in dealer markets that use open outcry, such as the Chicago Mercantile Exchange and the Chicago Board Options Exchange. But this floor/participant activity is difficult to capture and present to the market maker using an automated system.

So by automating the order routing and presentation of information to the market maker, the choices for message selection are different than simply emulating the content of manually-routed order messages. For example, an automated system can compute and present statistics of routed orders on a real-time basis. These statistics could include current trends in orders[8] and a comparison with order trends in other markets, and could become incorporated into the decision support system made available to market makers.

Another development includes the use of private firms that offer trade information services. Data vendors such as ADP, Telekurs, Quotron, and Reuters get executed trade information and computed statistics directly from the exchanges, which they pass on to market participants. This market-based approach has worked extremely well for the dissemination of trade information because it encourages vendor firms to develop a wide variety of information systems, which provides market participants with more options in assembling their own system. A market-based structure (i.e., based on the market for information services) also can be adapted within order routing systems to establish a market for market maker information services. This option fosters more innovation in the development and use of market maker information services, and it may result in more efficient markets.

However, the effect of the additional information made available by current technology can be difficult to assess. The identification of basket orders in the SUPERDOT system is one example. Typically, a SUPERDOT order displayed on a specialist terminal indicates the originating terminal. It does not, however, indicate whether the SUPERDOT order is part of a basket order that was entered using SUPERDOT's LIST processing option.[9] As described in Grossman (1990), this information is highly relevant because nonarbitrage-related basket trades have a lower probability of originating with investors who are informed about a particular stock. Without this information, the cost of transacting basket orders is higher for uninformed investors and lower for informed traders. By including the identity of basket orders, an opposite effect would be achieved. Consequently, deciding whether or not to include the identification of basket orders in SUPER-DOT depends on the resolution of these two competing viewpoints, as well as on other effects.

Order Routing Delays

Delays are another issue to consider because they have a detrimental effect on how well the market functions when prices are volatile. Delays hinder the price discovery function, fragment the markets, and make them far less efficient. Consequently, a faster response from all components of the market system—including the order routing system, the market making system, and the trade information dissemination system—is highly desirable. Unfortunately, however, delays in data transfer are generally inevitable.

From a technological standpoint, there are two sources of delay: the time it takes to propagate the order from origin to destination (propagation delay), and the time it takes to place the order on the communication medium (capacity delay). Propagation delay is a function of the distance between the origin and the destination of the message. Capacity delay is a function of communication capacity and intermediate processing.[10]

Capacity delay is a distinct disadvantage when fast response during periods of high volatility are required by the situation. Generally, periods of high volatility also experience high volume. One reason could be that a larger number of trades generated by heterogeneously informed investors results in more volatile prices, as happened following the October 1987 market break.

When loaded, the communication and processing systems that form the technical backbone of any order routing system behave like queuing systems. When capacity utilization increases, average capacity delay increases from a very small[11] to a very large value as the systems approach full-capacity utilization. In other words, delay in a high-volume period can arbitrarily worsen as more capacity is utilized. Investor surveys completed after the October 1987 market break by the SEC (1988) and the Brady Commission (1988) found that delays in market systems were a major cause of investor dissatisfaction. The only apparent solution to this delay problem is a partial one: increasing surplus capacity to mitigate the effect of high volume. Although this may be easy to implement technologically, this solution is not without economic problems, such as who should make the investment in spare capacity. The investment in surplus capacity by different groups of market participants differs across markets.

In the NYSE, surplus order routing capacity is built into the exchange-owned SUPERDOT system, into proprietary systems such as ADP, and into the communication lines leased by member firms and "upstairs" trading firms. These leased lines, in close physical proximity to the exchange floor, augment the market's order routing capacity. Therefore in this example, the exchange, the communication services firms, and the investors all support the investment in communication capacity.

In contrast, NASDAQ has no physical floor that serves as a physical focus for investment in communications so the exchange itself and the market makers finance the investment in increased communication capacity. Although some non-proprietary systems feed SOES, the volume is very small. Therefore on the whole, there is much less spare capacity in NASDAQ than in NYSE. The negative effect of this lack of spare capacity on investors also was evident in NASDAQ's inaccessibility during the October 1987 market break.

Propagation Delay

Normally, propagation delay is not crucial because, for example, the delay on a coast-to-coast message is only about one one-hundredth of a second. But to the extent markets globalize, propagation delay becomes more significant: the propagation delay on a message from Japan to the United States is about one-sixteenth of a second,[12] which is quite substantial during busy markets. By comparison, NYSE's SUPERDOT averaged more than 69 orders per second October 19, 1987, and more than 19,500 December SPZ contracts were traded during a one-hour period on the Chicago Mercantile Exchange the same date.

This level of volume indicates strongly that propagation delay cannot be neglected when price-time priority is established. Unfortunately, there is no technological solution for shortening propagation time on the increasing number of global messages. One solution developed for the GLOBEX system is to add origin-dependent, artificial delays to orders so that the sum of added delay and propagation delay is constant. This is a tradeoff between the small margin of market efficiency and proper priority—a tradeoff decision that can be made only by examining the economics of market making.

Location of Market Participants

Automated order routing reduces the need for buyers and sellers or their agents to be physically present at the market, which results in lower transaction costs because the communication system serves as a direct substitute for their physical presence. In other cases like NASDAQ's over-the-counter securities market, which is a dispersed market, there is no exchange floor.[13] OTC securities are supported by multiple market makers who compete for orders from different locations. These market makers are linked by data and voice communication systems. NASDAQ uses two primary channels of broker order routing: 1.) telephone to market maker and 2.) NASDAQ's Small Order Execution System (SOES). SOES accepts orders of up to 1,000 shares in NASDAQ/NMS securities and of up to 500 shares in other NASDAQ securities. SOES, along with telephone and proprietary order routing systems such as the Automated Execution System (AES) used by Shearson Lehman, make up the investor order routing system.

In some dealer markets data communication is used to replace direct physical communication between market makers. In such markets there are no 'exchange floors' that can serve as focus for communication investment by investors and other non-market making participants. As a consequence, these markets have less spare communication capacity that may be used during periods of stress such as the 1987 market break.

Technology Innovation and Its Impact on Markets

Information technology is changing in two important ways: there has been a steady decline in the price of hardware, and advanced software for aiding decision making and managing data has been developed. When increased competition in the communications industry is added to the equation, communication costs also decline—and they are expected to decline even further as a result of continuing technological innovations. The next step is for market participants to analyze how these changing trends in information technology will affect the market and assess the impact of these trends on the future economic behavior of market participants. Although communication processes and computing technologies are described separately below, they should not be considered independent factors: communication technology depends on computing technology for the development of new digital communication techniques, and data communication provides the input for computation.

Communication Technology

With the rapid development and deployment of ultra high-capacity optic fiber systems and with the phenomenon of increasing competition, communication costs are expected to drop dramatically in the next decade, as described by Arthur Anderson and Company (1986). This projection promises to affect every market mechanism in use today with both losses and gains in some form. For example, collecting fundamental and technical information will ultimately cost less; but the value of this information will decline correspondingly. The net impact on market efficiency, therefore, depends on the net of these two competing effects. Historically, greater market efficiency has resulted from the combined effects.

Another effect of reduced communication costs is larger spare order routing capacity. But the downside is that concomitant changes in order processes, such as the development of new program trading mechanisms, can negate the decrease in capacity delay because of the larger spare capacity. When these two effects are combined, at the very least a new level of order processing activity and a new capacity within the order routing mechanism results.

Reduced communication costs also affect market making. For instance, fixed market making costs are reduced. In the competitive, market making NASDAQ market, reduced costs encourage a larger number of market makers to participate and as a result, the market becomes more liquid.[14]

Reduced communication costs together with more communication technology options also have changed the ways by which trade information is disseminated. The ticker, which was introduced in the market before the light bulb was invented, has been supplanted by high-speed computer-to-computer data communications that have forced the ticker into second place as an information source. During high-volume periods like the October 1987 market break, the ticker was as much as two hours behind the high-speed tape. In contrast, the new technology consolidates trade information from multiple markets into one tape, which has a twofold effect: it reduces information costs and it improves market efficiency. As a result, shorter capacity delays in trade reporting enhances the implementation of program trading strategies. For these reasons, it is likely that market transactions will profit both from the wider consolidations possible, and the shorter time lag between the time of execution and the time of trade reports.

Computing Technology

The primary impact on computing technology is the continuous decline in hardware costs. They are declining by a factor of 10 for main memory every five years, for processors every seven years and for secondary storage every 10 years (see Gurbaxani (1987)). Three other impacts come from the new decision-support software that is usable by a much larger segment of market participants, from new data management programs, and from new applications of artificial intelligence. These enhancements in computing technology have a continuous affect on every aspect of decision making within the market mechanism.

One effect is the change in portfolio management strategy within both individual and institutional investor groups. Not only does the new technology reduce the cost of acquiring and processing technical and fundamental information about stocks. In addition, new risk management techniques that depend on the immediacy and computing power of these new systems have dramatically changed the market as well. Although some observers believe these trading practices increase volatility and decrease individual investor participation, the evidence is not unequivocal. At least part of the increased volatility results from greater market efficiency. With the increasing availability of inexpensive hardware and software plus more market data, individual investors have much greater access to the markets than ever before.

During the 1980s, one area of crucial software development was transaction management. In a data management system, transaction management subsystems guarantee that transactions are executed, that they are executed with a pre-specified priority scheme, and that a sufficient record of the transaction is retained so that it is recreatable and traceable. In addition, these transaction management systems provide location transparency; that means users can be oblivious to the location of the computing center. These features, therefore, are directly useful to the order routing systems in the financial markets: they mitigate the effects of dispersed markets such as NASDAQ, they provide transaction information for surveillance, and they enforce priority schemes. Excluding the function of immediacy, the advantages inherent in automated order routing stem directly from transaction management.

Conclusions

Order routing plays an important role in the market mechanism to the extent it provides input to the market making process. The two facets of order routing systems, economics and technology, are co-dependent. For example, the use of technology to identify basket orders is constrained by the effects of the economic behavior of market participants. Features that are desirable from an economic standpoint, such as low delay during volatile trading periods, are difficult to attain technologically. So the solution to these and other problems requires a joint technological and economic perspective that can be put to use not only in analyzing existing systems but also in developing new order routing systems that result from innovation in information technology.

Endnotes

1   A market order is an order to buy or sell a specified quantity at the market price, whatever that might be. A limit order, on the other hand, is an order to buy or sell a specified quantity at a given price or a price better than the given price. Currently, SUPERDOT has an upper limit on the order size it accepts. Post-opening market orders for up to 2,099 are accepted in all stocks. The size limits for more liquid stocks, for limit and pre-opening orders are different. This and other information about the NYSE can be found in the NYSE Fact Book (1988) published annually by the NYSE.

2   The SEC Report (1988). Footnote 66, at 7-21.

3   On an average day in 1986, 10% of the daily trade volume was program-trading related. In some half-hour periods during the market break of October 1987, over 40% of the trade volume was program-trading related. Over half of this volume was a result of portfolio-insurance related trades.

4   An example of a system that routes orders to runners is the BOOTH program at NYSE.

5   NYSE's SUPERDOT has an automated execution service called the Immediate Reporting Service. Orders of up to 1,099 shares in some selected stocks are eligible for this service. If the spread is less than one-eighth of a point and the NYSE has the best quote as compared to others from the ITS, the order is executed right away. Other orders of less than 1,099 shares are assigned the current quote as a reference price and are displayed on the specialist display book. If the specialist does not rescind the execution within two minutes, the order is assumed to have been executed at that reference price.

6   Approximately 25% of SUPERDOT's order flow comes from ADP, which routes orders from institutional investors and brokers.

7   These represent the "when," "who," and "where" issues of order routing, respectively. "Why" is beyond the scope of this chapter.

8   Statistics of executed trades are already available to investors, dealers, and market makers. Order statistics are different than trade statistics because it is ex-ante information and not all orders result in trades.

9   Prior distribution of basket trades by the specialist across terminals and knowledge from the originating terminal does provide some information.

[10] The following example illustrates the concepts behind the two delays. Hypothetically, a message has to be sent from Station 1 to Station 2 by placing the message on the side of a train that travels at a fixed speed. The time taken to transfer the message includes the time for the first coach to travel from Station 1 to Station 2 (propagation time) and the time between when the first coach passes the observer on Station 2 and when the last coach passes that same observer (capacity delay). Propagation delay is proportional to the distance between the two stations. Capacity delay depends on the capacity communication medium, which is the message capacity of each coach side in this case.

[11] This small value is the time taken to serve a single order.

[12] The propagation delay is 1/16 of a second (two round trips—one for data and the other for acknowledgement) if terrestrial lines are used and about 1.4 seconds if satellite links are used. Although satellite links have higher propagation delay, they can have much higher capacities.

[13] NASDAQ regulations require at least two market makers for the initial listing of a stock. At least one market maker is required to continue listing. In 1986, every NASDAQ security had an average of eight market makers.

[14] When fixed costs are lower, a smaller share of the market order is enough for a market maker to make normal returns. Consequently, this results in a larger number of market makers in equilibrium. Details of this analysis can be found in Ho and Macris (1985).

Additional References

Arthur Anderson & Co., "Trends in Information Technology: 1986," (1986).

Brady, Nicholas, "Report of the Presidential Task Force on Market Mechanisms," U.S. Government Printing Office, (January, 1988).

Grossman, Sanford, J., "Trading Technology and Financial Market Stability," this volume.

Gurbaxani, V., "Software-Hardware Tradeoffs and Data Process Budgets," Ph.D. dissertation, University of Rochester, (1987).

Ho, T.S.Y. and Macris, R.G., "Dealer Market Structure and Performance," *Market Making and the Changing Structure of the Securities Industry*, Amihud, Y., Ho, T.S.Y.. and Schwartz, R.A. Eds., (Lexington, 1985).

New York Stock Exchange, "The NYSE Fact Book 1988," (March, 1988).

United States Securities and Exchange Commission, "The October 1987 Market Break: A Report by the Division of Market Regulation," (February, 1988).

REGULATORY ISSUES

Regulation and the Automation of Information Dissemination and Trading in the U.S. Securities Markets

David S. Ruder
U.S. Securities and Exchange Commission

Alden S. Adkins
U.S. Securities and Exchange Commission[*]

Automated information dissemination and trading systems have developed during the last three decades at an accelerated pace.[1] In 1963, the SEC's Special Study of the securities markets noted the possibility that trading in the over-the-counter markets could benefit from automation and that exchange markets could be improved by the introduction of automated systems.[2] In 1975, Congress directed the SEC to "facilitate the establishment of a national market system for securities."[3] It found that:

- New data processing and communications techniques create the opportunity for more efficient and effective market operations;[4]

[*] The views expressed are those of David Ruder and Alden Adkins and do not necessarily represent those of the Securities and Exchange Commission, Commissioners, or Commission's staff.

- The linking of all markets for qualified securities through communication and data processing facilities will foster efficiency, enhance competition, increase the information available to brokers, dealers and investors, facilitate the offsetting of investors' orders, and contribute to the best execution of such orders.[5]

Developments since 1975 have resulted in automated systems in the U.S. securities markets for:

1. Dissemination of current quotation and last price information;
2. Routing of orders to selected markets;
3. Execution of securities transactions;
4. Market surveillance; and
5. Clearance, settlement, and payment.

Not only do such automated securities systems exist, but they are connected to and affected by other important markets in the United States and abroad. For instance, development of a futures market for trading derivative index products has made the connection between futures and stock markets both obvious and important.[6] Also, market linkages between U. S. securities markets and similar markets in Canada, Europe, and Asia emphasize the coming development of actual global trading systems.

These systems permit a useful analysis of the way the SEC regulates automation. It must review automation developments to see that investor protection exists and that the structural soundness of our markets is maintained. It also must exercise its regulatory authority in ways that will accommodate growing innovation in automated securities markets.

Automation in the U.S. Securities Markets

Automated Information Dissemination

Prior to the late 1960s, the principal information concerning securities trading available on a "real-time" basis[7] was the trade information disseminated through the stock tickers of the Amex and the NYSE. Real-time price information[8] was not available from regional exchanges or from the over-the-counter market, and real-time quotation[9] information was not available from either the exchanges or from the over-the-counter market.

In 1968, the National Association of Securities Dealers, Inc. (NASD) began to develop an automated quotation dissemination system.[10] This system, implemented in 1971 as the NASDAQ (National Association of Securities Dealers Automated Quotation) system, offers real-time electronic entry and dissemination through video display screens of market maker quotations in over-the-counter securities. The system has evolved to include real-time price information for the larger, more active OTC stocks.[11] The NASD also is currently considering providing real-time quotation information for smaller "pink sheet" stocks.[12] NASDAQ now is linked internationally with the Stock Exchange Automated Quotation (SEAQ) system of the International Stock Exchange (ISE) and with Singapore's automated quotation system.[13]

Concurrent with the development of the NASDAQ system, the nation's securities exchanges began to install automated systems for display of price and quotation information called the Consolidated Transaction Reporting and Quotation Systems.[14] Today, current prices and quotations from the floors of all U.S. securities exchanges are displayed electronically, both on exchange floors and on video display screens available to brokers and other users. But despite the availability of automated display systems, trading techniques on most exchanges continue to utilize the traditional personal auction trading method, in combination with automated trading for smaller orders.[15]

The Consolidated Transaction Reporting System, which became operational in 1974 and is governed by an intermarket agreement under SEC rules,[16] consolidates real-time trade reports from all markets, including the regional exchanges and the OTC market. The reports cover all securities listed on the NYSE and the Amex, and certain securities listed on regional stock exchanges. Reports from each market are collected immediately after execution, transmitted electronically to a central processor, and promptly disseminated. Reports from the various trading markets on each security are disseminated in the sequence received. This system improved on the stock tickers of the NYSE and the Amex, not only by consolidating trade reports but also by providing for a high-speed line[17] that disseminates real-time information without delays even during periods of very high volume.

In 1978, again under an intermarket agreement and SEC rules,[18] the Consolidated Quotation System became operational. This system consolidates quotations from among all markets trading NYSE and Amex securities, and certain regional listings; identifies the best bid and offer in each security from among all these markets; and disseminates that information.

While options price and quotation information dissemination is not subject to the SEC's consolidated trade and quotation rules, the SEC has insisted on real-time options price and quotation reporting. As a result, an options quotation and trade reporting system was established in 1975 by the options exchanges under an intermarket agreement promulgated under SEC rules.[19] The system is governed by the Options Price Reporting Authority (OPRA).

Today, the Consolidated Transaction Reporting and Quotation Systems makes U.S. equity and options markets an excellent source of real-time information and they are regarded as being as transparent as any in the world.[20]

Automated Order Routing

In addition to providing information to the public, the information dissemination systems have provided the base necessary for the efficient operation of automated order routing systems. Until the late 1960s, order routing was accomplished by telephone and pneumatic tube, and execution was effected by voice—either over the telephone, as in the over-the-counter market, or in person, as on an exchange.[21]

Beginning in 1969 with the creation of the Pacific Stock Exchange's automated order routing and execution system, U.S. markets have developed a variety of systems for the automated, electronic routing of orders directly from off the floor to a location on the floor where execution can take place. Or, in the case of the OTC markets, orders can be routed from brokers directly to dealers or to a centralized execution facility.

In addition to the internal order routing systems of the various markets, the Intermarket Trading System (ITS) facilitates the routing of orders between markets. By providing each market with the capability of routing orders to other markets, this system allows orders to be routed to the market having the best quotes.[22] ITS also enhances the ability of regional exchange specialists to compete with primary markets by providing them with an efficient method for transmitting excess positions to other exchanges.

Limited international order routing arrangements also exist between U.S. and foreign markets, but the systems have not prospered. The Toronto Stock Exchange terminated its link with the Midwest Stock Exchange (MSE) and with Amex. An order routing link between the Boston Stock Exchange and the Montreal Stock Exchange also exists, but the volume of trading is small.[23]

Order routing systems have brought efficiencies to U.S. markets primarily because they permit speedy transmission of orders. The most significant of the exchange systems is the NYSE's system for automated routing through its Designated Order Turnaround (DOT) system, called SUPERDOT.[24] In the 1970s, the NYSE developed SUPERDOT to route small orders electronically from brokers off the exchange to the specialist.[25] To accommodate program trading,[26] the NYSE in 1982 adapted the SUPERDOT system to allow the instantaneous routing of orders to the floor in a large number of different securities.[27]

Execution difficulties for both small and large orders have sometimes resulted when specialists have been confronted with waves of program orders, as occurred on October 19 and 20, 1987.[28] In response to these concerns, the NYSE instituted procedures to provide preferential routing of small customer orders if the Dow Jones Industrial Average (DJIA) moves 25 points.[29] In addition, the NYSE implemented an application of SUPERDOT that withholds program trade orders in an electronic "sidecar" for five minutes if the DJIA moves approximately 96 points.[30]

Automated Order Execution

Starting with the Pacific Stock Exchange's Comex System in 1969, regional exchanges now compete with primary markets by developing small order execution systems that provide automated routing and computerized execution of small customer orders, generally at the best intermarket quote for a security.[31] When a broker off the exchange floor sends small customer orders (e.g., 1,099 shares) to the specialist on the floor of the regional exchange, the specialist is usually given an opportunity to improve on the best intermarket quotation.[32] If the specialist chooses not to improve, the system automatically executes the order at the best ITS quotation, generates trade comparison reports, and transmits last price reports to the consolidated tape system.

In the over-the-counter market, volume surges in 1982 drove the NASD to add a Small Order Execution System (SOES) to its NASDAQ system. SOES was put into operation in 1985, and recently was supplemented with a limit order execution capacity.[33] Surges in index options volume and competition in multiple listings of options have spurred similar innovations in the options markets.[34] As a result of these developments, small order execution on equity and options markets now is largely automated.

The Cincinnati Stock Exchange (CSE) and the NASD have extended automation to orders of all sizes. The CSE system, or National Security Trading System (NSTS), is linked with other markets in ITS and is the only fully automated U.S. exchange.[35] The NASD recently implemented its Order Confirmation Transaction (OCT) system, which provides the opportunity for computerized automated negotiation. Following the computerized exchange of information, a broker-dealer now can execute a trade with a market-maker through a keyboard stroke.[36] Significantly, however, the volume on the CSE remains low, and NASD's keyboard execution still requires the market-maker to agree to the size of the transaction.[37]

Other Developments

In addition to these automated information, routing, and execution systems, other notable developments have occurred. First, the increasing development of so-called "proprietary trading systems," which are information dissemination and trading systems developed by private entities that are not registered as self-regulatory organizations. The first major operational proprietary trading system was Instinet, which came into existence in the late 1960s.[38]

Instinet was a response to the institutionalization of markets and increasing institutional demand for a way to trade directly, without the intervention of a broker-dealer. Today, it has evolved to the point where it provides automated trading capabilities as well as information dissemination.[39] In addition, Instinet has a Crossing Network that provides for the automated entry of orders for baskets of stocks, and for the automated matching and execution of such orders against orders entered into the system on the other side of the market, to the extent they exist. Jefferies and Company developed a similar system, called POSIT.[40]

Another example of a proprietary trading system is the Delta Options system, which received a no-action letter from the SEC allowing it to operate without registering as an exchange.[41] The Delta Options system involves the electronic collection and dissemination of quotations, and the clearance and settlement of trades. Delta Options is in large part a blind brokering system in which system users input quotes on an anonymous basis through an intermediary, or so-called blind broker, to see the quotes of other users of the system, and to execute against those quotes through the blind brokers. In addition, the system allows direct negotiation of trades by system users. It does not involve automated or computer-generated executions.[42]

The Amex and the NASD are developing automated systems to accommodate active secondary trading among institutions in securities that are not registered with the SEC.[43] These systems, which do not provide automated routing or execution, respond to increasing institutional demands for active trading markets for privately placed securities. The SEC has proposed a rule that would formalize the legal treatment of such trading.[44]

Finally, other developments are occurring both internationally and in other markets that may have competitive effects on U.S. securities markets. Most recently, the Chicago Mercantile Exchange received approval for an after-hours, automated futures trading system.[45] The Chicago Board of Trade is likely to follow suit, and as a result, the futures markets in the United States will consist of a combination of open outcry, physically centralized markets during normal hours, coupled with after-hours computerized trading.

Internationally, automation also has taken hold. The 1986 Big Bang conversion of the U.K. markets to screen trading is the most visible symbol of these developments.[46] The ISE has just introduced an automated small order execution system.[47] Automation also is an increasingly significant aspect of other foreign markets, most notably the Toronto Stock Exchange, the Tokyo Stock Exchange, and foreign derivative markets.[48]

Summary

Automated information dissemination systems, order routing systems, and small order execution systems are firmly established in U.S. securities markets. These developments have improved the informational efficiency of the markets, increased the speed with which customer orders are executed, and expanded market capacity. While the October 1987 market break exposed weaknesses in the capacities of these systems, the various automated systems have been enhanced, and more enhancements, particularly in the program trading area, are in prospect.[49]

While there is evidence of movement toward fully automated systems, particularly in derivative markets abroad,[50] it seems unlikely that either U.S. or world markets will move toward a totally automated trading system. Despite automation developments, trading on the NYSE with its physically centralized auction market has proven to be very durable. Even in Japan, with its highly automated Computer-Assisted Order Routing and Execution System (CORES),[51] most of the Tokyo Stock Exchange's total volume is in the stocks that still are traded on the Exchange floor, in the face-to-face auction system.[52]

The reasons for the durability of face-to-face and telephonic trading are not obscure. Simply put, most traders are not willing to guarantee firm prices for orders of large size. The size problem is exacerbated by the fact that automated execution allows professionals to react quickly to news regarding a stock or the market, and to "pick off" a dealer before it can revise its quotations. Fully automated trading systems are not likely to attract substantial order flow in active trading markets, unless the size problem and its automated aspects can be solved.

If there is a trend, it would seem to be in the combination of automation with more traditional systems, as exemplified by the integration of SUPERDOT into the NYSE's auction processes, and the integration of SOES and OCT with telephone negotiation in the NASDAQ market. Perhaps the most interesting question about the future of U.S. securities markets is not whether our markets will be automated fully, but whether the exchanges and the NASD will institute after-hours trading systems in response to increasing demand for global 24-hour trading systems for world-class debt and equity securities. While it is likely that automated information dissemination and order systems will continue to evolve to meet this demand, the same size problem that exists in U.S. markets makes it likely that global systems will not include substantial automated execution components.

SEC Regulation of Automation

Regulatory Framework

In the United States, the SEC continues to play a vital role in facilitating market automation. As a matter of process, suggested changes by securities exchanges or the NASD (generally referred to as self-regulatory organizations, or "SRO's") to their internal automated systems are submitted to the SEC, which publishes the proposals for comment, and reviews and approves or disapproves the proposals under its authority per Section 19(b) of the Act. Links between a U.S. SRO and a foreign exchange are processed in the same way because these links involve a U.S. SRO's operation. Intermarket systems such as ITS generally are governed by intermarket plans established under SEC Rules 11Aa3-1 and 3-2. The process for changing these systems is similar to changing SRO's, involving notice and comment, review, and approval or disapproval. The SEC also has the authority to amend SRO rules and intermarket plans.[53]

The Commission has been responsive to desires for procedural speed and flexibility in introducing automation.[54] The principal procedural issue has been the opportunity afforded by the Section 19(b) process to the competing exchange and the NASDAQ markets to copy the proposed automation changes of their competitors. To date, the SEC has not deferred approval of an automation proposal by these competitors to give the originator lead-time in introducing an innovation:[55] its policy is that innovation will be stifled, not enhanced, by delay.

Substantive Standards

Section 19 of the Act requires the SEC to approve rule change proposals that are consistent with the requirements of the Act. It draws primarily on Section 6 (National Securities Exchanges), Section 15A (Registered Securities Association), and Section 11A (National Market System) for these requirements.

Sections 6 and 15A require that an SRO be able to enforce member compliance with SEC rules and with the federal securities laws and rules, provide fair representation to members, protect investors, impose no unnecessary burdens on competition, and "perfect the mechanism of a free and open market, and a national market system."[56]

In Section 11A, Congress found that new data processing and communications techniques can make markets more efficient. So it established as affirmative goals "fair competition" among and within markets, the availability of quotation and transaction information, and a mandate to the SEC to help establish a national market system. While Congress wanted the national market system for securities to be a "linking of markets through data communication and processing facilities," Section 11A does not dictate the specific contours of the national market system. Instead, it gives to the SEC the general task of helping to structure a national market system for securities in a general way, without detailing the characteristics desired by any one group.

Several principles emerge. First, the SEC should not be extreme in its attitude toward technological advances. It cannot be entirely passive toward technological changes because federal securities laws require it to protect investors and to foster fair, orderly, and competitive markets. At the same time, the task of facilitating a national market system with "new data processing and communication techniques" suggests that it should support technological innovation. Use of the word "facilitate" also suggests that the SEC should not actively design and impose technology on the markets. So while centralization through information dissemination and intermarket order routing seems a clear minimum ingredient of a national market system, imposing specific technologies and trading systems on the markets seems to be inconsistent with the premise of Section 11A, which is that the national market system should encompass diverse systems and enhance competition.

What is called for is a pragmatic approach by which the SEC fosters, encourages, and cooperates with the securities industry in developing new technological developments that improve the market's efficiency, while taking steps to see that these developments do not threaten the structural soundness, competitiveness, or fairness of markets.

Application of Standards

Assuring Soundness

Section 11A's admonition that "the securities markets are an important national asset which must be preserved and strengthened" identifies the SEC's obligation to see that technological change introduced into the marketplace is functionally sound and workable. Therefore in reviewing automation proposals, the SEC seeks to ensure that the introduction of new systems and products will not overwhelm the capacity of U.S. markets. The breakdown of some order routing and execution systems during the October 1987 market break illustrates the desirability of continued SEC attention to systems capacity matters.[57]

Similarly, in reviewing proposals for links with foreign markets, the SEC has focused on regulatory soundness by requiring that surveillance sharing agreements with foreign markets accompany such links. The SEC also has worked out Memoranda of Understanding with the regulatory authorities of foreign nations where the linked markets are located.[58]

In addition to capacity and surveillance questions, the SEC encounters public protection issues in its review of automation proposals. In its review of automation proposals, the Commission has considered issues that include: the lack of protection for public limit orders;[59] the capability to execute public customer limit orders against each other;[60] the failure of Phlx's automated system to provide the specialist an opportunity to improve current ITS best bid;[61] the effect on the overall price efficiency of executing small orders at the quotes;[62] and the effect on competition of allowing regional exchanges to execute based on primary market quotes.[63]

Accommodating and Promoting Change

Consistent with statutory goals, the SEC has been flexible and responsive in reviewing automation proposals, while at the same time indicating its willingness to force the implementation of desirable changes. The introduction of automated trading systems by SRO's, while subject to SEC review and approval under the same standards as any other SRO changes, has been accomplished in an accommodating manner in general. When substantive issues have emerged, the SEC has avoided interference with the rapid introduction of change.

For example, in reaction to increased volatility that was attributed to index arbitrage, the NYSE in 1988 sought SEC approval for a pilot rule that would prohibit the use of its automated order routing system for index arbitrage if the DJIA moved 50 points in a day. The SEC expressed serious doubt about the effectiveness of this pilot,[64] and about the intermarket effect on pricing efficiency of seeking to inhibit arbitrage in this way. Nonetheless, the SEC accommodated the NYSE's judgment that it was appropriate to reduce volatility by limiting automated index arbitrage order routing temporarily, concluding that such an SRO judgment is permitted by the Act.[65] With the encouragement of the SEC, the NYSE later replaced this approach with preferential order routing for small orders, with "sidecar" procedures for program trades and with coordinated circuit breaker rules.[66]

The SEC also evidenced a flexible approach to technological change when it discussed at a public meeting a proposal to adopt a rule dealing with proprietary trading systems (15c2-10). Under the SEC's tentative proposals, these systems would be required to submit rules and procedures for review, as exchanges do. And like exchanges, they would be subject to SEC oversight over any limitation on access to their services that might be anti-competitive. The rule review process, however, would be streamlined, and these systems would not have the same governance structures that the Act requires of exchanges.[67]

The SEC also has an important role to play in promoting technological change. A recent example of the SEC's willingness to suggest such change is its recommendations in response to the market break, which include the creation of basket trading products and procedures, and the automated dissemination of real-time program trade information.[68]

The SEC's recommendation that the NYSE create systems or products for trading baskets is designed to promote a more liquid market for portfolio trades and to relieve specialists in individual stocks of the large liquidity demands created by occasional waves of portfolio-related orders.[69] Automated technologies undoubtedly will be a part of these procedures, particularly in light of the need to promote the participation of upstairs firms in the NYSE's basket trading market. The capital of upstairs firms will be as important to the liquidity of these markets as it is to the block trading market. So automation technologies will be needed to obtain the maximum degree of involvement in the NYSE's basket markets by the upstairs firms.

The SEC also recommended that real-time information about the amount of portfolio trading be publicly available to alert market participants to price movements caused by adjustments to entire portfolios rather than by information strategies relevant to a particular security.[70] Dissemination of this information can occur through the Consolidated Trade System.

Another application of existing automation technologies that could bring more useful information to the market is the electronic dissemination of information about the price and size of limit orders contained in the NYSE's specialist book. The specialists' limit order books are the aggregation of limit orders—orders to buy or sell at specific prices—left with the specialist for execution at various prices away from the current market. The availability of automated information dissemination technologies and systems makes the dissemination of information on the specialist book technically feasible today. In particular, the automated dissemination systems exist and most of the limit order books on the NYSE now are kept in electronic format. As a technical matter, it would be relatively easy to disseminate information about the contents of the book.

The dissemination of this data at and prior to the opening would be particularly helpful. For one, it could induce market participants to send in orders to absorb imbalances that often exist at the opening. So the pre-opening publication of limit order imbalances could be a supplement to the pre-opening and reopening procedures in use on the NYSE today.[71]

While market forces alone might eventually lead the exchanges in these directions, the SEC's leadership in this area can be a constructive force. Using a combination of public statements and its rulemaking power, the SEC also played an important role in the 1970s by requiring consolidated trade and quotation reporting,[72] in the 1980s by prohibiting the dissemination of representative best bid and ask quotations,[73] and by mandating last-sale reporting to the over-the-counter market.[74] Although at the time the SEC's suggestions were perceived by some broker-dealers as intrusive and unnecessarily burdensome government regulation, these innovations proved to be a tremendous benefit to the markets.

These examples of the SEC's positive approach to technological change not only demonstrate its special interest in information dissemination, but also suggest that the SEC is willing to use rulemaking to accomplish desirable change.[75] While the SEC has an interest in the trading systems used by the markets, in the past SEC efforts to promote new trading systems have not always proved successful.[76] So on balance, an important issue is the role that should appropriately be played by the SEC in developing automated trading systems.

As a practical matter there are ultimate limits on the technological changes the SEC can or should force on the markets. The real genius of the federal securities laws, and particularly Section 11A, resides not in the authority it provides to force change, but in the flexibility that it permits and promotes. This attitude of flexibility reflects the fact that the real strength of our securities markets comes from the peaceful, albeit competitive, coexistence of diverse systems. So under 11A and other sections of the Act, all of the various automated systems and trading approaches described above are tolerated and encouraged, from exchange auction principles, to over-the-counter dealer systems, to automated small order systems, to automated confirmation systems, and even to black box systems where particular markets and participants are comfortable with such systems. While there may be circumstances that justify the SEC's use of authority under Section 11A to require certain systems, such circumstances will be the extraordinary exception, not the rule.

Conclusion

Over the past 20 years, markets in the U.S. and abroad rapidly have become more automated, and this trend is likely to quicken and increase rather than diminish. This has been largely a positive development, with customer executions and overall market capacity greatly enhanced. The SEC's chief role will continue to be assuring the soundness and fairness of technological systems, and encouraging and facilitating the markets in moving forward.

Endnotes

[1]   In Chapter 3 of this volume, the authors describe the principal information dissemination and order execution and routing systems in use in U.S. and foreign markets today, as well as notable systems in use in futures markets.

[2]   *See* Special Study of Securities Markets, Report of the Special Study of the Securities and Exchange Commission (1963), Reprinted in H.R. Doc. No. 95, 88th Cong., 1st Sess. (1963), Pt. 2 at 358 and 678.

[3]   *See* Section 11A(a) (2) of the Securities Exchange Act of 1934 (Act).

[4]   Section 11A(a) (1) (B) of the Act.

[5] Section 11A(a) (1) (D) of the Act.

[6] *See* "The October 1987 Market Break," A Report by the Division of Market Regulation, U.S. Securities and Exchange Commission (February, 1988) ("SEC Staff Report"), Chapter 3.

[7] "Real-time" information is information about a trading event available immediately or soon after the event, rather than at the end of the trading day or later.

[8] "Price" information or a "trade report" consists of an indication of the actual price at which a trade is executed, without adjusting for commissions or markups and markdowns.

[9] A "quotation" consists of an indication of the price at which a dealer is willing to buy (bid) or sell (offer).

[10] *See* M. Simon and R.L.D. Colby, "The National Market System for Over-The-Counter Stocks," 55 *George Washington Law Review* at 34-38 (1986).

[11] *See* Securities and Exchange Act Release Nos. 17549 (February 17, 1981) (adopting rule 11Aa2-1 under the Act).

[12] *See* Securities Exchange Act Release No. 2. 25949 and 26545 (August 2, 1988 and February 14, 1989).

[13] *See* Chapter 3.

[14] *Id.*

[15] *See infra*, text accompanying notes 31-34.

[16] *See* Restatement and Amendment of Plan Submitted to the Securities and Exchange Commission pursuant to Rule 17a-15 under the Securities and Exchange Act of 1934 (available on file at the SEC); and Rule 11Aa3-1 and 11Aa3-2 under the Act.

[17] *See* Chapter 3.

[18] *See* Plan submitted to the Securities and Exchange Commission for the purpose of implementing Rule 11Ac1-1 under the Act (available on file at the SEC); and Rules 11Aa3-2 and 11Ac1-1 under the Act.

[19] *See* Plan for Reporting of Consolidated Options Reports and Quotation Information (available on file at the SEC); and Rule 11Aa3-2 under the Act. *See* Chapter 3.

[20] "Transparency" is the degree to which current market information is publicly available.

[21] While the technology developments described in this paper are truly revolutionary, the telephone and the telegraph were equally dramatic changes in their own times. Thus, a paper published in 1922 could say in reference to international arbitrage: "Few features of Wall Street life so irresistibly appeal to the imagination as this extraordinary business, conducted in the various world markets over the flashing cables with a speed vastly more rapid than the roll of the earth." "The Stock Exchange as an International Market," quoted by James M. Davin in his Handbook (NASDAQ, 1987).

[22] *See* Chapter 3.

[23] *Id.*

[24] *Id.*

[25] *Id.*

[26] The term "program trading" as used here means trading in portfolios of securities rather than in a particular security. *See* SEC Staff Report, *supra* note 6, Chapter 3.

[27] *Id.*, at 7-19 - 7-20.

[28] *Id.*, Chapter 3

[29] *See* Chapter 3.

[30] *Id.* At the same time as the NYSE instituted these new SUPERDOT applications, the NYSE also adopted coordinated intermarket "circuit breaker" procedures that call for the NYSE and other securities and futures markets to halt trading for one hour if the DJIA falls 250 points. *See* SEC Act Release No. 26198 (October 19, 1988).

[31] *See* Chapter 3.

[32] The Philadelphia Stock Exchange's PACE System for stocks and the options automatic execution systems do not provide this opportunity. *Id.*

[33] *Id.*

[34] *Id.*

[35] *Id.*

[36] *Id.*

[37] *See* discussion of size concerns *infra*, text accompanying notes 50-52.

[38] Autex, a system for disseminating indications of trading interest in block transactions, also was developed at this time.

[39] *See* Chapter 3.

[40] *Id.*

[41] *See* letter from Richard G. Ketchum, Director, Division of Market Regulation, Securities and Exchange Commission, to Robert A. McTameney, Esq., Carter, Ledyard & Milburn, dated January 12, 1989. The Division's no-action letter has been challenged in District Court. *See Board of Trade of the City of Chicago and Chicago Mercantile Exchange v. SEC*, No. 89-0332 (D.D.C. February 7, 1989).

[42] *See* Chapter 3.

[43] *Id.*

[44] *See* Proposed Rule 144A, Securities Act Release No. 6806 (November 11, 1988).

[45] *See* Chapter 3.

[46] *Id.*

[47] *Id.*

[48] *Id.*

[49] For a description of the capacity problems encountered by the markets during the October market break, *see* SEC Staff Report *supra* note 6, Chapters

7-9. For a discussion of the ways in which the markets have improved their capacities, *see* October 19, 1988 Memorandum from Richard G. Ketchum, Director, Division of Market Regulation, to Chairman David S. Ruder, on file at the SEC.

[50] *See* Chapter 3.

[51] *Id.*

[52] In 1988, approximately 74% of the share volume on the Tokyo Stock Exchange was accounted for by the 150 stocks traded on the floor in the face-to-face auction system. *See* Tokyo Stock Exchange 1988 Fact Book, at 36.

[53] *See* Section 19(c) (3) of the Act and Rule 11Aa3-2(c) under the Act.

[54] *See* letter from Richard J. Charts, Assistant Director, Division of Market Regulation, SEC, to the SRO's, (February 4, 1983).

[55] *See, e.g., id.*

[56] Sections 6(b)(5) and 15A(b)(6) of the Act.

[57] For the capacity recommendations of the SEC after the market break, *see* SEC Staff Report, *supra*, note 6 and "Recommendations of the Securities and Exchange Commission in Response to the October 19, 1987 Market Break," contained in February 3, 1988 testimony of Chairman David S. Ruder before the Senate Banking, Housing and Urban Affairs Committee ("SEC Market Break Recommendation").

[58] For a description of these agreements, *see* B. Becker, "Global Securities Markets," 6 *International Tax & Business Lawyer*, at 242 (1988).

[59] *See* SEC Act Release No. 21695 (January 28, 1985) (order approving CBOE's automated execution system pilot).

[60] *See* Chapter 3 and SEC Act Release No. 26476 (January 19, 1989) (order approving NASD limit order system pilot).

[61] *See* Chapter 3 and SEC Act Release No. 19859 (June 9, 1983).

[62] *Id.*

[63] *Id.*

[64] Index arbitrage is possible without automated order routing. Considerable arbitrage occurred during the NYSE pilot, even after the NYSE invoked its rule.

[65] *See* SEC Act Release No. 25599 (April 19, 1988). Another recent example of the Commission accommodating an SROs reduction of the availability of an automation system is the Commission's approval of the NASD's proposal to prohibit professional traders from using SOES. *See* SEC Act Release No. 26261 (December 15, 1988).

[66] *See supra*, text accompanying notes 28-30.

[67] The SEC will publish this rule proposal for public comment.

[68] *See* SEC Market Break Recommendations, *supra* note 49.

[69] *Id.* at 12.

[70] *Id.*

[71] *See* Chapter 3.

[72] *See supra*, notes 16 and 18.

[73] *See* Rule 11Aa1-2(c)(2)(vi)

[74] *See supra* note 11. In addition, the SEC encouraged the creation of NASDAQ, *see supra* note 2.

[75] Another example of the SEC's recent endorsement of automated consolidated trade and quotation information as a goal of international markets. *See* "Regulation of International Securities Markets," Policy Statement of the United States Securities and Exchange Commission, (November, 1988).

[76] For example, in 1976 the SEC requested comment on the possible characteristics of a composite limit order book ("CLBO"). *See* SEC Act Release No. 12159 (March 10, 1976). In 1978 it urged the markets to submit a plan to create such a system. *See* SEC Act Release No. 14416 (January, 1978). Due to resistance from the markets, the SEC eventually abandoned this initiative. *See* J. Seligman, *The Transformation of Wall Street*, (Houghton, Mifflin, 1982), at 527-530.

When Financial Markets Work Too Well: A Case for a Securities Transaction Tax

Lawrence H. Summers
Harvard University

Victoria P. Summers[*]
Harvard University

Technological and institutional innovations have radically transformed financial markets in the U.S. and around the world, permitting and encouraging spectacular increases in the volume of securities trading of all kinds. In 1960, 766 million shares were traded on the NYSE, while in 1987 more than 900 million shares changed hands in an average week. More shares were traded on the lowest volume day in 1987 than in any month in 1960. And more shares changed hands in the first 15 minutes of trading on October 19 and 20, 1987 than in any week in 1960.

Increases in trading have been even more spectacular in other markets. In 1960 or 1970, there were no organized markets in derivative securities. Today, the dollar value of contracts traded on the stock market futures market alone significantly exceeds the volume of trade on the stock market itself—and the volume of trade in stock market futures is nearly equalled by trade in index

---

[*] A version of this paper appeared in the *Journal of Financial Services Research* (3:1989).

options. And these explosive increases in trading volumes have not been confined to corporate equities. While the value of shares traded on the NYSE averages less than $10 billion a day, the daily value of trade in government bonds averages more than $25 billion and the daily value of trade in foreign exchange approaches $300 billion. Today, there is every reason to expect trading volumes to continue increasing. Already, the NYSE is preparing itself for a one-billion-share day. And with increasing international linkages among markets, an inexhaustible variety of securities are tradable 24 hours a day.

In the narrow sense of permitting trade to take place between consenting adults, these statistics make it obvious that our financial markets have become much more efficient over time. Unloading a one-million-dollar portfolio of stock easily might have cost $10,000 or more in 1960; but today a functionally-equivalent transaction can be carried out in the futures market for a couple of hundred dollars or less. To a great extent, it is reductions in trading costs that have allowed volume to skyrocket so dramatically.

Despite the tremendous increases in transaction efficiency, the contribution of the U.S. financial markets toward overall economic performance has come under growing attack in recent years. Liberal critics of contemporary institutions like Robert Reich complain of the rise of "paper entrepreneurs" who devote their talents to winning zero sum games by trading financial assets rather than by creating wealth. From a different point on the political spectrum, Treasury Secretary Brady has confessed to a growing feeling that "we are headed in the wrong direction when so much of our young talent and so much of this nation's resources are aimed at financial engineering, when the rest of the world is laying the foundation for future growth."

Even some active participants in the markets complain that the excessive trading pace gives rise to excessive volatility. First Boston's Albert Wojnilower fears that: "The freeing of financial markets to pursue their casino instincts heightens the odds of crises . . . Because unlike a casino, the financial markets are inextricably linked with the world outside, the real economy pays the price."

Concern about the consequences of rapid turnover in financial markets is hardly new. In one of the most famous chapters of *The General Theory*, Keynes questioned the benefits of more liquid and smoothly functioning financial markets:

> "As the organization of investment markets improves, the risk of the predominance of speculation does increase. In one of the greatest investment markets in the world, namely New York, the influence of speculation is enormous. Speculators may do no harm as bubbles on a steady stream of enterprise. But the position is serious when enterprise becomes the bubble on a whirlpool of speculation. When the capital development of a country becomes the by-product of the activities of a casino, the job is likely to be ill-done. The measure of success attained by Wall Street, regarded as an institution of which the proper

social purpose is to direct new investment into the most profitable channels in terms of future yield cannot be claimed as one of the outstanding triumphs of laissez-faire capitalism, which is not surprising if I am right in thinking that the best brains of Wall Street have been in fact directed towards a different object."

He continues the same passage by suggesting a possible remedy for the problems caused by excessive speculation:

"These tendencies are a scarcely avoidable outcome of our having successfully organized 'liquid' investment markets. It is usually agreed that casinos should in the public interest be inaccessible and expensive. And perhaps the same is true of stock exchanges... The introduction of a substantial government transfer tax on all transactions might prove the most serviceable reform available, with a view to mitigating the predominance of speculation over enterprise in the U.S."

Fifty years after Keynes, the U.S. today is one of the only major industrialized countries which does not levy a significant excise tax on the transfer of financial securities. Such taxes raised more than $12 billion in Japan in 1987, and several billion in the United Kingdom despite its smaller stock market capitalization.

Given concerns about financial engineering and a large federal deficit, it is hardly surprising that the idea of imposing some form of Securities Transaction Excise Tax, (STET) has received serious attention in recent years. James Tobin (1984) has urged adoption of such a tax to curb excessive volatility in international financial markets.

Former House Speaker Jim Wright proposed a .5 percent tax on all securities transactions. An alternative approach to curbing speculation advocated by Felix Rohatyn and Warren Buffett, among many others, is the use of a sliding scale according to which capital gains taxes are levied at different rates depending on how long an asset had been held.

It is a propitious time to analyze the economic and administrative issues raised by proposals to use the tax system to curb speculation. There are strong economic efficiency arguments to be made in support of some kind of STET that throw "sand into the gears" to use James Tobin's 1984 phrase about our excessively well-functioning financial markets. For one, the efficiency benefit from curbing speculation is likely to exceed any cost of reduced liquidity or increased capital costs that arise from taxing transactions more heavily. The Japan and Britain examples suggest that transaction taxes are feasible administratively and would not unduly interfere with our international competitiveness in selling financial services. International cooperation and coordination in setting STET rates would increase the ability of all nations to tax financial transactions fairly.

In the following analysis, the Panglossian efficient market's view of how financial markets operate is first contrasted with the way they work in practice.

It focuses on 1.) excessive volatility caused by destabilizing speculation, 2.) the diversion of human and capital resources away from more socially profitable pursuits into the financial sphere, and 3.) the impact of rapid financial turnover on the way corporate investment decisions are made. It also examines the extent to which these problems can be addressed by taxes that curb speculation, and the possible adverse economic effects of a transaction tax.

Then international experiences with transaction taxes are described; also considered are the historical U.S. experience as well as the tax rules currently directed at discouraging speculation by mutual funds. Many operational aspects of a U.S. STET are reviewed, with the conclusion that such a tax would be workable and could yield significant new government revenues. Finally, concluding policy observations are offered.

How Well Do U.S. Financial Markets Function?

American financial markets are extremely successful in the narrow sense of facilitating the free trade of a huge variety of securities. Capital market participants today enjoy a degree of flexibility that would have been inconceivable even a decade ago. Large institutions are able to reallocate their portfolios between stocks and bonds in a matter of hours. Well-developed futures and options markets enable investors to hedge all kinds of risks. Starting with relatively little capital, it is now possible to take over all but the largest companies within a matter of weeks.

The difficult question is how well do U.S. financial markets perform their ultimate social functions: spreading risks, guiding the investment of scarce capital, and processing and disseminating the information possessed by diverse traders. Financial innovators and their academic champions argue that facilitating trading necessarily contributes to economic efficiency. Therefore, they see innovations that reduce trading costs as clearly beneficial. They regard the proposals of Keynes and Tobin to throw "sand into the gears" of financial markets as badly misguided.

The belief that facilitating trading improves the social functioning of financial markets is based on the acceptance of the efficient markets hypothesis. If prices in unfettered financial markets closely track fundamental values, goes the argument, then they will provide proper economic signals, guide investment appropriately, and facilitate the spreading of risks.

On the other hand, if easy trading encourages speculation that drives prices away from fundamental values, concern arises for the social functioning of financial markets. Excessive speculation that increases volatility would create rather than reduce risk, distort investment allocations, and limit the information content of asset prices. Clearly, tax measures that curb speculation would be beneficial.

To analyze this tax clearly, first, consider the available evidence on the market efficiency hypothesis, plus three possible adverse consequences of excessive short-term trading: increases in volatility, the excessive diversion of resources into rent-seeking activities, and the shortening of the investment horizons of corporate managers.

Do Prices Track Fundamental Values?

While it has never been popular among practitioners, the efficient market view that stock prices rationally reflect fundamental values has, until recently, commanded widespread allegiance from academic students of financial markets. The logic of efficient markets is compelling. Suppose a stock price diverged from fundamental value. There would be a profit opportunity for anyone who recognized this fact as long as the asset would return to fundamentals eventually. If the stock were undervalued, for example, efforts to profit by purchasing it would continue until its price was pushed up to the point where it was no longer undervalued. If one assumes that stock prices move quickly to eliminate easy profit opportunities, then it must be the case that prices closely mirror fundamental values. Furthermore, investors who drive prices toward fundamentals by buying low and selling high will prosper over time, while those who destabilize prices by buying high and selling low will lose money. Accordingly, "good money" will drive out "bad money" and markets will come to function better over time.

This logic has been, at least until recently, supported by a huge empirical literature demonstrating the difficulty of making predictable excess profits in the stock market. Jensen (1978) labeled the efficient market hypothesis as "the best established empirical fact in economics." More recently, the efficient market hypothesis and its implication that the tremendous volatility of stock prices reflects movements in fundamental values has been subjected to substantial question.

At the theoretical level, critics have pointed out that as long as assets are risky, either because of uncertainty about their future yield or because of uncertainty about future demand for them, risk-averse speculators will not buy enough to drive prices all the way to fundamental values. Furthermore, any tendency for good money to drive out bad money will be attenuated by the tendency of bad money to buy aggressively, taking on more risk but also generating higher returns. Critics also have demonstrated that prices can diverge substantially from fundamental values for long periods of time without creating profit opportunities that are statistically-demonstrable absent many decades of data.[1]

Three types of empirical evidence suggest the likelihood that a substantial fraction of the observed volatility in stock prices reflects something other than the arrival of news about fundamental values. First and perhaps most fundamental is the difficulty of isolating the news that drives stock prices, even with the considerable benefit of hindsight. Table 1, reproduced from Cutler, Poterba and

---

Table 1   Fifty Largest Postwar Movements in S&P Index and Their "Causes"

	Date	Percent Change	*New York Times* Explanation
1	Oct. 19, 1987	-20.47%	Worry over dollar decline and trade deficit; Fear of U.S. not supporting dollar.
2	Oct. 21, 1987	9.10%	Interest rates continue to fall; deficit talks in Washington; bargain hunting.
3	Oct. 26, 1987	-8.28%	Fear of budget deficits; margin calls; reaction to falling foreign stocks.
4	Sep. 3, 1946	-6.73%	". . . no basic reason for the assault on prices."
5	May 28, 1962	-6.68%	Kennedy forces rollback of steel price hike.
6	Sep. 26, 1955	-6.62%	Eisenhower suffers heart attack.
7	Jun. 26, 1950	-5.38%	Outbreak of Korean War.
8	Oct. 20, 1987	5.33%	Investors looking for "quality stocks."
9	Sep. 9, 1946	-5.24%	Labor unrest in maritime and trucking industries.
10	Oct. 16, 1987	-5.16%	Fear of trade deficit; fear of higher interest rates; tension with Iran.
11	May 27, 1970	5.02%	Rumors of change in economic policy. ". . . the stock surge happened for no fundamental reason."
12	Sep. 11, 1986	-4.81%	Foreign governments refuse to lower interest rates; crackdown on triple witching announced.
13	Aug. 17, 1982	4.76%	Interest rates decline.
14	May 29, 1962	4.65%	Optimistic brokerage letters; institutional and corporate buying; suggestions of tax cut.
15	Nov. 3, 1948	-4.61%	Truman defeats Dewey.
16	Oct. 9, 1974	4.60%	Ford to reduce inflation and interest rates.
17	Feb. 25, 1946	-4.57%	Weakness in economic indicators over past week.
18	Oct. 23, 1957	4.49%	Eisenhower urges confidence in economy.
19	Oct. 29, 1987	4.46%	Deficit reduction talks begin; durable goods orders increase; rallies overseas.
20	Nov. 5, 1948	-4.40%	Further reaction to Truman victory over Dewey.
21	Nov. 6, 1946	-4.31%	Profit taking; Republican victories in elections presage deflation.
22	Oct. 7, 1974	4.19%	Hopes that President Ford would announce strong anti-inflationary measures.
23	Nov. 30, 1987	-4.18%	Fear of dollar fall.
24	Jul. 12, 1974	4.08%	Reduction in new loan demands; lower inflation previous month.

	Date	Percent Change	*New York Times* Explanation
25	Oct. 15, 1946	4.01%	Meat prices decontrolled; prospects of other decontrols.
26	Oct. 25, 1982	-4.00%	Disappointment over Federal Reserve's failure to cut discount rates.
27	Nov. 26, 1963	3.98%	Confidence in President Johnson after Kennedy assassination.
28	Nov. 1, 1978	3.97%	Steps by Carter to strengthen dollar.
29	Oct. 22, 1987	-3.92%	Iranian attack on Kuwaiti oil terminal; fall in markets overseas; analysts predict lower prices.
30	Oct. 29, 1974	3.91%	Decline in short term interest rates; ease in future monetary policy; lower oil prices.
31	Nov. 3, 1982	3.91%	Relief over small Democratic victories in House.
32	Feb. 19, 1946	-3.70%	Fear of wage-price controls lowering corporate profits; labor unrest.
33	Jun. 19, 1950	-3.70%	Korean War continues; fear of long war.
34	Nov. 18, 1974	-3.67%	Increase in unemployment rate; delay in coal contract approval; fear of new mid-East war.
35	Apr. 22, 1980	3.64%	Fall in short term interest rates; analysts express optimism.
36	Oct. 31, 1946	3.63%	Increase in commodity prices; prospects for price decontrol.
37	Jul. 6, 1955	3.57%	Market optimism triggered by GM stock split.
38	Jun. 4, 1962	-3.55%	Profit taking; continuation of previous week's decline.
39	Aug. 20, 1982	3.54%	Congress passes Reagan tax bill; prime rate falls.
40	Dec 3, 1987	-3.53%	Computerized selling; November retail sales low.
41	Sep. 19, 1974	3.50%	Treasury Secretary Simon predicts decline in short term interest rates.
42	Dec. 9, 1946	3.44%	Coal strike ends; railroad freight rate increases.
43	Jun. 29, 1962	3.44%	". . . stock prices advanced strongly chiefly because they had gone down so long and so far that a rally was due."
44	Sep. 5, 1946	3.43%	"Replacement buying" after earlier fall.
45	Oct. 30, 1987	3.33%	Dollar stabilizes; increase in prices abroad.
46	Jan. 27, 1975	3.27%	IBM wins appeal of antitrust case; short term interest rates decline.
47	Oct. 6, 1982	3.27%	Interest rates fall; several large companies announce increase in profits.

(Table continues)

Table 1   Fifty Largest Postwar Movements in S&P Index and Their "Causes" (Continued)

	Date	Percent Change	*New York Times* Explanation
48	Jul. 19, 1948	-3.26%	Worry over Russian blockade of Berlin; possibility of more price controls.
49	Nov. 30, 1982	3.23%	". . . analysts were at a loss to explain why the Dow jumped so dramatically in the last two hours . . ."
50	Oct. 24, 1962	3.22%	Khrushchev promises no rash decisions on Cuban Missile Crisis; calls for U.S.-Soviet summit.

The last column is per the *New York Times* financial section or front page.

Summers (1988), describes the news events on the 50 days in the last 50 years when the largest market moves were observed. On many of those days, it is difficult to pinpoint any one event that had a major impact on fundamental values. The example of October 19, 1987 is particularly striking. It is difficult to imagine what news arriving on that day was sufficient to cause a 20 percent decline in the value of the American corporate sector.

This method of examining the role of news in stock market volatility is inherently subjective because there are always many possible factors that affect fundamental values. An even sharper test should be possible by observing simpler markets. For example, Roll (1984) examines the futures market in frozen orange juice, in which prices are determined substantially by predictions about Florida weather. This may be a simple market, but it still is not possible to account for a large fraction of observed volatility. Roll (1988) reaches a similar conclusion examining the relative movements of individual corporate stocks.

Perhaps the clearest evidence that something other than fundamental values drives stock prices comes from French and Roll's (1986) ingenious study of volatility over periods both when the market is open and when it is closed. It has long been observed that the market's variability between Friday's close and Monday's close is much less than three times as great as its variability between Monday's close and Tuesday's close. This is attributed comfortably to the fact that less relevant news is revealed on weekend days than on week days.

However, French and Roll examine volatility during a period in 1968 when the market was closed on Wednesday because of the pressures caused by heavy volume. Remarkably, they found that the market volatility between Tuesday and Thursday was approximately halved when the market was closed on Wednesday! If Thursday's prices always reflected news as of Thursday and nothing else, one would not expect the opening or closing of the market on Wednesday to have any effect at all on the price movements between Tuesday and Thursday. The implication is that Wednesday's trading is itself a source of volatility, with lasting effects.

A second indication that factors other than fundamental values affect stock prices comes from studies that compare stock price movements with fundamental value movements. Shiller (1981) developed a statistical method for comparing the volatility of stock prices with the volatility of fundamental values based on an examination of the time series properties of dividends. He concluded that the stock market was far more variable than could be rationalized on the basis of the observed behavior of dividends. Shiller's work has proven to be very controversial because of the difficulty in drawing inferences about the variance of fundamental values from the behavior of dividends. But other evidence is more clear cut.

Consider the example of closed-end mutual funds. Because the only asset of a closed-end mutual fund is its stock portfolio, which is easily valued, its fundamental value is evaluated easily. Closed-end funds typically sell for less than the value of the underlying assets and the discount on closed-end funds varies widely. Fluctuating discounts on closed-end funds are hard to square with the idea that prices always reflect fundamental values. In a similar vein, it is hard to see how fundamental values change as much as market prices change in many takeover transactions.

This is not intended to suggest that stock prices are unrelated to fundamental values or that they are driven only by speculation. The evidence suggests that the stock market probably is efficient according to the rather weak definition offered by noted financial economist Fischer Black: "We might define an efficient market as one in which price is within a factor of two of value, i.e., the price is more than half the value and less than twice the value." By this definition, almost all markets are efficient almost all the time. 'Almost all' means at least 90 percent. This definition obviously suggests the presence of substantial excess volatility in the stock market.

Does Speculation Contribute to Excess Volatility?

Even if the argument is accepted that stock prices are excessively volatile, it does not follow that this is a result of excessive short-term speculation. Indeed, contrary to Keynes, the argument is often made that reducing transactions costs reduces volatility by making markets more liquid. This makes it easier for sellers to find buyers and buyers to find sellers, and so reduces the pressure of demand on prices. At some point, this effect must dominate. If markets become extremely illiquid, as certain types of art or real estate do, prices will become extremely volatile. But it is unlikely that this happens to publicly-traded securities. Increased liquidity may not reduce volatility and may even increase it.

When examining the relationship between speculation and volatility, it is helpful to distinguish two types of speculative strategies. The first type, "value investing," involves negative feedback. Traders who purchase stocks by comparing stock prices with some relatively stable estimate of fundamentals normally find themselves selling when prices rise and buying when they fall—thereby tending to reduce volatility. Negative feedback also arises when traders rebalance their portfolios, buying and selling equity to hold a given fraction of their assets in the form of stocks. Or it arises when they operate as though the market overreacts to news.

The second type of trading strategy involves positive feedback, or buying when markets rise and selling when they fall. Positive feedback traders tend to increase volatility. Those who believe that "the trend is your friend" pursue positive feedback strategies, as do those who place stop loss orders or who use dynamic hedging strategies to insure their portfolios.

The nature of negative feedback trading strategies is that there is no need to trade frequently; assets that are purchased are expected to earn abnormally high returns in a manner of months or years, not days or weeks. On the other hand, frequent trading is the essence of positive feedback trading strategies. Think of investors who rely heavily on stop-loss orders, sell out when they get margin calls, or trade continuously as part of dynamic hedging portfolio insurance strategies. Any sort of curbs on short-term speculative trading are, therefore, likely to discourage positive feedback investing to a greater extent than negative feedback investing, and may reduce asset price volatility.

This argument can get more complex than is necessary to support the idea that increased liquidity leads to greater volatility. The issue of positive versus negative feedback trading strategies aside, measures that curb speculation can discourage investment by those whose information does not rely on fundamental values. Instead, these investors rely on judgments about the guesses of others. If they discourage such "noise trading," measures that curb speculation will contribute to reductions in volatility and improve the functioning of speculative markets. As Delong, Shleifer, Summers and Waldmann (1988) demonstrate, reductions in noise trading will cause prices to fluctuate less violently about fundamental values, both because there will be less speculative pressure on prices and because speculative pressures will be more easily offset given reduced risks from changes in noise trader demands.

As a matter of theory, the effects of liquidity on asset price volatility are ambiguous. The evidence cited earlier on the extent of price movements over periods when the market is open and when it is closed suggests that trading itself may be a source of volatility. The dramatic run of stock prices in the first three quarters of 1987 when investors reinvested their market gains and relied on portfolio insurance when the market started to decline—followed by the October crash—highlights the potentially adverse consequences of an environment in which speculation is too easy. Statistical studies such as Schwert (1988) inevitably find a positive relationship between turnover and volatility, through the direction of causation is far from clear. As already noted, turnover has increased very substantially because of declining transactions costs over the last several decades, with no concomitant decrease and perhaps a trend increase in volatility.

On balance, this suggests that there is little basis for concern that volatility would increase if short-term trading in financial markets were discouraged. There is, however, some basis for concluding that taxes which discourage turnover might reduce volatility in general and the risk of fluctuations similar to 1987 in particular.

Are Too Many Resources Devoted to Financial Engineering?

Perhaps the most frequent complaint about current financial market trends is that so much talented human capital is devoted to trading paper assets rather than actually creating wealth. The spectacle of one-quarter of the Yale senior class applying for a job at First Boston in 1988 generated more than a little comment nationwide.

Even after the crash, financial jobs remain extraordinarily popular among top business school students. The situation is very different in Japan where top graduates vie for positions in large manufacturing companies like Toyota, leaving less successful students to enter the financial services industry.

In many sectors where productivity increases have been far greater than in the overall economy—agriculture and manufacturing, for example—the share of employment declined. However, the demand for financial services seems to be so elastic that as Figure 1 demonstrates, the share of American employment in the securities industry has increased sharply over time. Despite sharp declines in commission rates and other trading costs, the total real transactions costs associated with securities trading have risen significantly in recent years as Figure 2 indicates.

Perhaps James Tobin (1984) is correct in his view that "the immense power of the computer is being harnessed to the paper economy not to do the same transactions more efficiently but to balloon the quantity and variety of financial exchanges."

It is striking to contemplate the cost of operating our financial system. What is at stake is the allocation of capital among U.S. corporations. These corporations had a combined income of about $310.4 billion in 1987. The combined receipts of member firms on the NYSE in that year was $53 billion. This figure takes no account of the costs borne by individuals and institutions in monitoring their portfolios, acquiring information about securities, or actually making investment decisions. Nor does it consider the costs that corporations incur to attract investors in their securities. It is not uncommon for chief execu-

Figure 1   Securities Industry Personnel, Percentage of the U.S. Labor Force (1978-1987)

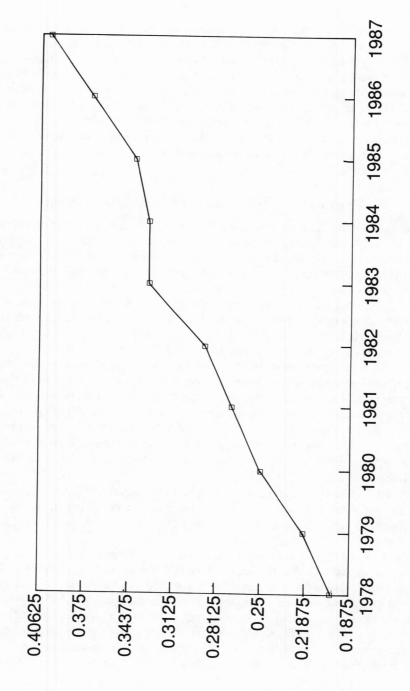

Note: U.S. labor force represents number employed in civilian labor force.

Figure 2   Income from Securities Commissions of NYSE Member Firms (in $ millions)

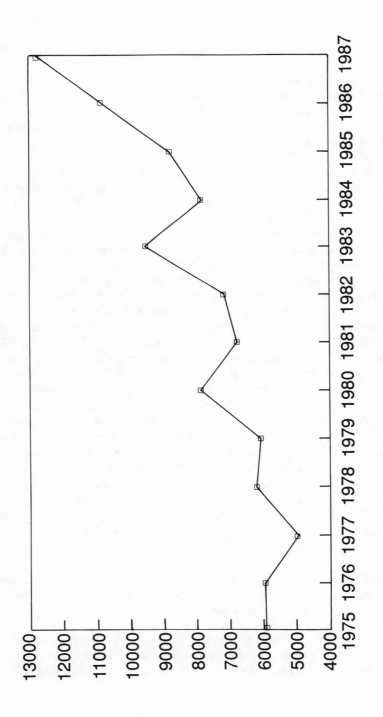

Note: Adjusted to 4th Quarter 1987 dollars; commissions for 1987 do not include 4th quarter earnings and are adjusted.

tive officers of major corporations to spend a week or more each quarter telling their corporate stories to security analysts.

Assuming that these costs are even half as great as direct payments to securities firms, it follows that the cost of operating our securities market was over $75 billion in 1987. This represented 24.2 percent of total corporate profits, and was only a little less than the $133.8 billion that the corporate sector paid in taxes during the same year.

Is this too much? If the lion's share of corporate investment comes from retained earnings, it is hard not to agree with Tobin's (1984) judgment: "What is clear is that very little of the work of the securities industry as gauged by the volume of market activity has to do with the financing of real investment in any very direct way."

It follows that there is a strong case for reducing the volume of resources flowing into trading activities. First, Tobin raises the consideration that "Every financial market absorbs private resources to operate and government resources to police. The country cannot afford all the markets that enthusiasts may dream up." It is true that many attempts to start financial markets fail, just as many new casino games fail to catch on. But the fact that some markets fail to meet the private-market test hardly establishes the precedent that they should be able to inflict the cost of regulation on the government.

There is, however, a more fundamental reason for being concerned about the diversion of human and capital resources into the trading of securities. While well-functioning securities markets produce risk-sharing and capital allocation toward high-value uses, it is true that speculative trading is a zero sum game in terms of direct effects. If A buys a stock from B because A has a good tip or good information of his own—or even a particularly trenchant analysis of his own—and the stock subsequently rises sharply, A has won a zero sum game. A's gain from trading is exactly matched by B's loss. Individuals each gain from acquiring information and trading on it, but much of the gains are at the expense of others. The social gains are much less than the private gains.

As Hirschleifer pointed out years ago, in such situations there is likely to be excessive investment in gathering information. To see this point more clearly, consider these questions:

- How does the social return to research directed at gauging track conditions at Churchill Downs compare with the social return to research directed at developing a better mousetrap?

- What about research directed at predicting Carl Icahn's next move, or anticipating General Motor's earnings announcement hours early, or finding patterns in past stock prices that help to predict future stock prices?

When a football fan stands up at the game, he sees better. When everyone stands up at the game, tall people see better and short people see less well than they did before. But overall, the game cannot be viewed any more clearly. The same is true when investors gather information to guide their trading on the stock market. But there is an important difference between the stock market and the race track: there is no advantage to knowing about track conditions. On the other hand, if individuals gather information and trade on it, stock prices reflect their information and perhaps even contribute to the efficient allocation of capital. This may well be an important beneficial effect of long-term investments. It is hard to believe, however, that investments made with a horizon of hours reveal much socially-beneficial information to the marketplace.

A transaction tax is a natural policy for alleviating this market failure. While it would not have much impact on long-term investors who invested on judgments about the true value of assets, it would have a significant impact by making it less attractive to invest in various short-term prediction activities. By encouraging investment research directed at long-term rather than short-term prediction, a transaction tax might help to solve the conflict noted by Keynes between the privately and socially most desirable investment strategies.

Does Excessive Speculation Shorten Managerial Horizons?

In *The General Theory*, Keynes stressed that most investors do not focus on gauging long-term fundamentals. Instead, they concentrate on assessing market psychology and the likely direction of short-run market movements. He attributed this to the temperament of those likely to go into money management and to the way in which money managers are evaluated. Keynes said those who are orthodox and wrong are often more richly rewarded than those who are unorthodox and right. Probably the most common complaint of corporate executives about financial markets is that the stock market forces them to take the short rather than the long view. The usual statement of the argument goes something like this: "Portfolio managers are evaluated, hired, and fired on the basis of quarterly performance. Therefore, they care only about maximizing the performance of their portfolio over the very near term. This makes them focus only on reported earnings and their near-term prospects. As a consequence, managers who are concerned about maximizing their stock price either in the interests of current shareholders or because they want to avoid being taken over, are forced to slight investment and manage short term earnings." Secretary of Treasury Brady has labelled changing this situation his highest priority.

The image is one of contagious myopia. Those who hire portfolio managers are myopic, therefore portfolio managers are myopic, therefore the managers of the companies in which portfolio managers invest are myopic. The argument linking these forms of myopia is less than transparent. For example, should not portfolio managers who are concerned today with long run performance nonetheless hold assets they think will perform best over the next week or month? Grant that portfolio managers care only about returns over a short horizon. Nonetheless, they care about the price at which they can unload their stock, which in turn depends on tomorrow's demand, which depends on expectations tomorrow of corporate performance thereafter.

Carrying this reasoning forward, it should be clear that a holder of corporate stock today, who anticipates selling to a sequence of future short-term holders, should be concerned about his company's profitability over the long term. And this is clearly true. Only a small share of corporate value represents the expected value of dividends or earnings in the very near future.

The connections between the horizons of portfolio managers and of corporate managements is a rich subject for future investigation. Two possible mechanisms are indicated, through which tax measures that discourage short-term speculative trading might work to lengthen managerial horizons.

First, if transaction taxes drive irrational investors who do not look beyond quarterly earnings reports out of the market, companies may be more willing to accept reductions in quarterly earnings that reflect investments long-term payoffs. Firms may take a longer view when their stock price is less sensitive to current market conditions. The difficulty is that driving any class of investors out of the market may raise capital costs, which discourages investment.

Second, as Lowenstein (1988) and others have argued, transaction taxes that tie shareholders to firms may induce shareholders to take a more active role in monitoring management, and in insuring that proper planning and investment activities take place. In Albert Hirschman's famous phrase, transaction taxes tend to substitute shareholder "voice" for shareholder "exit."

With significant transactions costs, it is possible that dissatisfied shareholders would seek to influence or displace corporate managements rather than simply to buy other companies. The importance of this effect is open to question. Even for relatively large passive investors, the free rider problem is likely to discourage efforts to control managerial behavior.

Third and perhaps most important, lengthening portfolio holding periods by discouraging speculation may well induce investors to focus more on fundamental values—on confronting "the dark forces of ignorance" to use Keynes' phrase—rather than on gauging market psychology. To the extent this change in investment practices was conveyed to managers, they might pursue different strategies. Or perhaps more plausibly, in the environment that would result if speculation were reduced, different types of managers would be selected to run major companies.

There is not much empirical evidence beyond abundant anecdotes about the importance of these mechanisms. And the available anecdotes do not always distinguish sharply between the consequences of rapid turnover in financial markets and the issue of takeover threats. A general sense that managers are more myopic in America than they used to be may be more relevant, and that stock market turnover has increased dramatically over time. In fact, the American stock market has relatively high turnover by world standards and American managers are thought to be more myopic than most.

Liquidity Considerations

These three economic arguments create a presumption that it would be desirable to curb short-term speculation if this could be done without adverse side effects. Consider the possible economic arguments against transaction taxes. First, they may reduce market liquidity, thereby discouraging investment and increasing the risks borne by the owners of capital. Second, by taxing investors, such taxes may reduce the supply of funds for investment.

The fundamental answer to the liquidity argument is that beyond a certain point, increased liquidity may cost more than its benefit is worth. As described later, transaction taxes are in place on most world stock markets without reducing liquidity in ways that create severe problems. Furthermore, even quite substantial transaction taxes would raise trading costs in the American market only back to their level in the 1950s, 1960s, and early 1970s when major liquidity problems were not evident. By avoiding the illusion of liquidity—liquidity that is not there when all investors try to move in the same direction, as in October 1987—transaction taxes actually may increase rather than decrease stability. At this late date, it is fair to throw the challenge back to the supporters of financial innovation. Trading opportunities have multiplied enormously. Whose risks have been reduced in the last 10 years? Whose access to capital has been augmented?

The concern that transaction taxes, like any tax on investment income, would discourage investment is a legitimate one. A first response is that transaction taxes could be matched by reductions in other taxes on corporate income so that the total tax burden on investment income is not altered. Even if this were not done, a modest transaction tax would not have a major impact on the return to the long-term investors who are the primary suppliers of capital. Nor would it have a major impact even if they are not the primary traders in financial markets. A tax of .5 percent on the purchase or sale of stock is not likely to stop an investor with a horizon of several years from investing in the stock market. Certainly any behavioral effects would be dwarfed by the effects of moving to the 28 percent capital gains tax.

Table 2   Transactions taxes and tax revenue

| Country | Tax | Tax Revenue as a Percent of | | |
		Total Revenue	GNP	Market Value of Equity
Canada	None	NA	NA	NA
France	0.3% below FFr 1 mill.	0.26%	0.12%	1.19%
	0.15% above FFR 1 mill.			
Germany	0.25%	0.14%	0.04%	0.28%
Italy	0.15%	1.10%	0.38%	6.10%
Japan	0.18% on dealers	1.42%	0.17%	0.34%
	0.55% on individuals			
Netherlands	0.5% below Dfl 1200	0.63%	0.32%	1.17%
Sweden	1.0% on sales	0.87%	0.36%	1.55%
Switzerland	0.15% (Swiss issuer)	2.33%	0.48%	0.94%
	0.30% (Foreign issuer)			
United Kingdom	0.5%	0.80%	0.30%	0.01%
United States	Document and stock transfer tax (State and Local)	0.17%	0.03%	0.08%

Source: Revenues and market capitalizations are for 1985. Transaction tax rates from Spicer and Oppenheim. *Securities Markets Around the World* (New York: John Wiley & Sons, 1988). *Revenue statistics* are from OECD. Revenue Statistics, various issues. Market values are from Morgan Stanley, *Capital International Perspectives*, various issues.

How Would A STET Work?

Most major industrialized countries impose some form of STET. As Table 2 indicates, these transaction taxes are in place in West Germany, France, Italy, the Netherlands, Sweden, Switzerland, the United Kingdom, and Japan, among other places. They represent a significant amount of revenue: in 1985, revenue collections ranged from .04 percent of Gross National Product in Germany to .48 percent of Gross National Product in Switzerland. This corresponds to a range of $2 billion to $25 billion in the United States. Similar figures are suggested by the comparisons of STET revenues with total revenues, and with the market value of outstanding equity.

A comparison of the administrative approaches used in other countries suggests a number of possible ways to structure a STET. The overall lesson to be drawn from international comparisons is that a STET can be made to work in a modern financial economy without insurmountable distortions, and without crippling the nation's securities industry.

Following is an analysis of certain aspects of the Japanese and British systems, as well as of the former United States documentary stamp tax imposed until the end of 1965. Issues raised by creating an administrable STET and their potential resolutions are addressed in detail.

The Japanese Tax

The Japanese transaction tax is situs based, imposed on the transfer of equity and debt instruments within Japan. It is an ad valorem tax, imposed on a base determined by the sale price of the instrument. The rate applicable to the transfer depends on the nature of the interest transferred. The rate applicable to debt interests, .03 percent, is one-tenth the rate applicable to equity interests, which is .3 percent (reduced from .55 percent in the 1988 tax reform). Derivative instruments that are not deemed to fall within the meaning of a "security"—for example, stock index futures—are not subject to the tax. National bonds, as well as privately-issued debt securities are, however, covered.

The tax is collected from the seller by the securities firm making the transfer. Certain transfers of covered securities, including gifts and some corporate mergers, are exempt. The securities transfer tax raised 1.7 trillion yen in fiscal year 1987-88, which converts to more than $12 billion in the United States.

The British Tax

The present British system of documentary transfer taxes was instituted in 1891. It was drastically revised in 1986 in order to widen the base of transactions that are subject to transfer tax and to lower the rate of tax applicable to many transactions. The original tax ("Stamp Duty") is a documentary stamp tax. It falls upon the issuance or transfer of stampable instruments. These instruments include corporate securities, although in 1988 Stamp Duty ceased to apply to the initial issuance of corporate stock. The 1986 Budget augmented the Stamp Duty by imposing the new "Stamp Duty Reserve Tax" (SDRT). This tax, despite its name, is not a stamp duty at all, but rather a pure transfer tax, designed to fall upon transfers of beneficial ownership of certain rights and securities which in the modern financial system may not be reflected in any "stampable" instruments.

The current British system has several notable features. Unlike the Japanese tax, the rate applicable to all taxed transfers is now the same, .5 percent of value. However, the British tax exempts pure debt securities. Exemptions are also are provided for options and futures traded on the Stock Exchange Traded Options Market and the London International Financial Futures Exchange, as well as for government gilt securities, purchases by charities, and bearer securities (although these are subject to a special higher "bearer instrument duty" upon issuance.) Securities subject to SDRT include stocks and shares and rights to stocks and shares in a United Kingdom company or in a foreign company that keeps a register in the United Kingdom. Because SDRT applies to transfers of beneficial ownership of chargeable securities, transfers in street name, or between brokerage accounts without changing the street name, are picked up. The tax is imposed upon nonresidents of the United Kingdom if their acquisition of chargeable securities occurs within the United Kingdom, through a broker or an agent there.

The potential to avoid the tax on transfers of beneficial ownership of U.K. chargeable securities by U.K. residents by making such transfers outside the United Kingdom is addressed under British company law. British corporations are in general required to maintain a corporate register of their stock within Britain. Thus, transfers of actual registered stock ownership must occur within Britain in order to be effective, and may therefore be picked up by the tax.

The development of modern financial instruments permitted the avoidance of this constraint, however, by permitting the transfer of beneficial ownership in an enforceable way without the need to transfer actual stock ownership. U.K. securities are transferred into a "depository" or "clearance system," and rights to the underlying stock then traded (outside Britain) through that system. The SDRT legislation dealt with these systems by creating a toll charge, at the rate of three times the normally applicable transfer tax, upon the transfer of chargeable securities into such a depository or clearance system. The subsequent transfer of the depository receipts or beneficial interests within the clearance system outside Britain is then free from SDRT. A similar charge applies upon the issuance of bearer instruments which are of a type which would have been subject to the tax if issued in registered form. These toll charges are intended to serve as a proxy for imposing tax on the unrecorded subsequent transfers of rights to British equity interests which, it was felt, could not be monitored or enforced in Britain.

The Former United States Documentary Stamp Tax

Until 1965, the United States imposed a federal stamp tax on the transfer of certain securities in the United States. Transfers of U.S. corporation stock outside the U.S. were exempt. The repeal of this tax occurred in the general repeal of almost all of the hodgepodge of federal retail and manufacturers' excise taxes which had grown up over the course of three decades. At the time, the repeal of tax on securities transfers was estimated to result in the loss of approximately $195 million annually, in 1965 dollars. The dollar volume of transactions on the NYSE has increased about twenty-fold since that time, so this tax would collect about $4 billion a year today.

The tax was imposed on the transfer and issuance of capital stock, shares in RICs (registered investment companies, also known as mutual funds), certificates of indebtedness, and rights to acquire these interests. Like the current Japanese tax, the rates of tax applicable to different types of interests varied. Interestingly however, the differences were reversed: the charge on the issuance or transfer of certificates of indebtedness exceeded the charge on the issuance or transfer of equity.

The tax contained an exemption for state and federal obligations, similar to the British tax. Foreign stock exchanged in the U.S. also was not subject to the stamp duty. Perhaps significantly for the current debate over the feasibility and wisdom of such a tax, transfers of U.S. equities that took place entirely outside of the United States were exempt from the tax. Certain exemptions existed for transfers in corporate mergers and consolidations; however, the issuance of new equity instruments in such transactions was, in general, subject to the tax. Transfers by gift and death were not exempt, nor were tax-exempt entities, in general, exempt from the stamp tax.

Designing a STET[2]

A number of questions currently are under consideration concerning the structure of a STET, including:

- What assets should be subject to a transaction tax?

- How should transactions taking place outside the United States by U.S. investors be handled? Does the answer differ depending on the nature of the asset being traded, i.e., whether the asset represents an interest in a U.S. entity or not? How should transactions within the U.S. by non-citizens be handled?

- What exemptions, if any, based on the identity of the persons transferring or receiving the assets should be permitted? Should any exemptions based on the nature of the transfer itself be provided?

- How and by whom should the tax be collected?

Assets Subject to the STET

Perhaps the most fundamental issue involved in the adoption of a STET is the type of assets that should be subject to the tax. Decisions must be made regarding the treatment of debt (as opposed to equity), of bearer instruments, of tax-exempt obligations, and of obligations of the federal government. The economic arguments discussed above suggest that a STET should cover the transfer of marketable securities or their equivalents. This means debt or equity interests in corporate or business enterprises in other forms, debt of governmental entities, rights to acquire title or beneficial ownership to such assets, and other financial assets. None of the considerations raised here suggest the adoption of a tax applicable to every contract for the transfer of other types of assets, such as documents of conveyance for real or personal tangible property, trust instruments, and others.

We see no argument for a blanket exemption from the tax for all debt instruments, though a lower rate for such instruments, such as is imposed under the Japanese transfer tax, may be appropriate because of the tremendous volume of trading in fixed income markets. A complete exemption for debt would merely exacerbate the existing problems under the income tax in distinguishing debt from equity interests. Further, an exemption for debt, even if it could be easily administered, would create additional distortions of capital structure in favor of debt financing. Although the use of a lower rate of tax with respect to debt instruments might arguably lead to these distortions as well, albeit to a lesser extent, the purpose of such a lower rate is actually to equalize the economic effects of the tax with respect to debt and equity, because of the much greater trading frequency and shorter average maturity of debt. A sliding scale for different forms of debt could theoretically be introduced to take more specific account of these differences, like the scale that was used for this purpose between differing maturities of debt under the former U.S. Interest Equalization Tax.

To some degree the omission of a blanket exemption for debt merely pushes back to another level the decision as to what instruments should be covered by the tax. If debt securities are covered in at least some forms, the issue arises as to which loan contracts will fall within the ambit of the tax. For example, should the issuance of a promissory note be taxable? What features of a bank loan for a corporate acquisition would distinguish it from corporate bonds in a way sufficiently significant to draw an administrable line? The issue of what debt should be chargeable is a very real one; this question was addressed repeatedly by the courts, including the Supreme Court, in the administration of the old U.S. documentary stamp tax. Then, the question was answered largely by reference to the degree and ease of marketability of the instrument in question. Such distinctions are neither impossible to make, nor unique to the transfer tax issue; distinctions between "securities" and nonsecurity debt contracts are formally drawn in both the income tax and the securities laws. For the purposes suggested here, a marketability test would be appropriate. However, it should be noted that this approach under the old U.S. documentary stamp tax led to a distortionary pattern of avoidance of the tax by the use of private financings through banks or other lenders in circumstances where debentures would otherwise have been used.

Assuming that readily marketable debt is covered by STET, there is still the question of whether or not government debt should be exempt. The old U.S. tax exempted federal, state, and municipal obligations. Similarly, the British system exempts transfers of government debt obligations. The Japanese, however, impose their transfer tax on national bonds. The distorted effects of allowing an exemption for government obligations are probably much lower than the distortions caused by exempting all "pure" debt from the tax. Such an exemption would, however, significantly reduce the revenue raised by the tax. And it might make the cost of capital to corporations somewhat higher than if the tax were imposed on government bonds as well as on privately-issued debt. Further, speculation in government obligations and government-backed obligations is probably at least as serious a problem (given the arguments in this chapter) as that with respect to privately-issued instruments.

It is clearly desirable to impose the tax on rights to acquire or to control, currently or in the future, assets which are themselves subject to the tax. It would seem that failure to do so could lead to widespread avoidance of the transfer tax by the use of economically equivalent derivative securities. Again however, the taxation of the transfers of options futures and other assets introduces considerable complexity. In particular, if STET is to be imposed on an ad valorem basis, the value of the right to acquire the asset must itself be weighed. While this is easy with traded options, it becomes more difficult with futures and more exotic instruments and rights. (As we have seen, the British exempt financial futures and options from their transaction taxes and the Japanese exempt derivatives such as stock index futures.)

Finally, such issues as whether currency and commodity futures and options should be subject to STET must be addressed. With commodity futures, the question is whether or not such rights should be subject to STET when a contract for the transfer of the underlying tangible asset itself would not be subject to the transfer tax contemplated. Perhaps a rule can be drawn which distinguishes between rights to which delivery of the commodity itself may be taken or required, and those more purely financial assets to which this could not happen.

Other issues arise: a serious valuation problem for such assets as foreign currency futures; enforceability issues that result from the lack of inherent connection between such financial futures with the U.S.; and the ability to acquire and sell such assets on other markets with little inconvenience or cost. Further, the use of these futures raises another question: should hedging transactions be subject to STET when the acquisition and disposition of positions hedge against changes in the value of certain assets used in or produced by an active trade or business?

Issues Raised by International Markets

The global marketplace raises several issues that must be addressed in the creation of a workable STET. First is the possibility that such a tax would harm the competitiveness of the U.S. financial industry, both with respect to trades and investments by U.S. persons and by foreigners. Second is the question of whether trades occurring "outside" the United States but involving U.S. persons should be taxed. Finally, the mechanism for and feasibility of enforcing the tax in the context of trades occurring outside the U.S. markets must be resolved.

Perhaps the principal objection raised to a STET by its opponents is that such a tax would cripple the United States securities industry by driving much of the activity of the U.S. financial markets offshore. We tentatively conclude that fears regarding a drastic reduction in the size of the U.S. securities industry are unwarranted. As the significant revenue collections realized from similar taxes in many other countries attest, such a tax can actually be enforced without resulting in the elimination of national stock markets. Trading in derivative securities and commodities may, however, pose a greater problem in this regard. Evidence for this may be found in the exemption from transfer tax of certain of such products in both the United Kingdom and Japan, as well as, for example, the downfall of the small Sweden Options and Futures Exchange, attributed by some to the Swedish government's decision to increase turnover taxes on options transactions. The imposition of a significant STET would clearly exert market pressure to move trading beyond its reach; the question, which has not yet been definitively answered, is whether such a tendency would be sufficiently great to prevent the tax from raising significant revenue or to harm U.S. competitiveness in financial services.

At least two possible approaches to this problem present themselves. First, and perhaps most ambitious, harmonization of the STET structure and enforcement among the financial center countries would minimize the potential gains from shifting trading to those nations. Of course, the possibility would remain for tax-haven countries to provide sanctuary in this case as well as in the case of direct taxes. Second, the STET could be imposed upon transactions occurring outside the United States but involving U.S. persons as principals, on a residency, rather than a situs, basis. This would minimize the advantages of such offshore trading. Conversely, with respect to the competitiveness of the U.S. markets for foreign participants, transactions by foreigners within the United States could be partially or wholly exempted.

As a theoretical matter, we conclude that the STET should be imposed upon any transaction involving a U.S. beneficial owner, regardless of the location of the transaction. Such an approach, if it were administratively feasible, would minimize the attractiveness of offshore trading of U.S. assets by such persons and would increase the revenue raised by the tax. Avoiding a shift to offshore trading of U.S. assets is important for reasons other than protecting the competitiveness of the U.S. securities industry. One of the goals of imposing a STET is to curb speculative trading, through the imposition of an extra marginal cost on each trade. This goal clearly would not be achieved merely by moving the location of such trades. Furthermore, the United States has additional interests in regulating the markets for domestic assets and their derivatives, which would be undermined if those markets moved beyond U.S. jurisdiction to a greater extent than they already have.

Several considerations support the view that trades in non-U.S. assets by U.S. persons should also be taxed, whether here or abroad. First, of course, is the revenue issue. Second, in interlinked markets the United States may be concerned with excess volatility not only of the U.S. stock market but of world markets; excessive speculation by U.S. persons in those markets may contribute significantly to such volatility. The connections between the world's markets were made dramatically apparent during the events of October 19, 1987. Finally, the definition of a "U.S. asset" would add an additional layer of complexity to the STET system. For example, should publicly traded debentures of a wholly owned foreign subsidiary of a U.S. corporation be considered different for this purpose from similar debentures of a domestic subsidiary doing business abroad?

Nonetheless, such taxation of foreign assets would be a departure from past U.S. practice, as well as that of most other established STET systems. Furthermore, inclusion of foreign transfers of assets, especially in the case of non-U.S. assets, is likely in some cases to subject such transfers to a double STET, that of the United States and of the country where the trade takes place. This could be addressed through a treaty or credit system, or, alternatively, that result could be allowed. Double taxation of offshore trading would certainly serve as an additional disincentive to moving parts of the U.S. securities industry out of the United States.

It would be possible to exempt from the tax either or both the transfer of U.S. assets or foreign assets on U.S. markets by foreign persons; this approach would minimize the anti-competitive nature of the STET with respect to the use of the United States as a world financial center. We conclude, however, that the registration of foreign stock or debt on U.S. markets or the use of U.S. markets or brokers by foreign persons should subject trades in such assets or by such persons to the STET. The STET is not an inappropriate price to pay for access to the U.S. markets. Furthermore, the fact that a speculative trader has his tax residency outside the United States will not serve to limit the destabilizing effect of his frequent trades which (as argued above) increase U.S. market volatility. Finally, providing exemptions for foreign assets or trades by non-U.S. persons through U.S. markets or brokers would merely complicate further the already complex administrative issues surrounding the imposition and enforcement of a new STET.

While a tax structured as just outlined would be theoretically preferable, such a structure does raise a number of issues that would have to be resolved to implement the tax. These international considerations can be dealt with in several ways. First, any transfer made through a U.S. broker, regardless of the identity of the principal or the nature of the asset, could be collected in the normal course, as described in the following section. This method would not, however, pick up transfers effected through foreign affiliates of U.S. brokers. Second, the tax on any transfer of equity recorded on a register kept in the United States (whether the principal register or a duplicate) could be enforced by prohibiting the transfer agent from effecting a change in registration without evidence of payment of the tax.

The transfer of beneficial interests on behalf of U.S. persons by non-U.S. brokers, agents, or clearance services without transfer of registration of legal title to the actual assets does raise significant enforcement problems. These transactions would probably have to be subject to voluntary reporting. Capital gains realized by U.S. persons on transactions occurring outside the United States is required now in the income tax context. It is no less likely that the STET would be reported and paid as that the income tax on such gains would be paid. While a certain amount of avoidance will be inevitable, large institutional investors, in particular, are probably unlikely to fail intentionally to report legally taxable transactions. (Although tax-exempt investors such as pension funds are not now subject to capital gains taxes on these or most other market transactions, pension funds are required to file certain annual reports which could be expanded to include reporting regarding the STET.)

The spectre of offshore mutual funds organized to trade on behalf of U.S. persons in foreign assets raises the prospect of avoidance, since the non-U.S. entity itself would be conducting the trading. A very similar problem was addressed in the income tax area with the 1986 creation of the so-called "Passive Foreign Investment Company" (or "PFIC") rules. These rules alone may have been enough to restrict the use of such offshore funds by U.S. investors who are aware of them. However, a similar system of rules in the case of the STET could be used. Such a scheme would impose a very high tax on the investor upon the receipt of distributions from the fund or on liquidation of his interest, which would serve as a proxy for the foregone STET which should have been incurred by the U.S. investor during the period in which he held the fund. In order to avoid this penalty tax, the investor would have to make current periodic payments in lieu of a direct STET, based upon accounting by the fund to the investors regarding the volume of its trading on world markets.

The Transfers and the Investors to Whom the Tax Would Apply

The exemption of taxable asset transfers by gift, bequest, or inheritance probably would create little distortion with STET. Further, taxation of gifts and bequests would likely do little to reduce speculative trading. However, tax administration could become more complicated by the creation of an exemption, and the tax revenue raised could be diminished to some extent. Although an exemption for charitable donations could be added as a policy matter—it probably would be implemented best through a donor credit claimed on his income tax return— there seems to be no good reason to exempt such transfers.

Another position on STET has been that the transfer tax should not apply where stock or securities are issued or transferred on a tax-free basis in a non-taxable corporate acquisition or merger. However, the logic of the income tax exemption does not necessarily apply to the STET because it is premised on the view that the beneficial interest of the corporate participants has merely changed form, and that the transaction is not, therefore, an appropriate juncture at which to impose a tax on the increase in value of the beneficial interests in the target enterprise.

Exemptions should be made, however, for certain other transfers, including 1.) transfers of title only, in which beneficial asset ownership remains the same, i.e., the transfer to a grantor trust, 2.) transfers through fiduciaries or nominees where a single beneficial transfer occurs using multiple steps to a broker for sale or to the executor of a decedent's estate for subsequent transfer to the beneficiaries, and 3.) transfers of title or possession only when the asset is transferred as security for a loan.

One of the key questions raised by a STET is its application to tax-exempt market participants. The general rule should be that the tax-exempt status of the transferor or transferee is of no consequence for the imposition of the STET. It might well be argued that the discouragement of short-term, speculative trading is most important for these very investors. First, tax-exempt pension funds and other institutions account for a tremendous portion of the market's trading volume. Second, just as the short rule limiting certain tax benefits to mutual funds that churn their portfolios too rapidly protects retail capital investments in mutual funds, the retirement funds of the millions of workers who did not choose the investment vehicle or manager for those funds should have the limited protection against speculation afforded by STET. If the rationale makes sense in the mutual fund context where it has been incorporated within the law for 50 years, it also makes sense for pension funds and other tax exempt shareholders. While certain common law and statutory doctrines govern the investment decisions of pension fund managers, STET would create additional incentives in the appropriate direction.

Its ability to discourage speculation on the part of tax-free entities is an important STET virtue accomplished with taxable entities through the use of the short-term/long-term capital gains distinction. It may not be practical to extend the capital gains tax to such institutions; but if STET is collected from the broker who performed a given transaction, it could be applied to all transactions regardless of the investors involved. Finally, the application of the tax to mutual funds must be addressed. As noted, such entities are already subject to certain tax restrictions that depend upon the frequency of their trades. We conclude that transactions by mutual funds should be subject to the STET in a normal manner. A reduced rate could be applied to reduce the double taxation effect.

Collection of and Liability for the STET

The old stamp U.S. tax provided that legal liability for payment fell on all parties involved in a stampable transaction—but the parties could decide who among them would bear the economic liability. In transactions effected through brokers, the broker generally was responsible for collecting the tax and affixing the requisite stamps. Liability for the British SDRT falls to the transferee in any chargeable transaction; however, registered brokers are responsible for tax collection when they are involved in a taxable transaction. Transfers on the Stock Exchange are addressed through a central clearing mechanism as they are on the national exchange when subject to the old U.S. tax, which could be effected without the use of documentary stamps.

In the current electronic age, a collection mechanism that relies on documentary stamps would be hopelessly unwieldy. Instead, a system similar to the mechanism used for transactions on national exchanges under the old stamp tax could be put in place for the administration of a STET. All registered brokers who complete transactions subject to the tax could serve as tax collection agents in the same way they currently collect the small SEC transaction tax on every sale of shares.

The tax on transactions that are effected directly with the issuer of the instrument could be collected by the issuer. Collection for transactions effected among persons without the services of a broker could be enforced by requiring the transfer agent for the registered instrument to refuse transfer without evidence of tax payment or by tax collection by the agent. Persons holding securities in street name or otherwise as nominees could be required to collect and remit the tax when a transfer of beneficial interest in the assets from one principal to another occurs, even in the absence of a transfer of legal title or reregistration of the securities. When registered brokerage houses are involved, the completion of this duty could be enforced with SEC audits. Other taxable transactions would be relatively small in terms of economic effect, and would be enforced through individual filings and remittance of STET using a form that accompanies the federal income tax return.

Is It Too Late?

This examination barely has touched a few of the administrative problems that a STET would raise. It may be clear that the tax is feasible from its implementation in other countries, but the trend toward abolishing transfer taxes must be acknowledged.

In 1988, Britain abolished capital duties and retained transfer taxes. In 1986, the transfer tax rate was reduced simultaneously, however, with the introduction of SDRT. As noted previously, Japan also reduced its transfer tax rate. A proposed 1987 European Economic Community (EEC) directive, its fate still unclear, seeks the abolition of all transfer taxes in the European community as part of the unification of the continent. This directive was made after a decade of discussion and study of the harmonization of all transfer taxes within member states—a task that participants determined was extremely difficult, if not impossible. Clearly, this conclusion does not bode well for the feasibility of the suggestion that the U.S. STET should be harmonized with other nations' existing taxes.

To some extent, then, the imposition of a U.S. transfer tax at this time might be viewed as bucking the world trend. However, it is quite possible that the introduction of such a tax here could affect the actions of other countries. The issues that create support for a STET in the United States—revenue needs and concern with excessive speculation—are crucial to other major financial center nations as well: a harmonized system among these countries could reduce the potential for the offshore flight of trading activities significantly, could reduce market competition, and could provide a source of revenue that is easily administered. If a STET were imposed in New York, there is at least the prospect that the rush to reduce taxes in other financial centers would be slowed or reversed.

Conclusions

This analysis suggests that some form of STET, in curbing speculation, would have desirable economic effects and could raise a significant amount of revenue in the United States. STET's revenue potential will depend on its administration: A conservative estimate based on a .5 percent rate, with only a small allowance for revenues collected from assets other than stocks, suggests that $10 billion a year could be raised.

In considering STET as a revenue source, it is important to recall that while STET may improve economic efficiency, most other tax measures have adverse effects on incentives to work and save. But even if STET has no beneficial effect on the economy, it is an efficient tax relative to most alternatives. And because its ultimate impact would be felt by corporate stockholders, it would be highly progressive as well: more than half of all retail stock is held by individuals in the top one percent of wealth distribution.

Endnotes

[1] For general discussions of the theoretical validity of the efficient market hypothesis, see Shiller (1984); Kyle (1985); Black (1986); Summers (1986); and DeLong, Shleifer, Summers and Waldmann (1988).

[2] This section draws heavily on the JCT memorandum describing the workings of a STET.

Additional References

Black, Fischer, "Noise," 41 *Journal of Finance*, (1986), pp. 529-543.

Cutler, David M., James M. Poterba, and Lawrence Summers, "What Moves Stock Prices?," *Journal of Portfolio Management*, (Spring, 1989), pp. 4-12.

DeLong, J. Bradford, Andrei Shleifer, Lawrence, H. Summers, and Robert J. Waldmann, "The Economic Consequences of Noise Traders," Harvard University mimeo, (1988).

Fama, Eugene, and Kenneth French, "Permanent and Transitory Components of Stock Prices," 96 *Journal of Political Economy*, (1988), pp. 246-273.

French, Kenneth, and Richard Roll, "Stock Return Variances: The Arrival of Information and the Reaction of Traders," 17 *Journal of Financial Economics*, (1987), pp. 5-26.

Jensen, Michael C., "Symposium on Some Anomalous Evidence Regarding Market Efficiency," 6 *Journal of Financial Economics*, (1978), pp. 95-101.

Joint Committee on Taxation, "Staff Memorandum on the Imposition of Security Transaction taxes," U.S.: Government Printing Office, (1987).

Keynes, John Maynard, *The General Theory of Employment, Interest, and Money*, (Harcourt Brace, 1936).

Kyle, Albert, "Continuous Auctions and Insider Trading," 53 *Econometrica*, (1985), pp. 1315-1336.

Lowenstein, Louis, *What's Wrong with Wall Street: Short Term Gain and the Absentee Shareholder*, (Addison-Wesley, 1988).

New York Stock Exchange, *Fact Book*, (1988).

Roll, Richard, "Orange Juice and Weather," 74 *American Economic Review*, (1984), pp. 861-880.

Roll, Richard, "R-Squared," 43 *Journal of Finance*, (1988), pp. 541-566.

Poterba, James M. and Lawrence H. Summers, "Mean Reversion in Stock Prices: Evidence and Implications," 22 *Journal of Financial Economics*, (1988), pp. 3-26.

Schwert, G. William, "Why Does Stock Market Volatility Change Over Time?" NBER Working Paper, (1988).

Scott, Thomas and Nik Mehta, "The U.K.'s New Tax on Securities," *International Financial Law Review*, (December, 1986).

Shiller, Robert, "Do Stock Prices Move Too Much to be Justified by Subsequent Dividends," 71 *American Economic Review*, (1981), pp. 421-436.

Shiller, Robert, "Stock Prices and Social Dynamics," *Brookings Papers on Economic Activity*, (1984:2), pp. 457-498.

Summers, Lawrence H., "Does the Stock Market Rationally Reflect Fundamental Values," 41 *Journal of Finance*, (1986), pp. 591-601.

Tobin, James, "On the Efficiency of the Financial System," *Lloyds Bank Review*, (July, 1984).

Tobin, James, "A Proposal for International Monetary Reform," *Eastern Economic Review*, (1978), pp. 153-159.

When is a Marketplace a Market? Automated Trade Execution in the Futures Market

Ian Domowitz
Northwestern University

In passing the Commodity Exchange Act of 1974, Congress directed the Commodity Futures Trading Commission to determine the "feasibility of trading by computer."[1] In other words, automated trade execution might be permissible if it were implemented in a fashion consistent with other provisions of the Act.[2] As noted early on by Melamed (1977), this suggestion is one of the most significant statements in the Act, carrying with it revolutionary implications for futures markets.

Following is an investigation of the legal and economic difficulties of defining a market within a computer, given that a particular mode of trading and its associated locale are so entrenched that they are placed within the language and provisions of the Act itself. These issues have been investigated extensively by the SEC and others in the case of stock trading, in part because automated execution systems for stocks have been available for quite some time.[3] Although advanced electronic technology has been a fixture on futures exchanges for many years, the one major exception to this adaptation to technology has been the actual execution of trades.[4] This function is carried out by "open outcry" auction in a pit, a system that has been in place for over 135 years.

The SEC's original problem in regulating automated execution schemes was rather simple: the technology that has led to the development of such systems was in no way envisioned when Congress passed the Securities and Exchange Act of 1934.[5] By the time of the 1975 amendments, the potential of computer technology in financial markets was clear, and Congress effectively gave the SEC the "power to classify markets . . . in any manner it deems necessary or appropriate in the public interest . . ."[6] The SEC has dealt admirably with the problem of computerized trading since that time, and the current attitude is well exposited in Ruder and Adkins (1990). The SEC recognized distinctions among exchanges and automated trading systems early on, stating that automated systems have neither a trading floor nor a variety of other characteristics commonly associated with an exchange.[7] At the same time, the SEC did reserve the right to classify automated systems as exchanges or brokers under the Securities and Exchange Act.

The phrase "in the public interest" is central to the debate over whether or not an automated execution system qualifies as a market for futures trading. Section 3 of the Commodities Exchange Act (the Act) defines the public interest as 1.) reliable price discovery; 2.) broadbased price dissemination; and 3.) effective hedging against price risks. Section 5(g) states that any market must show that its activities are not contrary to the public interest. The first requirement of the public interest is covered here. The second is indispensable to the first, and the last should follow if the market is otherwise sound in price and quantity determination.[8]

The price discovery process is linked to the physical characteristics and locale of the market, the mode of trading, and some notion of effective competition. The first aspect refers to the necessity of having a floor or pit where traders can meet face to face, versus a market within a central computer facility accessed by possibly anonymous traders sitting at computer terminals located virtually anywhere around the world. The second aspect relates to a perceived requirement that prices be set via the open outcry auction system. This system is replicated or replaced by the algorithm programmed to generate transactions given a set of bids and offers input to the computer. The third aspect concerns the basic economic notion that free competition gives rise to the best possible pricing within any market. These three considerations obviously are not independent. The Act treats each one explicitly; but recognition of their interdependence is not only part of the document and its legislative history, it also causes problems of interpretation with respect to new trading systems.

The introduction of such mechanisms will begin with GLOBEX, the first major automated futures trading system in the United States.[9] GLOBEX is a vehicle for trading futures contracts outside regular floor trading hours in Chicago. The Chicago Mercantile Exchange submitted the basic organization and rules concerning the GLOBEX Trading System to the Commodity Futures Trading Commission (the Commission) in a series of letters beginning May 11, 1988.[10]

The GLOBEX system serves as an example of the regulatory issues underlying the introduction of computerized order execution into futures markets in general. It is considered here a laboratory for analysis, as opposed to looking at "ideal" systems that have been examined extensively in the past. The two major benefits are concreteness to the analysis and the ability to compare trading carried out under an existing known computer algorithm with what happens on the trading floor, by example.

When is a Marketplace a Market?

Imagine sitting in front of a video screen on which is a graphics display of a trading pit. The pit area is divided in two, with buyers on one side and sellers on the other. The images are marked by numbers identifying them as traders, with the size of the bid or offer marked in each image. The current best bid and offer are displayed on a screen within the video screen, in the center of the pit. Bids and offers are valid for only five seconds, and must be accepted immediately for trade execution. Real life traders enter bids, offers, and execution instructions from screens far removed from any trading floor. Is this a market?

If not, the London International Financial Futures Exchange is going to have some problems. The scenario described above is a capsule description of what the exchange is supposed to look and act like. There are two things to notice about this attempt to replicate a futures trading pit. The bid or offer is good "only while the breath is warm," at least in the computer's discrete time, and there is no automatic execution component. Although issues surrounding the actual process by which prices and quantities are set are not relevant for these two reasons, several of the arguments against computerized trading floors still apply to the setup described above. Given the historical development of financial markets in the United States within its legal and regulatory structure, it is not clear that a computer can embody a market in its fullest generality. The first issue concerns the preservation of the physical trading floor itself.

It has been forcefully argued that the floor is such an important element of a healthy futures market that its replacement alone could destroy the market.[11] Melamed (1977) lists several factors embodied by the pit system that contribute to market liquidity. These include 1.) the floor as a primary stimulus for ideas and opinions contributing to the price discovery process; 2.) the ease of access to the market provided by the trading pit; and 3.) the stimulative and incentive effects of the floor's atmosphere in contributing to competitive responses.

The first factor relates to localized information not readily available from quotation or other news services. Melamed links opinion formation directly to speculative activity contributing to liquidity and, therefore, to the viability of the market. Ease of access concerns participation by the relevant players. The notion is that on the floor, a member can go to a pit within seconds after conceiving an idea. In using this as a defense against computerized floors, the implication is that traders would somehow have to wait their turn at terminals in order to trade, losing this sort of immediacy. This need not be the case, however. In principle, GLOBEX can handle a virtually unlimited number of terminal hookups, a possibility not originally envisioned by floor trading proponents. The third factor above is rather broad, but it might be linked to the issue of participation in the market. A chapter in futures folklore is that traders are attracted to noisy pits. The noise represents an active market, and for those who have experienced trading on the floor, it is palpable. It is not at all clear what mechanism can replace this sort of stimulus in a computerized system, and certainly one cannot hear or see activity on the screen in the same way. This problem is exacerbated if the computerized system operates as a closed book, a point to which the analysis will return later.

Although the special characteristics of the trading floor are integral to the objections of traders to computerized floors, the CFTC's Regulation 1.38 states that:

"All purchases and sales of any commodity for future delivery, and of any commodity option . . . shall be executed openly and competitively by open outcry or posting of bids and offers or by other equally open and competitive methods in the trading pit or ring or similar place provided by the contract market."

There is no further guidance concerning the "similar place," but the language certainly introduces the possibility of replacing the pit system. In the same fashion, Section 2 of the Act reflects Congressional expectations that trading will take place on a centralized "floor," but leaves the precise nature of the floor open:

". . . [floor broker is] any person who, in or surrounding any 'pit,' 'ring,' 'post,' or other place provided by a contract market for the meeting of persons similarly engaged shall purchase or sell . . . subject to the rules of any contract market."

Other legislative history confirms such ambiguity with respect to the precise environs within which trading is to take place. In particular, an interpretation of the purpose of Regulation 1.38 can be found in a 1974 Senate Report:[12]

"The purpose of this requirement is to ensure that all trades are executed at competitive prices and that all trades are focused into the centralized marketplace to participate in the competitive determination of the price of futures contracts."

A centralized marketplace easily can be conceived of as a facility in which all relevant market information is available and which can be accessed by qualified trading professionals during commonly accepted trading hours. A computer qualifies as well as a physical pit under the law, it would seem. Counterarguments must rely on the relation of the physical facility to the actual mode of trading or the competitive process itself.

Relative to the competitive process, potential connections are close at hand. According to the original CME proposal for a computerized system,[13] a variety of information is to be recorded into the system—before an order is transmitted for execution—in addition to the order ticket requirement mandated by the CFTC's Regulation 1.35. The Chicago Board of Trade has claimed that serious time delays occur as a result, and that the outcome could be a continuous flow of unfilled orders.[14] If this is the case,[15] the result is a phenomenon known as "chasing the market." In other words, if a buy order is placed at the current offer and the market moves up, the order may not be filled due to the delay. A new order must be entered, and the same thing may happen, possibly several times, before execution occurs. On the trading floor, a trade can be executed the moment it enters the floor broker's hand in the pit as an order ticket. The physical environment itself allows for such immediacy, which in turn is an important element in the price discovery process.

The CFTC also has questioned the CME about the possibility of chasing the market in the GLOBEX system.[16] The CFTC noted that a person entering a market order is reasonably assured that the execution of that order will occur within a short time at whatever price is obtainable at the moment the order is received on the floor. The CFTC asked whether the same can be expected on GLOBEX, and whether a customer can miss execution at a competitive price and risk chasing the market without strategic bidding that would be unnecessary on the floor. The CME's response acknowledged the latter possibility explicitly; i.e., a strategy that requires bettering the current bid or offer is necessary to increase the probability of a fill for the order. And if the market price moves before the order is executed, forcing the market participant to input new information with a revised price, the new order may enter with a lower execution priority due to the nature of time-stamping and priority in the GLOBEX rules.[17] This further enhances the possibility of a customer chasing the market while attempting to trade by computer.

Chasing the market is a regulatory concern in yet another way. Section 15 of the Act directs the CFTC to "endeavor to take the least anticompetitive means of achieving the objectives of this Act . . . in approving any bylaw, rule, or regulation of a contract market." If a phenomenon such as chasing the market is a real possibility in a computerized trading system relative to existing floor trading, then it might be concluded that the automated system is less competitive than the traditional floor. The CFTC does have some history of disapproving a proposed type of trading session on the grounds that "decreased competition may impair the effectiveness and efficiency of the price discovery process and the ability of the market accurately to reflect the forces of supply and demand."[18] On the other hand, the CME has argued that its automated trading system enhances competition relative to the floor by providing virtually unlimited access to the market (no physical limitations on the number of terminals that can be connected to the main system) and by providing a perfect audit trail, by which it is easier to ensure overall competitive behavior in the market.

Open and Competitive: Information and Open Outcry Auction

The issue of competitiveness, or the lack thereof, cannot be divorced from the method of carrying out the trading process. There are two major regulatory aspects to be considered here. The first concerns the extent of price information and the second involves statutory requirements that trading in the futures markets be carried out by the method of open outcry auction.

These two issues are not independent when legislative history is examined. For example, in a Senate Report relating to the Act, it was noted that:[19]

"The actual trading of futures contracts takes place in the noisy, boisterous setting of an auction-type market . . . This system also provides ready access to the market for all orders and results in a continuous flow of price information to the public."

The language contained in Regulation 1.38 concerning "open . . . methods" as quoted earlier bears on the information content of trading and links this to open outcry methods. That regulation does state, however, that "other equally open" methods would be acceptable.

There is a precedent for at least one such method that relates directly to the type of information potentially available in an automated execution system. This method is called "posting" or "blackboard trading." The CFTC has defined posting as:

" . . . the practice of displaying a prevailing bid or offer which, while posted on a blackboard, is subject to execution should the necessary buying or selling interest develop in the contract."[20]

Such blackboard trading has been replaced almost completely by pit trading in the futures industry, but the practice still prevails for contracts in which volume is low. In practice, traders announce bids and offers to an exchange clerk. The clerk writes the price, quantity, and contract month on a blackboard, along with the traders' initials. Orders have priority according to price alone, i.e., the highest bid and the lowest offer have priority. If ties occur, orders are executed in the sequence in which they were posted. Trades are executed at the price of the standing (posted) order in cases where the best bid is higher than the best offer. Transactions are recorded on a separate blackboard in chronological order. This record includes the time of the trade, price, size, and the initials of the executing floor brokers.

This scenario obviously can be replicated on a computer; approved minimum standards for such posting are contained in CME Rule 522, providing explicit guidelines for design. The capsule description of the computerized London Exchange fits the description nicely, assuming that another screen could accommodate the audit trail of completed transactions. There is some question, however, as to whether current systems under consideration match all details of blackboard trading.

In particular, GLOBEX is a closed book system, at least initially.[21] GLOBEX displays the last sale price and quantity, the best outstanding bid and offer prices, and the quantity at those respective prices. This appears to contravene CME Rule 522, which calls for the posting of all bids and offers. The CME plans to display the 10 best bids and offers eventually, along with associated quantity data to satisfy the current precedent for blackboard trading.

A closed book system effectively displays only the intersection of supply and demand in the market, potentially producing less accurate pricing than a complete set of bids and offers. The lack of quantity information at various possible prices also makes it difficult to isolate market trends, which further detracts from the price discovery process. The issue from the regulatory perspective is, however, whether such a system is "more anticompetitive" than what currently exists on the floor. The CME claims that the GLOBEX system provides the same information about orders that is available in the pit, (noting that floor trading proceeds successfully on the basis of such information): the prices of the best bid and offer, and the quantities available at those prices. On the other hand, although a complete array of bids and offers is not necessarily displayed in the futures pit, every bid and offer made is for a specified price and for a quantity that is revealed to all other traders present.

This last point leads to the issue of the open outcry auction in comparison to a computer algorithm that controls the price discovery and quantity determination process. A reading of CFTC regulation 1.38 quoted above, or of section 4c of the Act that stipulates a set of prohibited trading practices, indicates that neither the Act nor CFTC regulations mandate a particular method for executing futures transactions. Although both of these citations refer to the open outcry auction process as the acceptable mode of trading, the common theme is "open and competitive" procedure. Section 4b of the Act, however, states that:

"Nothing in this section or any other section of this Act shall be construed to prevent a futures commission merchant or floor broker who shall have in hand, simultaneously, buying and selling orders at the market . . . from executing such buying and selling orders at the market price: provided that any such execution shall take place on the floor of the exchange where such orders are to be executed at public outcry across the ring . . ."

The legislative history behind this section may provide some guidance. This language was introduced during the 1936 Senate debate of the House bill which amended the Grain Futures Act. Its intent was explained in the context of a broker who may have the opportunity to buy contracts, possibly raising the market price, and then to sell contracts held at the same time for a better profit. The world "simultaneous" is important here; the orders to buy and sell come at the same time in this story. In particular:

"Under this amendment, if a broker gets two such [simultaneous] orders, he must offer them simultaneously on the floor at the market, so that the effect of one will not be felt before the effect of the other is felt. That is all there is to the amendment."[22]

Even such precise language may be tricky to interpret in the context of computerized floors. It appears that the open outcry requirement applies only to the crossing of orders. Can this situation even occur in a computerized market? From a purely technical standpoint, the answer is a qualified no. It is true, for example, that all GLOBEX orders are routed to a central computer and exposed to all other orders for execution. The CFTC seems to believe that this process obviates the open outcry requirement by doing away with the order crossing phenomenon.[23] GLOBEX does not even allow for simultaneity; there can be no ties with respect to order entry time in the system. This is a technicality, however. The CME defines order entry time as the time of acceptance and posting of an order at the host computer. Communications between a terminal and the central processing site are handled by a separate computer subsystem which presents orders serially to the host. Given simultaneous orders entered at the terminal (clearly the intent of any language referring to simultaneous orders within an automated system), the subsystem breaks ties by an unknown process in serially routing the orders. The process by which this is done most probably is connected to the computer's internal clock, which splits time into small fractions of a second. It is not at all clear that such small time intervals were ever to be the metric in deciding whether orders arrived "simultaneously."

On the other hand, the legislative intent referred to above concerns the broker. "Floor" broker may be a misnomer after the introduction of computerized floors, but computerization still requires the analogue. Situations undoubtedly occur in which "floor" brokers receive corresponding or simultaneous matching buy and sell orders. This cannot be considered an unusual event; the debate of 1936 demonstrates the relative frequency of such occurrences. In other words, order crossing can, indeed, occur counter to the CFTC's interpretation of the statute concerning computerized execution systems. Section 4b of the Act probably applies here.

In fact, in the context of its disapproval of the Commodity Exchange, Inc.'s (COMEX) straddle session in 1981, the CFTC found that section 4b was enacted in order to protect the public interest and that it reflects Congressional belief that the public interest would be protected by the open outcry requirement.[24] The CBOT has used this interpretation, among other precedents from the COMEX decision, to support a variety of objections to GLOBEX.[25] A close examination of the case suggests the overriding importance of the "open and competitive" requirement in CFTC regulation 1.38 as it relates to any trading practice, however. The CFTC is hardly vague about its standards:

"The clearest reflection of competitive market forces is the number of buy and sell orders in the market at a point in time and the manner in which those orders will interact to achieve an execution or series of executions at prices which represent the market's collective evaluation of a commodity's worth at each point in time."[26]

Competitive Benchmarks for the Floor and Machine

Given the CFTC's mandate and the definition of "the public interest," it is clear that the main issue in any debate over floor versus machine is the competitiveness of the price discovery process. Such debates in the past have centered around speculation within the workings of any computerized system, without a clear statement of the algorithm to determine prices and quantities or some notion of an objective standard that can be used to compare alternative systems, including open outcry auction. In Domowitz and Gardner (1990), the classical benchmark of Walrasian or competitive equilibrium pricing is used to provide such a standard. The purpose of this section is to summarize those results relevant to futures markets and to indicate the logical extensions to trading situations not considered there.

Price and quantity determination in a Walrasian auction occurs at the intersection of the market supply and demand curves. The mechanics involve a fictional auctioneer, who calls out tentative prices until the quantity of contracts supplied adjusts to match the quantity demanded. The price at which this equalization occurs is used to clear all trades. The quantity traded at that price is the number of contracts that would change hands under "perfect competition."

Domowitz and Gardner (1990) consider trading scenarios involving six traders bidding for and offering a single contract. Floor trading rarely allows convergence to the competitive price itself; the competitive price and quantity are reached only 14 percent of the time. If the competitive outcome is redefined to include the competitive quantity reached in a Walrasian auction and a price range that includes the competitive price, open outcry auction obtains the competitive benchmark 57 percent of the time.

Price indeterminacy is not possible within GLOBEX. The results are impressive: GLOBEX replicates the competitive auction 75 percent of the time under its rules for a closed book system. To use the CFTC's terminology, the Walrasian solution "represents the market's collective evaluation of a commodity's worth at each point in time." By that metric, GLOBEX provides excellent price discovery and quantity determination relative to floor trading.

The situation is different with orders that are too large to be absorbed by a single trader. On the floor, an order can be "broken up" and offered sequentially in pieces, or the trader can attempt to place the entire order within the spread, dividing it among interested competing traders. Breaking up an order in GLOBEX is accomplished through the use of a "secondary" quantity mechanism that allows the computer-assisted trader the luxury of not showing the entire order at once.[27]

Preliminary analysis of the case in which a trader offers the entire large order as a block yields similar results for floor and machine. The competitive outcome is obtained on the floor 50 percent of the time, while GLOBEX reaches this benchmark in approximately one-third of the cases considered. This analysis is more specialized than the analysis in the last chapter, requiring specific assumptions about how trades are divided among competing traders and the type of large orders entered into GLOBEX. As with all specialized results, some caution is required in their interpretation.

The situation worsens when the possibility of breaking up an order is considered. Few scenarios examined for the floor yield the competitive outcome; the competitive price, but not the corresponding quantity, is reached 25 percent of the time. Similarly, the use of the secondary quantity mechanism within GLOBEX results in Walrasian outcomes for 20 percent of the cases examined, although the competitive price is achieved 50 percent of the time. Removal of partial quantity by the floor trader or passively by a computerized mechanism excludes a portion of the supply curve necessary to yield competitive outcomes.

A reading of these results suggests that a computerized futures trade execution system is not necessarily any less competitive than the open outcry method. The benchmark used above is well established in the economic analysis of competitive pricing, but it is not the only possibility. Other standards that are richer in terms of strategic behavior might be developed and applied in future work. The important point here is that the determination of concepts such as "competition" across markets requires such objective standards.

Conclusion

It is a lengthy process to identify all the components contributing to, or detracting from, making a marketplace a market in the context of futures trading. The role of market orders is one important issue on a longer list. Market orders are considered important in a competitive market, but they are not allowed on GLOBEX, for example. The establishment of an opening price without a concurrent floor market is an exercise in automating the specialist, as considered by Black (1971) some time ago. Proof that a computerized system cannot be manipulated within the rules of the game would be desirable, and the list could go on.

In the end, markets create markets in a sense independent of computers or floor traders. The viability of computerized floors ultimately will be established by a simple market test: where does trading take place?

Endnotes

[1]   Commodity Exchange Act, Section 18, 7 U.S.C. (Supp. V, 1975).

[2]   The CFTC's office of General Counsel stated in 1982 that provisionally it perceived no absolute prohibition in the Act or other CFTC regulations to the designation of a wholly automated exchange as a contract market. It was acknowledged, however, that several provisions of the Act and CFTC regulations are based on traditional floor trading practices. *See* letter of December 15, 1982 from Dennis A. Dutterer, General Counsel, to Thomas A. Russo, also referenced in a memorandum of January 25, 1989 from the Division of Trading and Markets to the CFTC about the CME's proposed GLOBEX Trading System, on file at the CFTC offices.

[3]   The Pacific Stock Exchange introduced the first such system in 1969, now called SCOREX. A completely automated exchange, the Cincinnati Stock Exchange has been in operation since 1978; *see* SEC Release N. 19315, (December 9, 1982).

[4]   *See* Burmeister (1977) for a description of the CBOT's impressive electronic and computerized features, even as of 1977.

[5] The SEC itself noted this problem in 1969; *see* SEC Release No. 8661, (1969).

[6] Senate Report No. 75, 94th Congress, 1st Sess., at 7 (1975).

[7] *See* SEC Release No. 8661, (1969).

[8] There are some issues concerning the actual mechanics of hedging transactions such as spreads, for example. Melamed's (1977) defense of floor trading rested in part on the contention that effective spread transactions could take place only on the floor via specialized "spreaders." For a discussion of spread transactions within GLOBEX, *see* CME responses to Questions contained in CFTC letter dated October 6, 1988, Exhibit 1, question 29. The basic idea is to trade spreads as separate instruments.

[9] There was one other: the Intex Futures Exchange, a fully automated system based in Bermuda, was not successful. For a description, *see* SEC Release No. 23795, (1986).

[10] In the original submission, the system was called the PMT System; it changed the name on June 20, 1988. The original proposal is published in 55 *Federal Register* 25528, (July 7, 1988). GLOBEX was approved in February, 1989; *see* Memorandum from the Division of Trading and Markets to the CFTC concerning the CME's proposed GLOBEX trading system, (January 25, 1989).

[11] *See* generally the recorded transcript (as opposed to the written *Proceedings*) of the Conference on Automation in the Futures Industry, (June 15, 1977) on file at the CFTC offices.

[12] Senate Report No. 93-1131, 93rd Congress, 2nd Sess. at 16 (1974).

[13] Exhibit V, submission of May 11, 1988 to the CFTC, rule 571.

[14] *See* letter from Thomas R. Donovan, CBOT President, to Jean A. Webb, CFTC, (September 6, 1988).

[15] The CME believes that any such delays are minor (see the Donovan letter, *supra*, p. 13). The only delay formally addressed seems to relate to order confirmation after execution, however. *See* CME Responses, *supra*, Exhibit 1, question 31.

[16]   *See* letter from Andrea M. Corcoran, Director of the Division of Trading and Markets, CFTC, to Carl A. Royal, General Counsel, CME, (October 6, 1988), at 7.

[17]   *See* Domowitz and Gardner (1990) for rules governing Globex trading and its order execution algorithm. The CME's statement can be found in CME Responses, *supra*, Exhibit 1, at 25.

[18]   Refer here to the Commodity Exchange, Inc. proposed straddle session; *see* 46 *Federal Register* 23516, (April 27, 1981), and the discussion in the next section.

[19]   Senate Report no. 1131, 93rd Congress, 2nd Sess., at 16 (1974).

[20]   46 *Federal Register* 23519, (April, 1981). *See* also the case of *In re Henner*, Commodity Exchange Authority, Docket no. 161, (September 15, 1971), at 14-15.

[21]   *See* the Corcoran letter, *supra*, and the CME Responses, *supra*, at 24 and 30-31.

[22]   80 *Congressional Record* 7865 (1936).

[23]   *See* Memorandum From the Division of Trading and Markets, *supra*, at 52.

[24]   *See* Notice of Disapproval of Contract Market Rules, 46 *Federal Register* 23516, (April 27, 1981). Interpretation of section 4b is at 23518.

[25]   *See* the Donovan letter, *supra*.

[26]   *See* Notice of Disapproval, *supra*, at 23519.

[27]   *See* Domowitz and Gardner (1990) for a description of and rules governing such secondary quantities. The analysis which follows is not contained therein.

Additional References

Black, F., "Toward A Fully Automated Exchange," 27 *Financial Analysts Journal*, (July/August, 1971), pp. 29-35, and (November/December, 1971), pp. 25-28, 86-87.

Burmeister, R., "Current Status of Automation in Futures Markets," *Proceedings of the CFTC Conference on Automation in the Futures Industry*, on file at the Commodity Futures Trading Commission (1977).

Domowitz I. and Gardner, W., "How Automated Trade Execution Systems Affect Trading, Price Discovery, and Quantity Determination," this volume (1990).

Melamed, L., "The Mechanics of a Commodity Futures Exchange: A Critique of Automation of the Transaction Process," 6 *Hofstra Law Review*, (1977), pp. 149-172.

Ruder, D. and Adkins, A., "Automation of Information Dissemination and Trading the U.S. Securities Markets," this volume (1990).

C H A P T E R **12**

International Securities Regulation in a Global Electronic Environment

Alger B. Chapman
Chicago Board Options Exchange

By any measure markets have become increasingly global. The October, 1987 market break slowed this trend for a short time, but the pace has picked up again. At the same time, the symbiotic relationship among markets worldwide was brought home to investors with the major global revaluation of securities within a few days during the market break.

The emergence of global investment management i.e., securitization of the government and corporate borrowing process, the development of powerful international investment banking and brokerage firms operating around the clock, and the blurring of the lines among traditional functions of financial intermediaries has been driven by three phenomena.

First, the volatility that has emerged in currencies, interest rates, and inflation rates, and the dramatic swings in trade balances, have caused markets to interlink. Volatility has driven asset and liability managers to find new mechanisms by which to evaluate and manage the risk that has been created. Second, the dramatic shortening of the time frame within which information is available almost anywhere in the world, and the ability to analyze that information to create action plans, has been an outcome of the increasingly rapid change in the power and speed of computers and electronic data transmission. Third, financial market entry by a generation of quants who in earlier times might have been lured by the space program or Silicon Valley, has resulted in the rapid adoption of new technology by which to manage risk against investment objectives.

There are several global financial markets today—including currencies and U.S. government bonds—where financial instruments can be traded in the major financial capitals of the world in size. Other markets—like gilts, yen bonds, and institutional grade U.S. equities—are developing rapidly. In the last five years, a dramatic expansion of financial futures and options markets has occurred. The dramatic growth of futures and options on stock market indexes, futures on U.S. Treasury bonds, and futures and options on currencies has added new dimensions to managing the risks inherent in the large pools of institutional capital that have been created to provide for retirement funds and to assist investors and savers who feel lost in these rapidly changing, institutionally-dominated markets. Tables 1-6 provide a glimpse of the dramatic growth and internationalization of these markets. Table 7 shows the rapid growth of financial futures and options listed on exchanges around the world.

A Hypothetical Marketplace of the Future

There is a growing awareness of the need for coordinated regulation of global trading activity. The pace of change is increasing so rapidly that it is not unreasonable to imagine a highly sophisticated international marketplace where everything is traded but nothing is listed: an institutional marketplace linked by a sophisticated satellite transmission network, in which institutional traders communicate modem to modem, and bids and offers are taken by touching a screen to produce a locked in trade, with price and volume information disseminated to all participants.

In this hypothetical marketplace, trades are cleared and settled by a "WorldClear" system which links to existing clearinghouses electronically for national markets, and to Cedel and Euroclear. Daily net balances are reached for each participant, and then consolidated in the WorldClear system where money balances are settled and the transfer of financial instruments is accomplished by bookkeeping entry only.

National markets operate on the periphery of this hypothetical global system. Instruments of local interest trade just like current home markets in government securities, and corporate bonds and stocks. Home country securities with international interest trade in both the home and global markets.

This global market is dominated by several dozen international trading organizations, banks, and investment firms with billions of dollars of capital, and a trading rather than an agency business. In all probability, they also dominate major national markets.

An examination of the Eurobond and Forex markets gives us a real-world preview of the developing electronic global market. These markets are institutional, dominated by big, well-capitalized participants trading around the clock and operating with limited national government regulation.

Table 1   Eurobond Underwritings: 1979-1988 (in $ billions)

1979	16.5
1980	24.3
1981	27.5
1982	46.8
1983	47.2
1984	78.6
1985	134.5
1986	182.7
1987	143.1
1988	181.4

Source: IDD Information Service.

Table 2   International Equities: 1984-1988*

1984	236
1985	328
1986	472
1987	493
1988	508

* Stocks traded on at least one market outside the domestic market.
Source: Euromoney

Table 3   International Equity Transactions: 1979-1988 (in $ millions)

	U.S. Purchases and Sales of Foreign Stocks	Foreign Purchases and Sales of U.S. Stocks	Total
1979	10,051	43,887	53,938
1980	17,941	75,168	93,109
1981	18,925	75,542	94,467
1982	15,667	79,862	95,529
1983	30,327	134,130	164,457
1984	30,733	122,648	153,381
1985	45,664	159,049	204,713
1986	99,486	277,483	376,969
1987	187,416	481,407	668,823
Jan.-Sep. 1988	107,267	288,208	395,475
Annualized 1988	143,023	384,277	527,300

Source: U.S. Treasury Bulletin.

Table 4   U.S. Equity Mutual Funds with Foreign Investments: 1984-1988 (in $ millions)

	International Funds[1]		Global Funds[2]	
	Number	Amount	Number	Amount
1984	13	1,169.1	16	4,019.6
1985	24	2,486.0	19	5,450.6
1986	35	7,186.1	22	8,282.0
1987	47	6,982.3	34	10,449.2
1988	59	6,831.8	45	11,151.1

[1] Two-thirds or more of portfolio is invested at all times in equity securities in companies located outside the U.S.
[2] Portfolio may consist of any mix of U.S. and foreign equity securities.
Source: Investment Company Institute.

Table 5   International Investments of Pension Funds: 1975-1993 (in $ billions)

	Total	U.S. Pensions
1975	6	0
1980	21	3
1985	85	25
1988	217	62
1993	530	162

Source: InterSec Research Corporation.

Table 6   Futures and Options Exchanges Listing Financial Products: 1978 vs. 1988

Region	1978	1988
United States	6	14
United Kingdom	1	2
Continental Europe	1	8
Asia	0	4
Canada	2	4
Latin America	0	3
Austalia	0	2
Total	10	37

Source: Courtesy of James J. McNulty, O'Conner and Associates.

Table 7   Financial Futures and Options Listed on Exchanges

Region	1978	1988
United States	12	93
United Kingdom	1	27
Continental Europe	1	22
Asia	0	13
Canada	2	10
Latin America	0	20
Austalia	0	20
Total	16	205

Note: All equity options on individual stocks are counted as one product per each exchange listing equity options.
Source: Courtesy of James J. McNulty, O'Conner and Associates.

Growing Awareness of Regulatory Needs

Prior to October, 1987, international financial regulatory cooperation was driven by insider trading cases, money laundering situations, and the need for strong capital adequacy standards. Progress was slow, and few agreements were reached. Bank secrecy laws in many jurisdictions made meaningful progress difficult.

And a different ethos, country by country, has made it difficult to arrive at common standards. A perfect example is insider trading, which is not a crime in some countries. Where it is illegal, it is pursued with different degrees of diligence around the world.

Now, significant progress has been made by the central bankers' Cooke Committee, which has promulgated a 12-country agreement on bank capital adequacy standards.

The October, 1987 market break and its subsequent analysis convinced most market participants and regulators that coordination by national regulators is required in order to deal with systemic risk arising from the impact of globalization on national markets and on giant, multi-market investment organizations. The failure of one or two can impact everybody. Trouble in one market spreads to other markets like a virus and national regulators do not have an effective grasp on the activities of their investment firms as they participate around the world. Also, the jurisdiction of national regulators is limited in dealings with foreign domiciled investors and investment firms operating in their national markets.

As the markets continue to globalize, transactional activity in this expanded regulatory environment probably will surpass that which occurs collectively in national markets. As this happens, the impact of a failure on the system and the loss of ability to protect domestic investors from abuses in the global system will multiply. As a result, there will be an urgent need for coordination among national regulators. Through expanded coordination at the national level, market participants can be regulated, and unsophisticated investors can be protected and informed without imposing an international regulatory hierarchy to top off the pyramid—an unnecessary burden on the global market of the future. The market will be an institutional-professional market dominated by well-capitalized, multi-market participants. Each will have access to international markets and a place of home jurisdiction where regulation will apply.

Every meeting of international regulators and self-regulators focuses on this need for coordination and cooperation, to deal with the risks in and necessity for globalization. Groups addressing these issues include IOSCO, the OECD Working Group, the Group of Thirty, the F.I.B.V. and many others. Figure 1 is a partial list of agencies, organizations, and self-regulators that will be solicited to deal with these problems. Many other organizations are at work already with the SEC, the SIB, and the Ministry of Finance grappling with such problems as coordination, capital adequacy, insider trading, exchange of information, and memoranda of understanding.

An Ideal Regulatory Environment

Consider a hypothetical 21st century global market in which individuals have a small role and institutions dominate. Market trading occurs via an electronic network; and intermediaries are highly competitive and global, with very large capital bases developed during an extended period of consolidation. In this market, trading occurs on a world basis. Also assume an umbrella clearing system with continuous net settlements and a bookkeeping-entry-only receive and deliver system (a certificate-less society).

In this environment, the most pressing regulatory problems have been solved, for example:

- Disclosure rules are uniform internationally. The accounting rules for companies with trading securities are harmonized internationally so that ready comparisons can be made for analytical purposes.

- Information is readily available for easy participation in the global market.

- Trades are cleared under the umbrella of a central clearing organization, which is linked to clearing organizations in national markets.

- Intermediary positions are netted on a global position basis and ownership is transferred by bookkeeping entry.

Figure 1   International Regulation

Efforts to regulate international activity have been and are being made by professional and independent associations, regulatory agencies, clearing organizations, and self-regulatory organizations, including:

- Associations
  - Association of International Bond Dealers
  - Cooke Committee/Bank for International Settlements
  - Federation Internationale des Bourses de Valeurs
  - Group of Thirty
  - International Accounting Standards Committee
  - International Bar Association
  - International Council of Securities Dealers Associations
  - International Federation of Accountants
  - International Organization of Securities Commissions

- Regulatory Agencies
  - SEC memorandum of understanding with authorities in:
    - Switzerland
    - Japan
    - United Kingdom
    - Brazil
    - Canada
    - France

- Self-Regulatory Organizations
  - Amex—European Options Exchange (EOE) re: XMI
  - CME—Tokyo Stock Exchange re: Nikkei Futures
  - CBOT—Tokyo Stock Exchange re: TOPIX Futures
  - SIMEX—Tokyo Stock Exchange re: Nikkei Futures

- Agencies/Self-Regulatory Organizations
  - The SEC is considering uniform standards for foreign debt exemptions its SEC registration requirements. Exemptions allow futures and options on those securities to be marketed and traded in the U.S. Currently, exemptions are allowed on a case-by-case basis; 14 have been granted.

(Figure continues)

Figure 1   International Regulation (Continued)

The CFTC has allowed the first foreign futures options to be marketed in the U.S., selected products on the Montreal Stock Exchange, Sydney Futures Exchange, and SIMEX.

- Clearing Organizations
  Options Clearing Corporation (OCC) - EOE re: XMI
  International Securities Clearing Corporation (ISCC)
  Japan Securities Clearing Corporation (JSCC)
  ISCC - International Stock Exchange
  ISCC - CEDEL
  ISCC - Singapore Stock Exchange re: NASD-SESDAQ
      quotation link
  Euroclear

- Regulatory standards are coordinated among home country regulators and jurisdictional reach is negotiated for national regulators pursuing violators in their home markets.

- Capital adequacy standards are adopted by all participants, to be administered by regulators in the participant's home country.

These are a few of the characteristics of an efficient regulatory framework for a 21st century global market.

But where is the United States now? Clearly not far from the beginning. To date, there are few bilateral agreements and several nonempowered international organizations. But in moving toward a regulatory structure aimed at this new global market, each country already has the jurisdictional hooks on which to hang a regulatory scheme that protects its nationals by regulating the information flow and the intermediaries that operate within its jurisdiction. In addition to supporting bank and securities regulators, the United States can look to postal, telephone, and telegraph regulation as the means to gain jurisdiction over this new international electronic market, in which data transmission and real-time communication are its lifeblood.

Country-by-country regulation will push this market offshore or to a jurisdiction of convenience, which will be defined by the lowest common denominator of regulation. But this powerful electronic marketplace made up of institutional participants should not end up flying the flag of an insignificant locality by default. The system-wide risks are too great, because one or two major participants could bring the system down if capital adequacy standards are not established cross-border.

Many of the traditional home market regulatory requirements may not be necessary because of the institutional character of the market. But coordinated home country regulation is a must to protect the global financial system from unexpected shocks. The history of global cooperation indicates that the task ahead is extremely difficult. However, even in a world where cooperation in protecting the environment or feeding the starving is slow and difficult, the World Health Organization and GATT are important examples of the global effort needed to prepare for the 21st century. Similarly, where national security is involved, alliances such as NATO have been effective.

The Tasks Ahead

Now consider a few of the tasks that should be performed along the way. Within each national market, most of these issues have been difficult to bring forward to state-of-the-art status. Imagine the complexity of answering these questions and of moving these underlying issues to an acceptable common level in order to function in a global market.

Accounting: What is a common standard for measuring the performance of companies with traded securities in the global market? How can this standard be identified?

Auditing: What is the common set of audit standards relative to these companies? Are there accounting and audit standards for determining the capital adequacy of participants in the global market?

Taxes: What approach should be used to assimilate different methods and levels of taxation in each nation? Taxes alone can drive the market to a flag of convenience, similar to the development of the Eurobond market.

International Clearing: Should the common clearing entity be an umbrella linking all clearing organizations, to arrive at global, one-account clearing? How is this achieved?

Risk Management and Capital Adequacy Standards: It became evident after the events of October, 1987 that capital adequacy and risk management standards need to be developed further and strengthened. The dramatic market moves of that period were met without failure by all but a few, relatively minor participants. Though the system suffered from a liquidity crunch, it was spared the added burden of a major financial failure. Fortunately, these events happened at the end of an unprecedented five-year bull market in which capital, built through retained earnings, provided a cushion for the market break shocks. We may not be so lucky next time.

Other Issues: As finance practice has changed and the lending process has become securitized, large global players are assuming major balance sheet risk in the form of trading positions and bridge loans. There is a clear need for clearer focus on these potential dangers. And surveillance and enforcement become more difficult in a global environment. In crossing national borders, one man's crime becomes another man's profit opportunity. The tradition of legally hiding capital for flight, or from the tax collector, is alien to the U.S. and to many other common law-based nations.

National Versus International Interests

The process of arriving at coordinated regulation of the global market and its participants will involve an unusually high level of cooperation. National interest will stay in the forefront, naturally. But there must be coordination and negotiation in an environment that will be open to change, where participating regulators can anticipate change and be pro-active in working with major market participants.

Regulators of the home countries of the major capital markets (the U.S., Japan and the U.K.) could form a task force to be advised by senior representatives of the major market participants. They, in turn, could form advisory groups on specific subjects. This group could establish goals and objectives that lay out the critical path to an optimum system of regulation for the new and growing global markets. The other pieces can be added later: advisory groups of accountants and lawyers, for example, making their contributions where appropriate.

In summary, the working group must be small enough to make progress, but large enough to represent those nations and markets with the biggest stake in its success.

Additional References

Arthur Andersen & Co., *The Globalization of the International Financial Markets: Implications and Opportunities,* Chicago, (1988).

Bank for International Settlements, *Recent Innovations in International Banking,* Basel, (1986).

Grundfest, Joseph, *Regulating the International Capital Markets: A New Perspective*, paper presented to the Chartered Association of Certified Accountants, London, (1987).

KPMG, *The Capital Explosion: A Worldwide Quest For Money*, (Amsterdam, 1986).

Securities and Exchange Commission, *Internationalization of the Securities Markets*, Washington, D.C., (1987).

Symposium: The Internationalization of the Securities Markets, 4 *Boston University International Law Journal*, (Winter, 1986).

THE CONTRIBUTION OF
TECHNOLOGY TO
SPECIFIC MARKETS

The Contribution of Technology to Financial Markets: A View from NASDAQ

John Wall
National Association of Securities Dealers, Inc.

There should be a plaque in the center of Wall Street to honor its biggest deal maker and it should be dedicated to technology. Telecommunications technology brought Wall Street to Main Street. It brought the market to Americans with capital, and in the process, technology built—and continues to maintain—America's network for the trading of securities. Technology also will be the backbone of the global securities network.

But technology has done something far more significant: the burst of technological inventiveness after the Civil War pressured us to come up with a way to finance these bright ideas. Our response was to invite wide-open participation in the process of capital formation.

Trying the Obvious

Great inventions seem to spend at least some time as side shows. They are curiosities before they become tools of progress. Samuel Morse invented the first telegraph that worked in the middle of the 19th century. But for some time, the invention was an oddity, a neat gadget that Wall Street businessmen could see demonstrated for a quarter.

Nevertheless, Americans have a keen eye for the obvious. Once a clear use for Morse's invention was found—to telegraph stock information—it promptly was put to use. Combined with the networking genius of Western Union, Wall Street was soon connected to every major city. The invention of the ticker tape in 1870 and the telephone in 1876 improved the market's outreach significantly. Constant refinements to Charles Babbage's "analytic engine," the computer, have revolutionized the world, and the securities markets with it.

Global Potential

As telecommunications technology advanced from telegraph to telephone to computer, it made possible what was once just an interesting philosophy: the idea of decentralized stock trading, where buying and selling securities is not limited to an exchange floor, but can occur anywhere in the world and at any time.

The National Association of Securities Dealers Automated Quotation (NASDAQ) system proved it was technologically feasible to lift trading from its exchange floor confines and take it anywhere. It took almost 40 man-years of design to get the NASDAQ system up and running because it is a complex system, and refinements take place continually.

But once the technological barrier was broken, screen-based trading systems have flourished, and links between systems have multiplied. The International Stock Exchange in London, for example, switched to a screen-based system in 1986. But even before that so-called "Big Bang," London had an automated quotation system called the Stock Exchange Automation Quotation (SEAQ) system, which was modeled after NASDAQ and shares quotation information with it. The Stock Exchange of Singapore now is automated and linked trans-Pacific with NASDAQ; Japan is about to automate its over-the-counter trading; and other European markets seem ready to embrace screen-based trading as well.

Stock markets do not operate around the clock—yet. But a joint venture of Reuters and the Chicago Mercantile exchange called GLOBEX indicates that continuous trading is possible. With GLOBEX as a guide, nonstop trading is bound to happen.

Technology also has helped immeasurably by reliably regulating the capital-raising process. Sophisticated computer systems are used by NASDAQ; real-time information is available constantly. Every trade can be compared to every quote update and tested to determine if it has been executed within acceptable parameters. Concise audit trails can be reconstructed quickly and reliably. The National Association of Securities Dealers (NASD) is able to detect trading aberrations and pursue disciplinary cases faster and with greater vigor.

The growth of the securities industry in terms of both share volume and new products is so large that it is inconceivable that the United States could do business today the way it was done a mere two decades ago. Then:

- There were only a handful of firms with automated recordkeeping systems.

- There was no National Securities Clearing Corporation.

- There was no NASDAQ.

- There was little, if any, capability for a registered representative to call up customer account information on an on-line basis.

- There were no sophisticated automated trading strategies in place to guide buy and sell decisions in the not-yet-developed standardized options programs of the exchanges.

- There was no composite quotation system or intermarket linkages.

- There were few, if any, internal order routing systems or automated execution systems such as the Small Order Execution System (SOES) or the Designated Order Turnaround (SUPERDOT) system.

- There was no working design like the NASD's electronic bulletin board to automate the "Pink Sheet" market.

- There was no design for an orderly system to manage the trading of securities among financial institutions, a design that now exists in the Private Offerings, Resales, and Trading Through Automated Linkages (PORTAL) system, the NASD's initiative to create a NASDAQ-type environment for this private placement market.

- There were few desktop terminals linking salespeople with price information to communicate with clients; there was a ticker tape for price information.

Today's sleek NASDAQ workstation makes the first Bunker Ramo model look prehistoric. The system crackles with features: it displays a continuous stream of real-time data; it shows quote and trade information in multiple formats; it notifies subscribers when a security breaks a specified last-sale price or bid/ask parameter; a personal ticker allows the subscriber to view changes in the inside markets, executions, individual market quotes, or volume parameters for up to 300 securities; and it can list immediate reports of the day's trade executions. It also can follow the trading of a foreign security such as Jaguar in its home market in London and as an American Depository Receipt (ADR) traded on NASDAQ in the United States; it even allows automatic intercontinental execution and confirmation over the NASDAQ communications link with the SEAQ system in London.

The NASDAQ workstation operates four times faster than the NASDAQ dealer terminals it replaced. But it barely stays ahead of the demands placed on market makers in the NASDAQ market. Efficient as it is, and after only two years in production, it will be consigned to the same museum as the first NASDAQ terminals because it is about to be replaced by digital feeds.

Technology has revolutionized stock markets, and has made life easier for the millions of investors in those markets. It also has changed the execution process for the investor. Before NASDAQ, here is how over-the-counter (OTC) stocks were bought and sold. A broker would call with a story: what was good or bad about a stock. The price of the stock would be checked. If the broker talked with his client in the morning, the price would be checked by looking at the newspaper of the night before. If the price range seemed acceptable and the client wanted to make a trade, the broker would send an order slip to the Trading Department and they would get on the phone to three market makers for the best price.

This used up a lot of time; and sometimes if the first price was the best, by the time the trader called back to take it, the price had changed. The Trading Department, having executed a trade with a market maker, would then notify the broker and he would call the client back to confirm the order and price.

Here is how things work today.

The broker calls his client with a story. The client checks the price on his PC, using software supplied by his firm. Then he decides how many shares he wants and sets a price limit. He inputs the order into his PC. It is sent to the broker's firm, verified, and checked against financial limits placed on the client's account. Having passed the firm's tests, the trade then is held in the firm's computer file. When the NASDAQ market reaches the client's limit price, the order is sent to NASDAQ's Small Order Execution System. It is automatically executed against the trading firm having the best price, reported to the tape, sent to clearing, and returned to the firm's computers. The trade then appears on the client's PC, indicating the details of the execution. The entire execution process takes just seconds, without a phone. And the client can switch on his PC at night using software that marks his portfolio to the market each day. With a couple of key strokes, he can find out how he did that day.

Automated Confirmation Transaction (ACT)

For the more complex and larger orders that require telephone negotiation to complete, the NASD has developed the Automated Confirmation Transaction (ACT) Service. In 1989, ACT technology rendered same-day comparisons on 100 percent of NASDAQ trades. ACT's real value is in risk management: market participants know the day of a trade whether the details of trades for stock that was bought or sold has matched and been accepted by the contra party.

ACT eliminates one of the biggest risks firms experienced during the October, 1987 market break. Even after firms bought securities from customers and sold blocks of securities to other market makers that week, and after they told customers that their orders had been transacted, they still remained at risk. Because of current clearance and settlement technology, they could not be absolutely sure that the details of the order they negotiated by phone matched the contra party's order. This remained uncertain for at least two days, and could have stretched for an additional two days. In fact, data for the week in October, 1987 show that about 70 percent of OTC trades did not compare during first review. ACT technology, and the same-day comparison it renders, eliminates this risk and permits firms to allocate their capital more accurately.

Clearance and Settlement

While technology is pushed to overdrive in market making, it remains underutilized and idling on other fronts. The clearance and settlement process must be improved before 24-hour trading becomes a reality. The technology to do so exists, but is only rarely allowed to strut its stuff. The same is true for deficiencies of the current international confirmation processes. There is too great a dependence on manual processing and telexes for transmission of instructions. There is a lack of centralized facilities for electronic, book-entry settlement of net positions with fails marked to the market. There is a lack of uniformity among different settlement and regulatory systems. Overhauling antiquated settlement systems is not easy. Under the weight of heavy expenses and differences of opinion, ideas that start with a full head of steam (the Taurus system of London's International Stock Exchange, for instance) can slow to a stop.

Efficient settlement systems do exist, like the fully-electronic settlement systems that exist in Denmark and Norway. A number of international systems under development hold at least the promise of a better global back office, including the International Bond Dealers TRAX system and the NASD's PORTAL system.

PORTAL

The design of PORTAL includes a linkage to the International Securities Clearing Corporation for the transmittal of settlement instructions through its Global Compass network to Cedel and eventually Euro-clear. When operational, Cedel and Euro-clear act as master custodians for the transfer and deposit of PORTAL shares placed and traded in the U.S. Transactions still will be settled individually, but certificates will remain immobilized in their home countries. Once shares are deposited into the PORTAL custody system, they will be subject to a standard, five-day settlement cycle that in most cases is not contingent on the settlement conventions of their home country.

Technology and Capital Raising

Americans owe another great debt to technology. Before there could be wide participation in the capital-raising process on a global or domestic scale, there had to be a demand for capital. Technology created voracious demand on an unprecedented scale.

A Paine Webber annual report noted a few years ago:

"In the seventy years before 1860, the U.S. Patent Office granted fewer than 40,000 patents. In the next thirty years, it granted 400,000. Invention piled on invention—the steel raise, the electric light, the rotary printing press, air brakes, refrigeration, the mass production of clothing—all in a single generation."

The sheer number of technological inventions requiring capital after the Civil War gave rise, almost by necessity, to the wonderfully simple idea of mass participation in the process of capital formation. America learned quickly that the really big money was not in the vaults of governments or rich people, but in the hands of millions of average Americans. With that idea, America's securities industry as we know it today was born.

Technology continues to generate promising new public stock offerings, which in turn spark investment that gives the securities industry its reason for being. To discover what is new in technology, don't look in *Scientific American*. Look at the daily stock tables for the NASDAQ market, where companies that make digital switches, numeric processing equipment, cellular phones, high performance workstations, voice-activated computers, artificial intelligence products, and more than most Americans ever imagined can be found. A handful of these technological ideas will flower into super-industries. Fiber optics and superconductivity hold almost unlimited promise for growth, and may generate countless smaller industries in their wake. In addition to creating significant job opportunities, companies that harness these ideas will make many investors wealthy.

It can be said without hesitation that technology has made NASDAQ what it is today: the third largest stock market in the world. It is a market that traded 31 billion shares in 1988, and is running close to the NYSE in share volume. The key to this growth is U.S. companies. Of the three principal U.S. stock markets, NASDAQ has the highest percentage of fast-growing high-technology and service companies, including:

- 84 percent of computer manufacturers

- 86 percent of computer and data processing firms

- 74 percent of electronic-component makers and telecommunications companies

- 87 percent of pharmaceutical and biotechnology companies

These companies are a key part of NASDAQ's future and America's future. Of the world's stock markets, NASDAQ owes the greatest debt to technology because it has catapulted NASDAQ into a sophisticated, global dimension with convenience, efficiency, visibility, liquidity, reliability, safety, and profitability.

Two Systems in Transition: Open Outcry and Electronic Trading

William J. Brodsky
Chicago Mercantile Exchange

There is no question that technology has had a tremendous impact on the financial markets within the last two decades. Not only are large institutions now the recipients of technology's benefits, individual investors now can access and utilize the conveniences that technology provides as well. Real-time prices for the capital, money, and foreign exchange markets are available around the globe through quotation vendors such as Reuters, Telerate, and Quotron, among others. As Marshall McLuhan wrote with uncanny foresight in his book, *The Medium is the Massage*, "The new electronic interdependence recreates the world in the image of the global village." When McLuhan first made this remark, he was an obscure media/communication professor at the University of Toronto. By the time of his death in 1980, he had achieved cult hero status.

Today we can say with utmost certainty that the financial markets are irretrievably linked by technology and mutual interest. That linkage will be facilitated by what could be perceived as the ideal trading system for the markets of the global village—GLOBEX, the automated transaction system developed by the Chicago Mercantile Exchange and Reuters Holdings Plc, which was approved by the CFTC in 1989.

In 1988, *The New York Times* ran a story about the supercomputer developed by Fujitsu Ltd. The company claims that this machine, the VP-2000, can operate at four gigaflops per second, meaning four billion floating point operations a second. A single cycle, or operation, of the Fujitsu processor takes four nanoseconds (billionths of a second). Available in 1990, this latest supercomputer serves as yet another example of technology's rapid advance. In the last decade alone, the world has experienced one breakthrough after another. Between now and the close of this century, there will no doubt be countless changes in trading systems, instruments, and techniques.

Trading systems are unquestionably the most visible and colorful aspect of the U.S. markets. The dominant form of trade on U.S. futures exchanges is the open outcry system, which has been the foundation of futures trading for over 100 years. There is little doubt that in North America open outcry will continue as the chief engine of liquidity well into the next century. But the trading floor will likely be much different by then.

For example, with the introduction of automated systems to route orders to the floor and to manage completed trades, the open outcry system becomes infinitely more efficient. Floor members have the ability to handle a greater volume of orders more quickly and accurately than was ever thought possible. For example, in 1989, the CME started a pilot program for an automated order routing system called TOPS, or Trade Order Processing System. TOPS is an order entry and fill reporting system that expedites the flow of non-arbitraged paper orders to the CME trading floor. It provides more timely order delivery and fill reporting, and allows fewer transcription errors. Additionally, it will provide more timely and enhanced interface into the CME clearing system for trade matching and will improve audit trails for customer orders. Ultimately, TOPS will allow efficient and accurate GLOBEX interfaces when it automatically passes the book of unexecuted orders from daytime trading hours to evening trading hours.

Outside the North American trading day, automated trading systems continue to be developed. The interest to date of such systems in Great Britain and in Japan, where the Japanese government bond futures market became fully automated, says that as new markets emerge and grow they are likely to be increasingly automated. As powerful as the open outcry system of trading is, there are alternatives available to encourage more active, liquid markets.

Until now, automated systems have been local in nature. But in the next decade, more sophisticated networks will emerge, like GLOBEX, to expand the horizons of any given market and directly encompass customers worldwide. The chief advantage of such networks is an unparalleled capacity to serve a global customer base efficiently and safely.

In addition to advanced trading systems, these networks are capable of transmitting the financial payments associated with trades. The ability to pay and collect from all traders in a timely fashion takes on increased importance as trading expands electronically. By employing the same network structure, the payment system efficiency is enhanced immeasurably. But such networking does not imply a single clearing agency worldwide. Instead, financial institutions such as clearinghouses remain distinct entities, using the services of the electronic networks to link customers worldwide.

As the amount of capital flowing across the international markets continues to increase, communication and cooperation across and among clearing houses also must increase in order to minimize the operational burden certain to be created by these huge cash flows. Because many multinational firms are clearing members of several exchanges, mechanisms can be developed to facilitate a degree of payment netting. This will make it possible to trade across many markets with minimal impact on the credit and exchange systems of individual nations.

The international banking system, and in particular the mechanics of central banking, must move quickly to keep up with the demands of global markets. For example, the Federal Reserve System of the United States can no longer expect to operate solely on a U.S. business-day basis. Many private banks already are operating on a global basis, 24 hours a day. So to meet the needs of these firms, the major central banks will have to match their availability.

Some commentators have argued that the financial markets ultimately will reach a point where there is only one global clearinghouse. Such an idea appears neither likely nor desirable. Strength lies in having a sufficient amount of financial diversification. Just as it is prudent to have more than one manufacturing firm in any given industry, having multiple clearinghouses worldwide will allow each to serve its main customers efficiently without being directly responsible for the financial risks of customers half way around the globe.

The technological revolution that has allowed trading systems to evolve toward greater automation also has spurred the development of new instruments —a trend which will persist over the next 10 years.

As the ability to analyze the pricing and risk characteristics of instruments has improved, the financial community has been quick to develop specialized products to meet the demands of diverse customers. Currency futures were followed rapidly by interest rate and stock index products. In addition to these innovative, exchange-traded instruments, there has been a proliferation of off-exchange products like repurchase agreements, "caps," "collars," SWAPS, Forward Spread Agreements, and others.

The lines between the exchange and off-exchange instruments will continue to blur. Professional traders will be able to choose from a vast array of instruments—some general and standardized, some customized to the users' needs. So financial integrity, or the ability of exchanges to provide guarantees in the clearing process, will be the pivotal difference more than ever. Traders will continue to rely on the exchanges for liquidity and for the creditworthiness that cannot be replicated in off-exchange markets.

Products that once appealed to customers in only one or two nations now have a worldwide audience. Global diversification and integration has just begun; in 10 years, there will be very few markets of any significance that are pure, single-country markets. The shift to global portfolios is an expression of the desire to diversify risk more completely than is possible with a single-country portfolio.

John Phelan, Chairman of the New York Stock Exchange, compares the global quest for the right hedge to "the surfer who travels the world looking for the perfect wave." Phelan once told *The Financial Times* that investors will continue to "go around the globe looking for the perfect hedge." And no wonder. Finance theory says that through diversification, average portfolio volatility can be reduced without lowering average return. The shifting values of foreign assets and various exchange rates imply risk; but with smooth flows of capital these features also can mean tremendous opportunity for more efficient risk management through diversification.

GLOBEX

GLOBEX is an electronic trading system that expands trading hours and opportunities for futures and options around the world. It is the CME's response to the increasingly global nature of the financial markets and the growing demand for 24-hour trading.

The concept of an automated futures exchange is, of course, not a new one. INTEX, the Bermuda exchange founded in 1981, never quite got off the ground. The New Zealand Futures Exchange, which opened in 1985, also failed to generate liquidity to any significant extent. The Swiss Options and Financial Futures Exchange (SOFFEX), which opened in 1988, has done somewhat better. And in 1989, the London Stock Exchange began offering automatic execution for trades of 1,000 shares or less on a pilot basis for its SEAQ Automated Execution Facility (SAEF).

The competitive advantage of GLOBEX seems to lie in a key ingredient which previous systems did not possess: liquidity. GLOBEX combines the best elements of electronic linkage and integrates them with the proven liquidity created by open outcry trading in the pit during regular trading hours. There is almost instant liquidity in the network because open orders pass from the CME's regular trading session into GLOBEX after regular trading hours.

The single biggest change in the future will be the way in which technology allows strong markets to reach out to a universe of sophisticated global customers. GLOBEX, for example, expands the community of traders. It involves traders more intimately with each market, and it is a focus that draws groups of traders that once were only loosely connected.

In approving the GLOBEX proposal, Commodity Futures Trading Commission Chairman Wendy Gramm said "innovation of this type is essential if the U.S. is to maintain its leading competitive edge and remain a leading provider of financial services to the world community."

GLOBEX draws the best from the present and marries it to the technology of the future. At the same time, it represents a giant step toward the creation of a true global exchange.

A 1989 article in *International Financing Review* observed that GLOBEX officially represents only an extension of the Merc's standard daylight trading hours. But with about 160,000 Reuters subscribers, the potential impact of the investor base gives GLOBEX much greater significance.

Eventually, any contract for which there is a widespread commercial need may be listed on the system because GLOBEX adds an attractive combination of stability, auditability, and increased liquidity to global futures trading. It provides an extremely reliable audit trail, credit checks, and instantaneous monitoring of position limits. GLOBEX reaches the world through a dedicated, high-capacity, interactive network linking mainframe computers to smart trading terminals built around 386 microcomputer technology. This network is devoted to GLOBEX and remains entirely separate from the Reuters Monitor network. It will rely on dedicated, fully redundant subordinate computers or "concentrators."

The firmly established liquidity of the CME's markets combined with the communications capabilities of Reuters Holdings Plc makes GLOBEX a formidable industry presence. Consider that as a financial news and information company, Reuters is the premier international financial communications organization in the world. Reuters has more than 160,000 screens worldwide, located in 170 cities. Reuters' service and maintenance force, covering 150 countries, is unsurpassed.

So like the CME and the futures industry, Reuters also is an innovator. Its transaction networks already enable dealers in stocks, bonds, and currencies to execute transactions via computer terminal.

It appears that the GLOBEX developers correctly envision that the time for the global marketplace has come, because this system embodies the manner in which the world of tomorrow will function. And others agree. CME joined with the Matif (France) by reaching an agreement. If former SEC chairman David Ruder's prediction that GLOBEX is "the wave of the future" proves to be correct, many other exchanges are certain to follow.

The Future of Financial Markets and the Role of Technology: The Impact of the GLOBEX System

Paul A. Tattersall
Reuters Plc.

In 1987, the Chicago Mercantile Exchange and Reuters announced that they had agreed to embark on a joint effort to develop and launch a fully-automated system for trading futures and futures options contracts. The two organizations immediately put the requirements for the system on paper. As those requirements grew, the system was developed in two phases to get basic capability on-the-air as soon as possible.

It is a measure of the importance that both Reuters and the CME attach to this system that a contract was not signed until 1988. System specifications proceeded side-by-side with contract negotiations; but each party saw the long run value of a successful launch and was careful to protect its interests in the future use of the system by others. At the same time, both the CME and Reuters understood the value each organization was bringing to this venture. Both parties wanted certainty of commitment, to contribute all that was needed for success. When the contract was signed, both committed to the other through the end of the year 2000. There was further agreement to extend the relationship beyond 2000 as the contract period begins to expire.

The relationship between Reuters and the CME is important because the agreement involves a task that neither organization probably could have completed successfully without the other. Considering how technology already impacts financial markets, it is significant to acknowledge that technology without the commitment of appropriate markets cannot be successfully implemented. By the same token, the support of the right markets by an around-the-world electronic system is not a task for the inexperienced.

It is clearly expressed in the CME-Reuters agreement that the CME is the designated marketplace and that Reuters is the provider of computer and communications services. So in the CFTC application to trade using GLOBEX, the effort to make and support that application was provided by the CME. Reuters deals with communications regulators around the world, but not with market regulators. Any decisions about what products are traded and under what terms and conditions are made by the CME with whatever approvals their decisions entail. After telling Reuters what they want the system to do, the CME cedes to Reuters the determination of how to implement those desires technologically. The hardware and the software belong to Reuters; creating market liquidity is the CME's responsibility.

Major GLOBEX Functions

To have the right to use a GLOBEX terminal, membership on the Chicago Mercantile Exchange is required just as it is now. Then in order to trade using GLOBEX, the trader must be a CME clearing member, or clear trades through a clearing member. In order to have a terminal, the trader also must be "sponsored" by a clearing member.

When a trader logs on to GLOBEX, he first has to satisfy certain authorization steps that permit access. Then he can view a screen displaying different functions and information in various windows. At the top of the screen is a trading window showing those commodities he followed the last time he used the system. Of course he can change the instruments he watches on his terminal at any time. For each of these commodities, he sees the best bid and offer in the market at the moment and the total quantity other traders are willing to trade at those levels. He also sees his own bids and offers for any of the commodities on the screen before him. And with the use of a toggle switch, he can see the book of bids and offers for any commodity in the system; he not only sees the best bid and offer, with quantity, but also the 10 levels of bid and the 10 levels of offer above and below the best price—with the market quantity for each level. This information is available only to the GLOBEX terminal user.

A trader can customize his trading window and the system brings the information to him that way until he decides to change it. The trading window is the place to execute trades, so the system also aids their execution. Other windows on the screen include a "mail box," in which the system informs the trader about such events as the execution of a trade. There is also a "ticker" window which, like today's electronic wallboard, lets the trader know what is happening in the whole market. And, there is an information window with data about relevant price movements in the cash markets. There is also a field on the screen where traders can enter a request for a quote, for example, on some option strike price that has very little activity. When a trade is done, a trade ticket is printed at the terminal of the relevant clearing member, not at the trader terminal unless the clearing member entered the trade at his own terminal.

The host system for GLOBEX is located in a Reuters data center in New York. GLOBEX terminals, of course, can be located anywhere, although telephone line costs make it most economical to locate the terminal near one of the major cities where Reuters has communications concentrators: initially, near Chicago, New York, London, Tokyo, and other cities around the world. The GLOBEX host system has a direct communications link to a CME computer in Chicago which is used to transmit a continuous stream of quotations information and clearing data. Whenever a trade occurs, or a new best bid or offer, the host system communicates that to the CME. The CME in turn, disseminates that information through its own facilities out to quotation vendors. As one of those quotations vendors, Reuters receives this information simultaneously with other vendors. The clearing data is forwarded to the CME clearing system to begin the normal process of clearing trades. Because this system provides electronic matching, the out trade problem is not present in the clearing of GLOBEX trades.

In addition, the GLOBEX system provides audit trails at each keystation and one for the host. Every day after the GLOBEX system has completed operations, Reuters produces a magnetic tape file of the host audit trail and sends it to the CME. This record and the ability to analyze an audit trail for each keystation gives the CME significantly improved information with which to complete its surveillance and compliance functions.

GLOBEX Instruments

The instruments traded initially on the GLOBEX system will include currency futures and options on futures contracts in British pounds, German deutschemarks, Japanese yen, Swiss francs, and Canadian dollars. The Eurodollar Time Deposit and Treasury Bill instruments will also be traded on GLOBEX. These contracts have genuine round-the-world interest and active cash markets during Chicago night time. Currently, there is a huge opportunity for a physicals market in these financial instruments because someone somewhere in the world is willing to exchange a cash position for a CME contract position. GLOBEX can attract a good deal of that Exchanges of Futures for Physicals (EFP) business by way of tighter spreads between bid and asked than are available today.

The interest in the CME instruments after regular trading hours was a major stimulus behind the CME's move toward electronic trading in the first place. Chicago had to find a way to protect its position as the leading world market in the instruments that trade on a 24-hour basis, and the solution was off-hours computerized trading. But market protection and market development were the driving forces.

In fact, the CME now looks at nighttime electronic trading as the best way to protect daytime open outcry trading for the foreseeable future. By staying open at night, the CME generates additional volume for the exchange, which in turn leads to more daytime open outcry volume. As long as the CME can maintain its position as the leading market for the contracts it trades, the very fact of being the largest, most liquid market assures the attraction of the majority of trading activity to those contracts.

Although GLOBEX is not the first electronic system for matching futures trades, its impact on futures markets is likely to be much more significant than any previous development has been. Basically, that is because the exchange is very large and the contracts traded on it are very liquid and very strategic. GLOBEX technology literally will enable the exchange to dominate the market around the world. As trading technology changes with GLOBEX, this new kind of trading will be used only as a complement to open outcry trading—not as a replacement. Electronic trading can demonstrate its strengths and weaknesses without having to impact the primary trading technology on which futures trading has been built. In the future, it should be possible to see whether or not liquid electronic markets are possible or whether or not they will fail without the proven capability of open outcry to generate liquidity.

GLOBEX expands the physical dimensions of the pit in terms of the distance between traders and the number of transactions the market can handle. Two traders at GLOBEX terminals in London and Chicago deal with each other as if face-to-face. As the trading volume grows in this electronic marketplace, the system will grow by adding computer equipment to increase capacity. A precise record of every transaction in this expanded pit already creates efficient follow-on processing, and reconstruction and review if required later.

It is true that trading techniques already are changing in this new environment. For one, it is impossible to garner clues from nervous habits or altered voice pitch because traders in the electronic environment are completely anonymous. And every order or action transmitted to the system is given an absolutely unique time stamp. As a result, it can be predicted confidently that orders are filled on a first-come, first-served basis at the best price. No one with a competitive trade to accomplish can be excluded from trading.

Incidentally, if a trader wants to take his orders out of the market immediately, he can hit either the hold or cancel buttons. Holding means his orders are taken out of the active transaction state but are left in the system for re-entry as active orders. The cancel instruction takes his orders completely out of the

GLOBEX system. Orders that have been held re-enter the active queue with an updated time stamp indicating a new priority sequence.

GLOBEX contributes to the stability of these futures markets because it is expandable as volume increases, because it keeps the market open round-the-clock, and because it enables it to react immediately to events that occur at any time. Economic or political events anywhere can affect a market, so it is probably best if the effect happens right away. On the other hand, if a cooling-off period seems advisable, the GLOBEX market can be shut down rapidly as the whole market or as any individual instrument.

One of the GLOBEX enhancements is a complex credit control system. Before a transaction is accepted for entry into the system, an assessment is made of the impact of successful execution of that transaction on the margin account of the trader. If this check indicates an unfavorable result, the transaction is rejected with a notice to both the trader and to his clearing member.

Another aspect which will enhance the impact of GLOBEX on the futures markets will be its adoption and use by other futures exchanges. Interestingly, these GLOBEX partners, with the CME, plan to allow cross-trading of their contracts among GLOBEX users. That means that a GLOBEX trader, say on the Matif in France, will be able to trade a CME contract provided he has an arrangement with a CME clearing member to clear the trade. Not only does GLOBEX enable the trading of one exchange's contracts around the world, it also enables the interrelationship of multiple exchanges in the same trading environment.

The importance of 24-hour trading grew exponentially in the second half of the 1980s. Most major financial corporations are represented by branches around the world. Financial transactions are supported by increasingly complex computer analyses. It seems fitting that the financial market environment is enhanced by a new level of worldwide financial futures capability in GLOBEX.

Index

A

Accounting, of traded securities, 205
ACT, 40n, 215
ADP, 34, 127n
ADRs, 34
American Depository Receipts. *See* ADP
American Stock Exchange. *See* Amex
Amex
    Auto-Ex system, 29-30, 41n
    AUTOPER System, 38n
    DOT, 26-27, 37n
    electronic collection of reports, 24
    EOE, 34
    index participation instruments, 82
    market making, 74
    PER, 27, 119
    trading links, 34, 136
Anonymity, 7
    in ideal trading system, 76-80, 87n
APT system, 7, 8
Arbitrage, 76
Asimov, Isaac, 13
Asset allocation, changes in, 61-62
Association of International Bond Dealers, 33, 43n
Auditing, of traded securities, 205
AURORA system, 7, 8
AUTOM, 41n
Automated Confirmation Transaction, 40n, 215

Automated Data Processing, 120
Automated execution system, 77-80, 83-84
Automated Options Market, 41n
Automated options order routing systems, 41n
Automated order routing, 136. *See also* SUPERDOT
Automated Pit Trading, 7, 8
Automated quotation and execution system, 76, 86n
Automated trade execution systems, 89-111, 137
    in futures trading, 96-99
    in open outcry auctions, 91-96
    in options trading, 99-102
    rules governing, 96-97
    in stock trading, 102-109
Automated Transaction Exchange System (TRAX), 33, 43n
Automation
    of information dissemination, 23-25, 34n, 133-135
    of trading in U.S. securities, 25-34
    See also Technology

B

Bank of New York, 15
Barclays de Zoete, 32
Basket portfolio, 75, 76
Basket trading, 31, 52-54, 82-83, 88n
BEACON, 26
Best and Trade, 32
Black Fischer, 159
Black Monday. *See* Crash of 1987
Boesky, Ivan, 18, 68
Boston Stock Exchange, 24, 25, 26
    trading link with Montreal Stock Exchange, 34, 136
Brady Commission, 69-70, 74, 122
Brady, Treasury Secretary, 152, 165
Broker order routing, 119-120
Brokers, 49
Buffet, Warren, 153
Business Week
    and confusion of index arbitrage with portfolio
        trading, 68-69

C

CAES, 38n

Capacity delay, 122

Capital adequacy standards, 205

Capital use, maximization of, 75-76

Carnegie, Andrew, 17

CATS, 4, 32, 42n

Centralized order flow, 81

Chicago Board Options Exchange, 72
    RAE System, 99-102

Chicago Board of Trade
    after-hours trading system, 32, 138
    computerized delays, 187
    RAES, 29-30, 41n

Chicago Mercantile Exchange
    after hours trading, 31, 138
    and Globex trading system, 96, 226
    and Reuters link, 71-72, 225-226

Cincinnati Stock Exchange, 24
    and automated order execution, 137
    and Globex system, 72
    NSTS system, 32

"Circuit breaker" procedures, 146n

Clearing organizations, 204

Closed book system, 189

Closed-end mutual funds, 159

CME. *See* Chicago Mercantile Exchange

Comex System, 137, 191

Commercial paper, 16

Commissions, decline of, 63-65

Commodity Exchange Act of 1974, 183, 184

Communication technology, 125

Competition, and technology, 18-19

Competitive outcomes, frequency of, 110

Competitiveness, of U.S. financial institutions, 20

Composite Tape Association, 80

Computer Assisted Execution Service, 38n

Computer Assisted Order Routing and Execution System
    See CORES

Computer Assisted Trading System (CATS), 32

Computerized trading. *See* Program trading
Computing technology, 125-126
Consolidated Transaction Reporting System, 24-25, 135
Consolidated Quotation System, 23-25, 80, 135
Content of order message, 121-122
CORES, 4, 7, 8, 10, 32-33, 42n, 139
Crash of 1987, 14, 16, 31, 37n, 72
    order routing delays, 122-123
    regulation need, 201
    significance of, 60-61
    structural changes before and after, 59-70
Cross hedging, 76
Crossing Network, 31, 137
Cross margining, 85n
Customer needs, meeting, 20-21

D

Data Network Service, 119
Delivery systems, 50-56. *See also* DOT
Delong, Shleifer, Summers and Waldmann, 160
Delta Options system, 31, 138
Deregulation, 69
Derivative instruments, 15, 73
    and hedging strategy, 73, 75, 76, 85n
Designated Order Turnaround System. *See* DOT
Division of Market Regulation, 37n
Documentary Stamp Tax, 170-171
Domowitz and Gardner, 191, 192
DOT, 4, 26-27, 37n, 50-56, 139. *See also* SUPERDOT
Dow Jones Industrial Average
    and preferential order routing, 27

E

Eastern European changes, effect on markets, 19
Electronic markets, 71-84
Electronic order delivery system. *See* SUPERDOT
Electronic order matching, 60
Electronic trading, 3-11. *See also* Information dissemination systems,
    automation of *and* GLOBEX
Equity trading, 66, 199-200

Eurobond markets
    automation of, 33-34
    and electronic global market, 198-199
Eurodollar markets, 66
European Economic Community, 179
European Options Exchange, 34
Exchange floor system, alternatives to, 65
Exchanges, automation of orders, 25
Exchange-traded futures and options, 88n

F
Final customers, 48, 49
Financial futures contracts, 88n
Financial markets
    functioning performance, 154-155
    resouces devoted to, 161-165
    and technology, 15-17, 47-57, 211-217
Financial services, and technology, 13-22
Floor trading, 110-111, 192n
Ford, Gerald, 72
Foreign markets, 32-34
Forex market, 198
FOX, 4, 9, 33
French, Kenneth, 158
Fujitsu Ltd., 219-220
Fungible options, 72
Futures exchanges listing financial products, 200
Futures trading and markets, 31-32, 72
    automated trade execution systems in, 96-99, 183-193
    CFTC regulations, 57n
    exchange-traded, 88n
    Globex system, 96-99
    and portfolio risk, 66

G
General Motors, 18
General news delivery system, 50
General Theory, 152-153, 165
German exchanges, 43n
Global competitive pressures, 9

Global electronic environment, international securities
      regulation in, 197-206
GLOBEX, 31, 42n, 65, 72, 87n, 96-99, 114n, 184-185, 212,
      219, 220, 222-223
   anonymity feature, 7
   as closed book system, 189-190
   diversity of, 6-7
   functions of, 226-227
   impact of, 225-229
   instruments, 227-229
   order book display, 8-9
   price indeterminacy not possible, 192
   and propogation delay, 123
Gorbachev, Mikhail, 19
Gramm, Wendy, 222
Group of Thirty, 14, 80

H

Harris and Gurel study, 112n
Hedging, 73, 75, 76, 82, 85n
Hirschleifer, 164
Hirschman, Albert, 166

I

Immediacy, 75, 86n
Index arbitrage, 148n
   and confusion with portfolio trading, 68-69
Index Futures Exchange, 42n
Index participation instruments, 82
Industrial Revolution, 13
Information dissemination systems, automation of, 23-25, 34n, 60
Instinet, 35n, 41n, 72, 119
   Crossing Network, 137-138
Inter-dealer brokers, 77
Interest equalization tax, 66
Intermarket Trading System. See ITS
International clearing, 205
International equities, 199
International links of stock exchanges, 34
International regulation, 203-204

International securities regulation, 197-206
International Stock Exchange. *See* ISE
INTEX, 65, 194n, 222
Investor order routing, 120
ISE, 32
    automated small order execution system, 138
    NASDAQ link, 135
ITS, 25, 28, 29, 36n, 40n
    and automated order routing, 136

J-K
Japanese brokers, as stabilizing factors during crash
        of 1987, 65
Japanese markets, 42n
    screen-based trading, 65
    See also Tokyo Stock Exchange
Jefferies and Company, 31, 138
Kaufman, Henry, 60
Keynes, John Maynard, 152-153, 165
Kleinwort Benson, 32

L
Large order execution, 8
Levine scandal, 68
LIFFE, 7, 185
Limit order file, 29
Limit orders, 26, 37n, 60, 118, 127n
Liquidity
    and automated trade execution systems, 90
    decline in, 63
    and proposed securities transaction tax, 167-168
    providers of, 65-66
LIST, 27
List order processing, 27
London Futures and Options Exchange, 4, 33
London International Financial Futures Exchange 7, 185
London International Futures Exchange system
        Automated Pit Trading System, 33
London Stock Exchange, 16
Lowenstein, Louis, 166

M

McLuhan, Marshall, 219
Major Market Index Options, 34
Margin, efficient use of, 81
Market makers, 48-49
  content of order message, 121-122
  in electronic age, 71-84
  over-the-counter, 75
  structure and problems of markets, 72-75
Market order, 118, 127n
Markets
  as information conveyors, 49-56
  technology innovation, impact of, 124
  as trade enablers, 46-47
Matif, 32
MAX, 26, 37n
Medium is the Massage, 219
Melamed, L., 183, 185, 194n
Message and Order Processing System, 119
Midwest Stock Exchange, 24, 25, 26. *See also* MAX
  link with Toronto Stock Exchange, 34, 136
Montreal Stock Exchange
  and BSE trading link, 34, 136
Morgan, J.P., 17

N

NASD, 23-24, 28-30, 40n, 74n
  development of ACT, 215
  development of NASDAQ, 134
  and PORTAL system, 215-216
  development of SOES, 137
  See also NASDAQ *and* SOES
NASDAQ, 23-24, 28, 29, 34, 102, 128
  development of, 134-135
  global potential, 212-215
  international links, 34, 135
  listing standards, 24, 35n
  regulations for market makers, 128n
National Association of Securities Dealers, Inc. *See* NASD
National Association of Securities Dealers Automated
        Quotation system. *See* NASDAQ

National Market System securities, 24, 28, 39n, 104
National Securities Clearing Corporation, 74, 80
National Securities Trading System. *See* NSTS
New finance, and technology, 17-18
New York Mercantile Exchange, 32
New York Stock Exchange, 14, 26-27
    batch system, 112n
    electronic collection of reports, 24
    market making, 74, 75
    order routing in the 1960s, 117-118
    See also SUPERDOT system
New Zealand Futures Exchange, 8, 33, 222
19-c-3 securities, 40n
NMS securities, 24, 28, 39n, 104
Nomura Securities, 65
NSCC, 74
NSTS, 32, 38n, 137

O
OARS, 26
OCT System, 29, 137, 139
October 1987 crash. *See* Crash of 1987
Opening Automated Report Service. *See* OARS
Open book, 111n
Open order book, 79
Open outcry auctions, 4
    automated trade execution systems in, 91-96, 188-191
    efficiency of, 220
    order routing, 121
OPRA, 25, 36n, 135
Options, 29-30, 88n
    automated trade execution systems, 99-102
    exchanges listing financial products, 200-201
Options Price Reporting Authority. *See* OPRA
Order book display, 8-9
Order Confirmation Transaction (OCT) System, 29, 137
Order execution
    automation of, 25-26
    innovations, 56-57
Order routing
    automation of, 25-27

broker order routing, 119-120
delays, 122-123
DOT system, 26-27, 37n, 50-51
investor order routing, 120
SUPERDOT system, 68-69, 83, 118
Over-the-counter market makers, 75
Over-the-counter stock, 39n, 102, 104

P

PACE, 26, 36n, 37n, 146n
Pacific Stock Exchange, 24, 25, 136
    Comex System, 137
    SCOREX, 25, 193n
Paris Futures Exchange, 9
Passive Foreign Investment Company rules, 176
Pension funds, international investments of, 200
PER System, 27, 119
Phelan, John, 222
Philadelphia Stock Exchange, 24, 25, 26, 41n
    index participation instruments, 82
    See also PACE
PORTAL, 30, 215-216
Portfolio insurance, 62
Portfolio management, index strategies of, 72
Portfolio trading, 66-67
    confusion with index arbitrage, 68-69
POSIT, 31, 138
Position risk, 73
Post Execution Reporting System (PER), 27
Price delivery system, 50
Price discovery, effect of automated trade execution
        systems on, 89, 91-96
Private Offerings, Resales, and Trading Through
    Automated Linkages (PORTAL), 30
Program trading, 27
    observations of, 52-53
    and stability of financial markets, 59, 67
Propagation delay, 122, 123, 128n
Proprietary trading systems, 30-31, 137-139

Q

Quantity determination, effect of automated trade execution
      system on, 89, 91-96
Quote delivery system, 50

R

RAES, 4, 29-30, 4ln, 99-102
    rules governing, 100
    SOES compared, 106
Registered specialists, 75, 83, 86n
Regulation, 19-20, 66, 201-206
Reich, Robert, 152
Retail Automatic Execution System. *See* RAES
Reuters Dealing 2000 system, 4
Reuters Information Systems, 31
    and CME link, 71-72, 225-226
Reynolds, R.J., 17
Risk arbitrage, 68
Risk, minimization of, 75-76
Rohatyn, Felix, 153
Roll, Richard, 158

S

SAEF, 32
Saitori, 33
Salomon Brothers, 64
Savings, effect of technology on, 16-17
Schiller, Robert, 159
Schleifer study, 112n
Schumpeter, 59, 69
SCOREX, 25, 193n
Screen-based automated execution system, 77-80, 83-84
SEAQ, 32, 34, 77, 212
    Automated Execution Facility (SAEF), 222
    NASDAQ link, 135
SEC, 24, 133
    regulation of automation, 10, 139-144

Securities Communication Order Routing and Execution
        (SCOREX), 25
Securities and Exchange Act of 1934, 184
Securities and Exchange Commission. *See* SEC
Securities Industry Automation Corporation (SIAC), 24-25, 80
Securities and Investment Board (UK), 34, 43n
Securities markets, automation of, 134-138
    information dissemination, 134-135
    order execution, 137
    order routing, 136
Securities Reform Act of 1975, 72
Securities regulation, 66
Securities Transaction Tax, 152, 153, 167-180
    assets subject to, 171-174
    collection and liability for, 178-179
    designing, 171
    in foreign countries, 168-170
    international markets, issues raised by, 174-176
    transfers and investors applicable to, 177-178
Self-regulatory organizations, 139-140, 142, 203
Shearson Lehman Hutton, 18, 21
Short sale rule, 81-82, 88n
SIAC, 24-25, 80
Singapore, trading links with, 34, 135
Singapore International Monetary Exchange, (SIMEX), 44n
SITUS, 30
Small Order Execution System. *See* SOES
SOES, 28, 39n, 102-109, 114n, 139
    automatic execution algorithm, 104-105
    broker order routing, 119
    development of, 137
    RAES compared, 106
SOFFEX, 4, 7, 33, 43n, 65, 222
Specialists. *See* Registered specialists
SROs, 139-140, 142
Standard & Poor's 500 Index
    fifty largest postwar movements, 156-158
    rise in funds, 51
    and side-car procedure, 27, 38n
    net program buy intensity vs. price change, 55
    volatility vs. program intensity, 54
STET. *See* Securities Transaction Tax

Stock Exchange Automated Facility (SAEF), 32
Stock Exchange Automated Quotation system. *See* SEAQ
Stock exchanges
    international links, 34
    See also names of individual exhanges
Stock index artitrage, 67-68
Stock index futures, 33, 67
Stock market crash of 1987. *See* Crash of 1987
Stock trading
    automated trade execution systems in, 102-109
    over-the-counter, 102-104
    SOES system, 102-109
"Sunshine trading", 79
Super Designated Order Turnaround system. *See* SUPERDOT
        system
SUPERDOT system, 68-69, 83, 118, 119, 120, 122
    automated order routing, 136
    Immediate Reporting Service, 127n
    limit on order size, 127n
    surplus order routing capacity, 123
    See also DOT
Swedish Option Market, 43n
Swiss Options and Financial Futures Exchange (SOFFEX),
        4, 33, 43n, 222
Sydney Futures Exchange (SFE), 32
System for Institutional Trading of Unregistered Securities
        (SITUS), 30

T
Tactical asset allocation, 62
Taxes, on traded securities, 203
Technological experimentation. *See also* Technology; and
        financial markets
Technology
    communication, 125
    and competition, 18-19
    computing, 125-126
    and financial markets, 15-17, 47-57
    and financial services, 13-22
    general news, price, and quote delivery, 50
    innovation, impact on markets, 124

and meeting customer needs, 20-21
and new finance, 17-18
order execution innovations, 56-57
order routing and delivery systems, 50-56
and regulation, 19-20
risk and solutions, 14-15
and savings, 16-17
Telerate, 72
TIFFE, 4
Tobin, James, 153, 161, 164
Tokyo International Financial Futures Exchange (TIFFE), 4
Tokyo Stock Exchange, 14, 33, 139, 148n
TOPS, 220
Toronto Stock Exchange (TSE), 32
    automated order routing, 136
    trading link with ASE, 34
Trade information systems
    Automated Data Processing, 120, 121
    Quotron, 121
    Reuters, 31, 121
    Telekurs, 121
Trade Order Processing System, 220
Trade and quotation reports. *See* Information dissemination
        systems, automation of
Trading, effect of automated trade execution on
    futures, 96-99
    options, 99-102
    stock, 102-109
Trading links, international, 34
Trading system, features of an ideal, 75-83
Trading technology
    and financial market stability, 47-57
Transparency, 135, 145n
TRAX, 33, 43n

U-V
Unbundled Stock Unit (USU), 18, 21
Uncompared trades, 74
United Kingdom
    quotation and trading system, 32
United States Documentary Stamp Tax, 170-171

Uptick rule, and index arbitrageurs, 70n
U.S. Steel, 17
Visa, 16
VP-2000, 219-220

W-Z
Walrasian auction, 91, 93, 96, 110-111, 191, 192
Wojnilower, Albert, 152
Wright, Jim, 153
Yen bond futures, 33
Zaitech, 59